A STUPID, UNJUST, AND CRIMINAL WAR
IRAQ 2001–2007

ANDREW GREELEY

A Stupid, Unjust, and Criminal War

Iraq 2001–2007

ORBIS BOOKS

Maryknoll, New York 10545

Founded in 1970, Orbis Books endeavors to publish works that enlighten the mind, nourish the spirit, and challenge the conscience. The publishing arm of the Maryknoll Fathers and Brothers, Orbis seeks to explore the global dimensions of the Christian faith and mission, to invite dialogue with diverse cultures and religious traditions, and to serve the cause of reconciliation and peace. The books published reflect the views of their authors and do not represent the official position of the Maryknoll Society. To learn more about Maryknoll and Orbis Books, please visit our website at www.maryknoll.org.

Manufactured in the United States of America.
Manuscript editing and typesetting by Joan Weber Laflamme.

Library of Congress Cataloging-in-Publication Data

Greeley, Andrew M., 1928–
  A stupid, unjust, and criminal war : Iraq, 2001–2007 / Andrew Greeley.
  p. cm.
  ISBN-13: 978–1–57075–732–7
  1. Iraq War, 2003—Religious aspects—Catholic Church. 2. War—Religious aspects—Catholic Church. 3. United States—Foreign relations—Iraq. I. Title.
  BX1793.G726 2007
  956.7044'3—dc22
                                                        2007018789

Contents

2003

2004

2005

2006

Contents

2007

Introduction

Even when fully justified, war is a dirty
business which can foul those who set out with
pure hearts and noble intentions and drives
combatants into desperate alliances, sometimes
in indecent company.
—Norman Davies
Europe at War 1939–1945

In the years since 1945, the Catholic Church has modified its teaching about war. The recent popes, while affirming that the traditional norms for a just war are still valid, argue that modern war almost never is just. The shift in papal teaching about war seems to be based on the conviction that the weapons of war now are so horrific that war itself is almost necessarily evil. Yet in terms of the number of people killed, the Thirty Years' War and the Napoleonic Wars devastated much of Europe, and some parts of Germany (like the Palatinate) recovered from the former only in the final decades of the 20th century. Nuclear war is unthinkable but still possible.

Moreover, the Vatican is probably influenced by the consensus among the prosperous and democratic peoples of the European union that war is no longer legitimate among them. Prosperity and democracy are strong inoculations against war. Similarly, the elimination of the death penalty in these countries may have influenced and been influenced by the church's more recent abhorrence of capital punishment.[1]

Perhaps the change in papal emphasis results from the fact that no one really wins wars. They usually begin with a mistaken assumption about length. In 1914, Germany thought its armies would reach Paris in thirty

---

[1] The *Wall Street Journal*, which has never seen a chance for American aggression that it hasn't liked, enjoys ridiculing Europeans for their lack of the "manly" virtues—small families, small armies, lack of support for their American allies, avoidance of intense economic competitions. The United States, it is implied, has to depend on allies who are cowards. A more charitable judgment would be that in the last century Europe saw enough war to want no part of it. From Europeans' point of view, American attitudes are those of cowboys in Western films.

days after mobilization of the army. Austria thought it would snuff out the Serbs in a couple of weeks. Russia thought it would destroy the German army in East Prussia in a single battle. President Lincoln thought it would require only six months for his seventy-five thousand volunteers to crush the Confederacy. In all three small wars of the second half of the 20th century American leaders firmly believed that vast military power would quickly overcome the peasant armies their troops were fighting. From the German thirty days to Paris to Donald Rumsfeld's flowers in the streets of Baghdad, miscalculations have turned various easy wars into catastrophe. Europeans perhaps have had enough experience with wars to understand that better than Americans. War is a very dangerous affair to be embarked upon only with extreme caution.

Harry Truman, Lyndon Johnson and Richard Nixon learned that lesson the hard way. Astonishingly George W. Bush did not learn it before the Iraq war started and seems not to have learned it yet. How many more times will the United States blunder into "small-scale wars" that cost thousands of lives (tens of thousands, if one counts the natives), diminish the prestige of the country, embitter the people, and finally destroy the administration.

I have gathered together these syndicated commentaries to demonstrate that someone writing out of the context of the Catholic just war theory, shaped by the last several popes, can use that theory to offer critical commentary on an immoral and unnecessary war.

There are five conditions in Catholic teaching for a just war:

1. The cause must be just.
2. All peaceful solutions must have been exhausted.
3. The means used must be proportionate.
4. The bad effects of the war must not exceed the good.
5. There should be a reasonable hope of victory.

In fact, the war in Iraq failed on all these criteria.

1. There were two public reasons for the war—Iraq had weapons of mass destruction and participated in the World Trade Center attack. Neither was true. The less public reason was to impose American democracy on Iraq. Given the history of the country, that was folly. President Bush to this day (April 2, 2007) links the Iraq intervention to the 9/11 attack.
2. The United Nations inspectors were not given a chance to finish their work.

3. Destroying the social, political and economic structure of the country far exceeded right proportion.
4. Anyone who knew anything about the history of Iraq knew that the various tribes would start killing one another.
5. Given the inevitability of tribal conflict, failure was inevitable.

I am not an ideological pacifist. I supported the Afghan war and lament only that the administration became too involved in Iraq to finish it. I grew up during World War II (or, as I would rather call it, the second phase of the Great War). The aggression of Imperial Japan and Nazi Germany left no choice. Alas, however, even a just war inevitably leads to actions that seem indefensible—the destruction of Japanese cities by fire bomb raids and then atomic bombs, the fire bombing of German cities by the Royal Air Force's Bomber Command.[2] It seems to be in the nature of wars that they bring out the worst in humankind. I can, however, imagine limited wars that are just, even some preemptive wars, but only if they are approached cautiously, with restraint and with full consideration of the possible negative consequences—an attitude that is very difficult for American leaders.

Yet such a response to challenges is not impossible in the political climate of the United States. Consider what would have happened if a man like George W. Bush had been president during the Cuban Missile Crisis. A lot of us would be toast. Instead of the drumbeat for war, the false intelligence, Mr. Cheney's fears about chemical weapons, General Powell's comments about biological weapons factories, the president's remarks about "yellow cake" uranium, the administration in 1963 did everything it could to calm the situation, to restrain its trigger-happy military, and to seize even the dimmest signal from the other side. Strength in such circumstances, it turns out, means restraint. Mr. Kennedy may have been flawed in some ways, but at the most dangerous time in the Cold War, he kept his cool. He didn't, perhaps, have to prove how tough he was.

The American people would have resisted the Iraq war if it were not for the climate of anger and fear generated by the attack on the World Trade Center. Administration officials like Donald Rumsfeld, Dick Cheney and Paul Wolfowitz were already on record in favor of a war with Iraq. Indeed, they wanted to blame Iraq for the World Trade Center attack. The

---

[2] Revisionist arguments have been made against both these judgments. If it had not been for the raids, millions of Japanese would have died in an invasion in which the whole population would have become suicide bombers. The RAF raids did destroy the will of Germany to resist. I find the first argument more persuasive than the second.

president, convinced that he was a wartime leader like Lincoln, was able to persuade a majority of the American people that an invasion of Iraq would be part of the "war on terrorism." Frightened and angry, most Americans were all too ready to teach the Arabs a lesson. Congress went along, and the punditocracy supported the decision.

Perhaps future historians will judge that the years after the World Trade Center attack were a time of acute neurosis for the American people, one whipped up by the media and used as an excuse for a foolish and dangerous war. In his final press conference before the war the president linked the invasion with the attack on the World Trade Center. None of the reporters challenged that link.

While the Catholic Church, both in Rome and in the United States, is opposed to preemptive wars and made that clear in the run-up to the Iraq war, it did not address itself explicitly to the war. Moreover, in matters such as going to war, the church usually leaves the decisions to the local clergy and laity. One cannot make the claim that it was immoral for Catholics in this country to support the war, especially at the beginning. Most changed their minds eventually. Did they do so soon enough not to be morally responsible? It is not up to me to say. For a sociologist who has studied both military history and the church's teaching on war and peace, it would have been immoral for me to remain silent, especially since I had in my column a platform from which to speak out.

I'm not sure how many priests denounced the war from the altar. They would have had a lot of trouble from their parishioners if they did. It is much safer to write a critical column than to preach against the war.

What right does a Catholic priest have to criticize the president, the hate mail asked, especially after the pedophile mess?

The only answer is that a priest has not only the right but the obligation to condemn a war that he thinks is unjust and immoral. The deplorable sex abuse mess the bishops have created is irrelevant (and I had written fourteen columns criticizing the bishops for their failures).

Moreover, I was doing nothing more than following in the footsteps of the pope and the American hierarchy. The *Wall Street Journal* had reprimanded the pope for intervening in the "war on terrorism." I was too small a target for it to bother with.

The hate mail poured in, though the favorable mail normally was larger. I'm sure my cardinal received many demands that he silence me. He did not. The *Chicago Sun-Times* heard similar demands. It did not either. The parish where I had worked on weekends for sixteen years suddenly had no openings for me in its mass schedule. I don't know whether there was a connection between that and my commentaries in Chicago papers, though some of the parishioners said there was. As the war became unpopular, the hate mail decreased. The theme, however, was the same. How could a priest be a front for liberal Democrats.

I admit to being a Democrat, though I opposed Lyndon Johnson's adventure into the Big Muddy. I'm a liberal too, though with a small "l". I'm a Chicago Democrat. We don't do ideology in Chicago. We don't do Republicans either for that matter. We were ejected from the Democratic Party in 1972 when the Democrats threw Richard Daley and George Meany out of the convention.

But the charge that I simply repeat the Democratic party line assumes that the war is a Republican war. I wonder how many Republicans want to claim credit now.

On occasion I'm asked why priests (including me) and the bishops don't speak out against the war. People must follow their own conscience in these matters. With a column I could think of no excuse to dodge a fight when I saw the slaughter of innocents (Iraqi and American) in a stupid war. I don't regret a single word. I wince every time I hear the daily number of casualties or see a full page in a newspaper with pictures of dead GIs or the PBS *News Hour*'s photos. These young men and women have had their lives cut short and tragedy has invaded their families never to go away, because our leaders fabricated reasons for an unjust war and the majority of our people cheered the decision.

And then there are the tens of thousands of Iraqis who have died because of our campaign to eliminate terrorism. How many terrorists did we get, I wonder.

Is the war "criminal," as my title suggests? It is up to God and not to me to judge the state of their consciences. But, objectively, is it a criminal war? I think so, but I don't expect any war-crime trials for those responsible—though such trials might be a useful experience for this country. We have tried others. Will we try our own? I doubt it.

I have no illusions that what I have written has influenced anyone to a change of mind. At best I may have reinforced the opposition of those who already had their doubts and of those Catholics who complain about the silence of the church—though I speak in these commentaries only for myself, *but in the context of what the church teaches about war.* I urge those who still support it to make their own case for the war in light of the church's criteria.

I am grateful to the *Chicago Sun-Times* for putting up with me and especially to John Cruickshank, Michael Cooke, John Barron and Steven Huntley of the *Sun-Times* and Ed Koziarski of the *Daily Southtown*, and to June Rosner for critical reading of the commentaries. And I'm grateful also to the cardinal.

Mindless revenge won't solve anything

The national cry for revenge is shameful. We Americans are presumably a people who do not believe in an eye for an eye and a tooth for a tooth. Yet many of our national leaders, most of the talking heads who have been babbling on television this week, and the mental defectives who repeat clichés on talk radio are demanding that we get even.

The desire to even the score is an understandable human reaction. Thousands of lives have been destroyed and thousands of families suffer from losses that will change their lives and in many cases ruin them.

Yet no one—certainly not the president or any of those around him—is promising that we will avoid action that might lead to the death of more innocents.

Moreover, who are "they" with whom we must get even—30, 40, even 100 fanatics? We must apprehend and punish criminals. Then what? Will we nuke Kabul or Baghdad? Will we blow Afghanistan from the 10th century back into the first? Will mass murder satisfy American blood lust? Do we want to become indistinguishable from our enemies? It would appear that many of us do.

The Pearl Harbor analogy is frivolous and dangerous. There is no militaristic enemy bent on conquering half the world. No mighty navy to sink. No brilliant air force to annihilate. No fanatical population to bring to its knees. We must capture a few terrorists, eliminate a couple of networks, improve our intelligence agencies. Indeed, if anyone is to be blamed for the tragedies in New York and Washington, it is Congress, which has not passed bipartisan legislation that would have improved our intelligence services. We hotly debate a dubious shield against missiles and skimp on funding to intercept terrorists. Perhaps the cries for vengeance we hear are a cover-up for that failure.

The too-easy use of the term "war" is scary. With whom are we to go to war? Iraq? Iran? Afghanistan? How will we fight them? Will we send combat troops into central Asia? Does anyone remember that the Russians tried that and it failed? Those who prate about "war" seem eager to have one.

President Bush knows full well that his legacy as president will depend on how he reacts. There are two models on which he might reflect. The first is that offered by John F. Kennedy, who, when everyone else had signed off on an invasion of Cuba, would not give the go-ahead to an impatient military and thus avoided World War III. The other is Lyndon B. Johnson, who did not stand up to the military and escalated the war in Vietnam. In the short run, restraint looks like cowardice. In the long run, it becomes a mark of greatness. In the short run, the use of overwhelming military power looks like decisive leadership. In the long run, it ruins a presidency.

There appears to be nobody around the president whom one could count on to counsel restraint. For all of Bush's fervent piety when he demands that God bless America, he does not seem to grasp that the religion to which he subscribes teaches that vengeance belongs to the Lord, not to us.

Also, he might follow the example of New York Mayor Rudy Giuliani and other leaders and warn against abuse of Muslim and Arab Americans.

The media babblers are telling us that Americans have lost their innocence, that the country will never be the same. Such claims are nonsense. The serious fear is that the American government will sink to the level of our enemies, and that a revenge-hungry public will support it.

September 23, 2001

An eye for an eye?

Since this country is apparently organizing its own jihad, its only holy war of vengeance, it is appropriate enough that we calculate precisely how many eyes are required to compensate for an American eye, how many teeth for an American tooth.

An American life is obviously worth more than an Afghan life, right? The Afghans are not Arabs, by the way; neither are the Iranians, but that doesn't matter. Afghans are poor, illiterate peasants. They live in caves and tents and survive by simple farming and grazing, much as their ancestors have done for thousands of years. About a quarter of them may starve to death this winter. They don't bathe very often or use deodorant. They are dirty, smelly, unkempt and uncivilized. They don't live very long. So clearly, one of their lives is not worth an American life. Nor is the death of one of their children a fit recompense for the death of an American child. Hence, we must establish for our revenge an appropriate ratio of value.

Let's say for the sake of an argument that we will have to kill six Afghans for every American who died in the terrorists' raids. That means our righteous revenge will require the death of perhaps 30,000 Afghans—well, round it out to 40,000. The U.S. military, which desperately wants to even the score for the damaged Pentagon, can easily dispose of 40,000 of them. We will have our revenge and the world will be a better place. Who will miss the smelly, dirty Afghans?

None of the 40,000 we kill may be terrorists. Indeed, the real terrorists have probably disappeared already. So we will have to kill a lot of the Taliban to make up for that, even if that means we create new terrorists.

However, our leaders have more in mind. Paul Wolfowitz, the deputy secretary of defense, has told the world that if a country doesn't cooperate with us, we will "end" that country.

That would be a real challenge for our generals. How does one go about ending a country? We would have to wipe out its government completely and any possible successors it might have. We could spray tactical nuclear weapons all over the Afghan countryside, killing millions of people, and still not collect any terrorists or Taliban leaders in our net. Then we would have to send in massive ground forces to do what the Russians or the Brits have never been able to: bring the Afghans under foreign rule.

So such a plan imposes another calculation on our revenge. How many American lives are we willing to spend to kill one terrorist? How many body bags with young American men and women will have to arrive at Dover Air Force Base before we begin to wonder whether we are accomplishing much with these tactics. It took 25,000 deaths for the country to turn against the Vietnam War (and 25,000 more during the Nixon years). Would that be enough this time? Or will the public decide it wants to reject the war it so enthusiastically supports now?

Our leaders tell us that we will have to "sacrifice," by which they mean partly that we will have to slip a little in the direction of a police state, but more that a lot of young people will have to sacrifice their lives, even if a strategy of "ending" countries doesn't work.

President Bush has taken advantage of the fury of Americans to decide that we will fight the first war of the new millennium and that he will be a successful war president, indeed the Franklin Roosevelt of the new millennium. The final result may well be that he becomes the Lyndon Johnson of the new millennium—a man who used the wrong strategy and the wrong model and the wrong motivation for a new kind of conflict, one that required a more deft, nuanced and sophisticated strategy than unilateral American brute force.

It would be much wiser of him to remind the bloodthirsty element in our population that vengeance still belongs to God and that He will repay. God is not likely to approve of a country that tries to usurp His role, especially if we repeatedly invoke His blessings on our revenge.

September 30, 2001

We're still babes in woods of the world

The talking heads have been busy these last couple of weeks telling us that there is an "end of American innocence." It's hard to know what they mean because they are always talking about the end of something or the other. If they mean that the optimism and expansiveness that are at the core of American culture are ending, then they're flat out wrong. These characteristics are indelibly stamped on the American soul and will never go away as long as there is an America. If they mean that Americans now know that terrorism can creep into our society, I think we've known that at least since Oklahoma City.

However, there is another kind of innocence that should have ended long ago but has survived into the present and indeed in the Bush administration has notably increased. The name of it, for want of a better word, is unilateralism—the conviction that the United States can do anything it wants in the world and everyone else had better get out of the way.

Our foreign policy, if one wants to call it that, in the last eight months has meant backing out of treaties and agreements, walking out on meetings, and "consulting" with our allies by telling them what we're going to do whether they like it or not.

Many Americans like this kind of foreign policy. It is tough, macho and, one should excuse the expression, Texan. However, now we are in the embarrassing position of having to ask others for help at the same time we're telling them what to do. We must listen to their reactions and take their concerns into account. We are not doing a very good job at it because our leaders are not overly possessed of the humility required to build coalitions. In fact, we are trying to build a unilateral coalition, one in which all the members do what we want them to do.

In a marvelous irony, one team of American diplomats is in Moscow asking about air bases in the former Soviet republics that border Afghanistan from the north, and another team is there trying to impose our missile-shield scheme on the Russians. No one in Washington sees the irony in this. Not only do we ask the Russians for assistance after a half year of pushing them around, we now ask them for assistance while pushing them around. There are, of course, some people around the president who reject completely the notion of building a coalition. They want us to continue our unilateralism.

The president's rhetoric is no help. While it plays to the hyper-patriotism and blood lust that are sweeping our society, it scares most of our potential and actual allies. The use of the word "war" scares them because they fear some massive and brutal American military attack that will kill thousands of people and make matters worse instead of better.

The president's cowboy language about "dead or alive" and "smoke 'em out and get 'em" also scares a lot of people on both sides of the Atlantic because it suggests an inexperienced and shallow leader deciding the fate of the human race as if he were a sagebrush hero in a Hollywood film.

Moreover, his invitation to all the nations, including the Islamic ones, to join our crusade against terrorism boggles the mind. It's like asking Jews to join a pogrom. Not to realize what the word "crusade" means to Muslims is an intolerable display of superficiality. The people around him have no idea how to program the leader of the free world on what to say and what to do in a time of crisis.

We knew when we elected him (though actually we didn't elect him) that we were getting a president who was inexperienced in foreign policy, who in fact had rarely been out of the country and never to Europe. Now the cry is that we have to stand behind him and be loyal, no matter how inept he might be. Too bad for the Muslims if they don't like the word "crusade." We can still do and say whatever we want. We can call the campaign on which we have embarked a war (like we call the campaign against drugs a war), even if it does not describe what the campaign really will be like and scares our friends. We're America, God bless us!

That innocence is still very much part of our life, God help us all.

October 7, 2001

Blaming God for disaster won't help us

Where was God?

Many Americans are angry not only at all Muslims and all Arabs but also at God. Where was He when those planes were hijacked? How could He permit such terrible things to happen?

The questions miss the point. One could just as well ask where God is when a premature baby, desperately fighting for life, can't quite make it. Or when a drunken truck driver wipes out a whole family. Or when each of us must die.

Why does God permit death? That's the proper question.

A number of theologians have asked how one can believe in God after the Holocaust. The more fundamental question is how one can believe in God after the death of a single child.

Where was God on Sept. 11? He was somewhere (which in His case is everywhere) grieving for His suffering children. Like every good parent God mourns for His children. We don't know enough about God to understand what His sadness is like or how it happens.

But God is sad, so the scriptures tell us repeatedly, even if theologians have a hard time explaining it. As a Russian mystic says, when a little baby cries, God weeps. What is God's weeping like? One can speak of the sadness of God only in metaphors, because one can speak of God only in metaphors.

Paul Murray, an Irish Dominican poet, puts it this way: He who has no need of our gifts, who gives us all that we bring, still needs us so that if one of us should cease to exist he would die of sadness.

For reasons that we do not and cannot understand fully, God cannot prevent death, though He can triumph over it, no matter how horrible it is. Like any good parent He will eventually wipe away all His children's tears. That is all we have in this life and in the face of death.

Blame God for death if you want and if it makes you feel good. Demand to know why He stood silent at the "worst disaster in American history" (conveniently forgetting such incidents as the battles of Antietam or Cold Harbor). Make God the enemy just like the Arabs and Muslims we have to kill. You know what?

That won't help you for one minute.

Nor does it help to claim God as our ally in the "war" our foolish leaders promise and plan. You may be able to create a God who will lead us into battle, a God who will bless America on demand. But when you put that God in an American uniform, you'll find out that you have created Him in our own image and likeness and that this God is not God at all but a blasphemous idol.

The real God is mysterious. If He weren't mystery, He wouldn't be God. We cannot fit Him into our categories, our plans, our ideologies, our wars of revenge. God is not the Roman god Mars. He is not a god of battle.

To make matters worse, He loves our enemies too. He "weeps" at their deaths as He "weeps" at ours. They are His beloved children just as we are. The rain of His mercy falls on the just and the unjust. Nor is it wise to claim that our cause always is just. If we are to follow in the path of the God of Christians and Jews, we must probe tentatively and uncertainly to make sure that we have not created the path in our own name instead of His. We must seek justice; we must prepare to defend ourselves. But we must not hate. We must not become like our enemies.

We must also be prepared to forgive. This may be what a correspondent tells me is "Jesus drivel." OK, perhaps it is. But those who prate the Lord's Prayer trippingly on the tongue should reflect on its words. We forgive others because we are forgiven ourselves and thus manifest God's forgiveness in the world. That does not mean that we abandon the quest for justice and self-protection, but it does mean that we understand that hatred and revenge are not options.

That's Jesus drivel too, perhaps, but those of us who claim to be of Jesus must pray with him: "Father, forgive them, they know not what they do."

And if we don't, then we have repudiated the essence of Jesus.

October 14, 2001

Europe struggling with Muslim "invasion"

VIENNA, Austria—This cultivated, blasé, tourist-jammed city—whose streets are alive with the sound of music—is an excellent place to consider the third Islamic invasion of Europe.

The first invasion was stopped at Tours in France in 732 by Charles Martel.

Islam fell back to Spain, where it held on for 700 years and constructed a civilization far superior to any in Europe for most of those centuries. Its people discovered algebra and rediscovered Aristotle before the Catholic theologians of Europe.

The second invasion was halted here in Vienna in 1683, in what, to quote the Duke of Wellington on another battle, was a very near thing. After the fall of Constantinople in the mid-15th century, the Turks pushed north into the Balkans and routed the Serbs and the Hungarians. Twice they raced north to the Imperial Capital, the second time almost taking it. France and Spain, the pope and the Prussians, the English and the Scandinavians were otherwise occupied. If Vienna fell, there was little chance that the Turks could have been stopped short of the English Channel. The Polish army, however, commanded by King Jan Sobieski, arrived in the nick of time and sent the Turks reeling back. They were never a threat to Europe again. Austria repaid the favor by participating in the next century in the dismemberment of Poland with Prussia and Russia.

The third invasion is now. More than 10 million men and women of Islamic faith live in Western Europe today. They have not come as armed invaders seeking to take political power. Rather, they are poor people seeking jobs and the good life for themselves and their families and hoping to preserve some of their heritage while they do so.

No one really wants them. In this country an anti-immigrant political party is already part of the government. In other countries opposition has increased dramatically. A cardinal has asked the Italian government to ban any more Muslim immigrants. Yet Western Europe, where low birth rates have created a serious shortage of labor, needs them. Like all immigrants, the Islamic arrivals—Turks, Moroccans, Pakistanis, Algerians—are relegated to the fringes of society. Some are involved in crime. Their young are restless and alienated. Their neighborhoods are considered dangerous at night. These descriptions are not unlike the descriptions of the Irish and Italians and Poles in the United States in the 19th and early 20th centuries.

The official policy is that these immigrants be integrated into the host societies and become good Austrians, good French, good Germans, good Britons, while retaining a "humanistic" version of Islam. Leaders of the host societies and of the immigrants have endorsed this goal, perhaps with unrealistic optimism.

According to a copyrighted article in the *International Herald Tribune*, Moroccan youths demonstrated joyously in the Netherlands at news of the Sept. 11 massacre in the United States. The Dutch government considered calling out the army to put down the demonstrations. A newspaper poll showed that 20 percent of the Moroccans in the Netherlands were delighted by the murder of so many Americans.

Thus 80 percent were opposed to it, a finding that shows the dilemma of the European governments. Most Muslims in their countries want no part of a holy war against the West. But some, especially among the young people, are angry and cannot be completely trusted.

Europe cannot expel the new invaders, because it needs them to do the dirty work in European society and because most of them are not criminals.

Yet some of them either are or are willing to be. And many Europeans hate them—all the while decrying American racism. At least the European police seem to be able to keep an eye on them. They quickly picked up suspects in France, England and Germany after Sept. 11. The FBI, stumbling and bumbling as always, had done nothing about a CIA warning concerning two of the hijackers.

Europe and the United States share common problems: How does one deal with immigrants among whose number might be a tiny number of dangerous religious fanatics, and at the same time preserve the values that fanatics like Osama bin Laden want to destroy? How does one also cope with the racist haters from within? Yet if the West can facilitate the integration of Islam, it will be richer and better for having done so.

October 28, 2001

As memories of tragedy fade, life goes on

A favorite cliché of the talking heads during the past couple of weeks is that life in the United States has changed forever because of the World Trade Center tragedy. One is permitted to doubt that self-serving prediction, which establishes our era and us as unique in American history. The more complicated reality is that human societies do their best to forget about tragic experiences and to proceed with the ordinary activities of life. They do so not because of insensitivity but because there is no other way that life can go on—and life must go on. Not much will change, because people forget.

One of the most striking examples of this phenomenon was the Spanish influenza epidemic in the fall of 1918. About 200,000 Americans died, out of a population that was at that time only about 100 million—two out of every thousand Americans. My mother told me that she remembered riding home on the Jackson Boulevard bus and seeing crepe on half the houses on the block. One night she went right to her room, collapsed on the bed, and said to herself, "I have the flu." She was, she said, too tired to care whether she lived or died. The next morning she woke up, weak but still alive.

The flu struck rapidly. Soldiers on the parade ground at Camp Leavenworth keeled over suddenly, dead before their bodies hit the ground. It attacked especially the young and healthy (my mother was 24). The death rates increased so rapidly that there was fear that most Americans would die. Then, just as suddenly as it started, it stopped—perhaps because it had already killed those who did not have some kind of at least partial genetic immunity. More Americans died of the flu than died in the war. Worldwide, 20 million people died.

Yet it was quickly forgotten, especially by those families who had lost no one. As I was growing up, I heard an occasional reference to a relative who had died "during the flu." Only 20 years later, my own contemporaries had never heard of it. Life went on. America went into the Jazz Age and the Roaring '20s in a burst of euphoria that was unprepared for the Great Depression (the tragic effects of which on so many people are now also largely forgotten). People prayed for the relatives who died of the flu, but eventually these were merged with other dead relatives. As Jesus said with harsh realism, "Let the dead bury their dead." Life has to go on.

Some will say the flu was caused by a virus, the World Trade Center mass murder by human agents. However, both were the result of irrational forces that sometimes break into the human condition. There is no other way human society can respond to mass disaster—wars, volcanic eruptions, hurricanes, famine, plagues, sudden death. The immediate relatives—spouses, children, parents—don't forget. Eventually, alas, they die too, and all that is left are vague memories of tragedy.

Seven million Germans died in World War II, and somehow Germany revived. In 1358, one-third of Europe (30 million people) died of the plague. In less than half a century, Europe entered the most prosperous time until then in its existence, the Renaissance.

More Americans died in the Civil War than in all our other wars put together. We remember them, if we do at all, only on Memorial Day—or when we see films such as "Gettysburg," which can only approximate the horror of those days. Humans have no choice but to forget as best they can, even in the midst of grief.

This may seem heartless and, these days, with the memories of jets crashing into buildings and anthrax sent in the mail, impossible. Yet it is almost certainly what will happen. The World Trade Center dead will be memorialized. We will pray for them and their families. Except for the immediately bereaved, life will go on because it must. Grief and anger cannot go on forever, although pain and loss can and do.

In years to come, Americans will not want to remember this time. Those who were supposed to protect us—the FBI, the CIA, the airlines— let us down. Indeed, they acted like blind fools. Congress could not mobilize itself even to pass an airline security law. Our leadership, doubtless unintentionally, fed our panic. National anger and the desire for revenge substituted for wisdom. All these phenomena are understandable, perhaps, but nothing to be proud about in years to come.

November 25, 2001

Our greatest threat comes from within

It is ironic that on this weekend when we offer thanks for all the blessings our country has received, there is a whiff of fascism American style in the air. The precious freedoms that the Pilgrims came in search of and that the founding fathers confirmed are under systematic assault from hardright Republicans who apparently are ready to use the present crisis as a pretext for abrogating freedoms that they've never really liked.

The right of habeas corpus has been suspended, lawyer-client immunity has been suspended, the right to a speedy trial has been suspended, the right to trial by jury has been suspended. The right to be free from unreasonable search and seizure has been suspended. The right of access to presidential papers has been revoked.

More than 1,000 people are in jail without being identified or charged or indicted by grand juries. The government eavesdrops on lawyer-client conversations. Military tribunals will try captured persons suspected of terrorism (as a prelude to their certain execution). Five thousand legal immigrants are being rounded up for "voluntary" questioning by the FBI.

President Bush, unlike most of his recent predecessors, who have been only too eager to make their papers available to historians, wants to tie his up in red tape.

There are three defenses offered for these violations of our heritage:

1. Previous presidents have taken similar extra-constitutional steps.
2. They are necessary to protect us from terrorists.
3. Only aliens are subject to most of the violations of the Constitution.

No one would deny that previous presidents, including some very great ones, played fast and loose with the Constitution. However, those who point to Lincoln's military tribunals fail to report that most of the convictions (which on the record were patently unfair) were later reversed or pardoned.

The issue, however, is not whether other presidents violated the Constitution; the issue is rather whether they ought to have. No one argues seriously today that Franklin Roosevelt did the proper thing when he herded Japanese Americans into concentration camps.

No evidence has been adduced to show that these draconian measures will make us one bit safer from terrorists. We are told that we must trust that our leaders know what they're doing. Yet one must wonder if such measures are not a way to cover up for the failure of the FBI to prevent the terrorist attacks, to collect enough evidence to indict those who worked with the terrorists, to apprehend other potential terrorists, or to figure out who is sending anthrax through the United States mail. The arguments against jury trial for arrested terrorists is that they have come into this country to kill Americans and are not entitled to the rights of American citizens. In other words, they are guilty till proven innocent.

Finally, it is all right to suspend the Constitution, we are told, because the immediate targets are foreigners. Indeed, it is all right to "profile" 5,000 young men from mostly Islamic countries for FBI interviews because they are not citizens. When the liberties of foreigners are threatened, it is implied, the liberties of the rest of us are not put in jeopardy. Only a fool would believe that. The people in charge just now would not hesitate a second to go after American citizens if they thought it was a good idea. Witness presidential adviser Condoleezza Rice's successful effort to censor CNN from presenting interviews with Osama bin Laden.

Even more fundamentally, however, it is simply wrong to assume that the Constitution creates rights for American citizens that need not apply to foreigners. There are, as the Declaration says, certain inalienable rights with which the creator has endowed us, rights that are inherent in human nature. The Constitution does not create these rights. It merely confirms and validates them.

I suspect that most people, whipped into a frenzy of fear and anger by the media, don't care that, when we violate the rights of a young Arab against whom there is no suspicion, save that he is young and Arab, we endanger the rights of everyone. When good does evil in its fight against evil, it becomes indistinguishable from that evil. The closet fascists among us, however well-intentioned they may be, are far more serious threats to us than the followers of bin Laden. They would, given half a chance, destroy the American soul.

December 16, 2001

Christmas can conquer fear of death

Christmas is a major anti-death festival. It asserts the power of light over darkness, hope over fear, life over death.

At Christmas (and during the other midwinter festivals of the various religions), we celebrate the belief that life is too important ever to be anything but life.

However, this Christmas is blighted by the fear of death, which has taken possession of the souls of so many Americans.

Al-Qaida will get you if you don't watch out.

The World Trade Center attacks were a success beyond all possible expectations of the terrorists. The attacks not only killed several thousand Americans but also plunged the nation into paralyzed fear. Many Americans have stopped buying, they have stopped traveling, they are unconcerned about a massive attack on their constitutional rights, they tolerate the Keystone Kops who do "security" at their airports. Americans are, to sum up, scared silly.

To make matters worse, the lugubrious leaders of our country are doing their best to keep us scared. We are now in our third "warning" of a "credible threat." They don't know what the "threat" is, they don't know where it will occur if it does, but nonetheless we should be "alert" for it. How can one be alert for something that is so vague?

Al-Qaida will get you if you don't watch out.

One suspects that the warnings are a substitute for efficient intelligence services—to cover the fact, for example, that the FBI has no trouble finding perpetrators of anthrax hoaxes but has no idea who's sending real anthrax in the mail.

The president keeps telling us that we should get on with our lives and demeans his office by participating in silly television ads. Yet he never reminds us that, statistically, our life expectancy has hardly changed at all.

Al-Qaida will get you if you don't watch out.

What are the chances that al-Qaida really will get you? It is not unlikely that they will attempt another terrorist act before Christmas. The odds that a given person will be killed in it are substantially less than the chances of being knocked off by a drunken driver or a gun-toting crackhead or by a lifetime of smoking or by the effects of obesity.

Yet one hears no cries that the tobacco and gun and alcohol companies are terrorist organizations and that they should be "smoked out" by special forces and B-52 raids.

Al-Qaida will get you if you don't watch out.

Don't bother, however, to be alert for the threat from tobacco and guns. Indeed, our ineffable attorney general is very careful to protect the rights of terrorist suspects (all young Arab immigrants, in his view) to own guns.

We are all going to die sometime. No one wants to die, no matter how long life has been. Every death is a horrible tragedy. Whether al-Qaida gets us with a bomb or whether lung cancer or breast cancer gets us or whether our whole family is killed in a highway accident, the result is the same: a tragic and senseless end. Which of us can by worrying about it add a single hour to our life?

Our lives are only very slightly more at risk today than they were before Sept. 11. Hence, our fear of immediate death ought at the most to be only very slightly increased. The only sensible way to live in a time of terror is to keep repeating, "Everyone has to die sometime."

Christmas tells us not that there is no possibility at all that al-Qaida will get us. Nor is it the business of the midwinter festival to calculate exactly how infinitesimal are the chances that it will get us.

Rather, it is the purpose of the trees and the cribs and the lights and the candles and the carols and the electric trains and midnight mass and Hanukkah candles to tell us that death has no power over us—that we shall all be young again, we shall all laugh again, we shall all play again at the foot of the Christmas tree with the happy little children we will then be.

So we better be good for goodness' sake, good to all the loves in our life, open, generous, faithful and trusting. Laugh so that they will laugh with you. Goodness, you see, is stronger than evil—in the long run, much stronger.

Al-Qaida can't get us because, finally, it can't take away the life that Christmas reflects for us.

So be good for goodness' sake!

December 30, 2001

War on terrorism truly is a holy war

Instead of dropping bombs and killing innocent people, the cliché insists, the United States should deal with the "underlying causes" of anti-American resentment in the Muslim world. It should ask what are the reasons that so many Muslims all over the world hate and resent us. Americans should ask whether American injustice and oppression have created such emotions. If we back off from these underlying causes, then the hatred will abate.

This is the constant mantra of pseudo liberals, clergy (especially priests in England and Ireland), academics, journalists, European intellectuals, and wise men and women all over the world. Such comments are cheap grace, a strategy for sounding both profound and superior in dinner-party chatter, faculty-lounge posture, and outraged letters to the editor. It is innocent of thought and meaning. There is but one way that Americans could stop being the target of virulent hatred from Islamic extremists: We would have to stop being infidels and convert to Islam. They want to kill us because the United States is the most powerful nation in the world and is a nation of infidels. The power of America belongs by right to Islam.

Therefore, death to the infidels! Death to Americans!

This sentiment runs among Muslims on a continuum from zero to the sheer delight some feel at the deaths on Sept. 11. I can make no estimates of the distribution along this continuum. I assume that most Muslims are at or near zero. However, among fundamentalists and their clerics such sentiments are strong. There's nothing we can do about it, save to convert to a belief in Allah (who, by the way, is for Muslims the God of Abraham). Islam for such extremists is not only a religion, it is a nation, indeed, the nation of God. As the nation of God, it should be the most powerful nation in the world. That it is not, and America is, does violence to the will of God.

When one begins with such a premise, one does not find it hard to see God's will in killing Americans. Osama bin Laden is not a madman but only a perfectly logical devout fundamentalist Muslim who sees America as having usurped the role of power that belongs to Islam. I hasten to add for the benefit of those who read hastily and inaccurately that most Muslims accept neither the premise nor the conclusion. My point is that resentment of America is widespread among Muslims, and there is nothing we can do about it save for abandoning our infidelity. Islam, they believe, was once the greatest nation in the world. After the failure of the Turks to capture Vienna, Austria, in 1683, it went into a decline caused by the oppression of the Christian West. It has been chopped up into many artificial states created by the West to enforce this oppression. Finally, the oppression has become intolerable. It is time for all good Muslims to rise up and strike down the oppressors.

Death to the infidels! Death to all Americans!

Hence the so-called war against terrorism is a religious war in the strict sense of the word. The terrorists are driven by a rigid interpretation of a religious tradition that is not shared by most who believe in the tradition (and from the point of view of the terrorists are themselves infidels). They may talk about the rights of the Palestinians, but, should Israel disappear tomorrow, resentment of the United States would not diminish in the slightest. Moreover, the appeal of the terrorists to those who are horrified by what they do is the appeal of all fundamentalists: No one can accuse them of not being serious about their religion.

Doubtless the United States has not done as much as it can to reduce the hunger, the disease, the misery in the world. However, that is not the cause of the holy war against us. The cause is our infidelity. Those who fatuously cry for an investigation of "underlying causes," not being very religious themselves, cannot believe that others would be so deeply committed to a religious vision that they would kill thousands of people because they were the enemies of Allah. It is not clear to me that our intelligentsia and our leadership really understand this belief. It is not sufficient to dismiss the people who hold it as "evil."

January 11, 2002

U.S. failed to heed lesson on terrorism

Of the many ways the present time is different from the time after the attack on Pearl Harbor, one is that today there is almost no cry for an investigation of how we were caught by surprise. Before the Christmas recess, Senators Joseph Lieberman (D-Conn.) and John McCain (R-Ariz.) introduced legislation that would mandate an investigation. Their suggestion attracted no attention in the media and has been forgotten. We don't know why we were caught by surprise and don't want to know. And God bless America!

In 1941 and 1942, everyone wanted to know why the Japanese surprise attack was so successful. Today we seem content with the president's condemnation of the terrorists as evil. Enough said. In fact, it would appear that the same mind-set that left us unprepared for the attack on Pearl Harbor also left us unprepared for the World Trade Center attack. In both cases the people and their leadership were blinded by a mix of arrogance, ignorance, stupidity and racism. In both cases bureaucratic incompetence blinded the decision makers to what was about to happen. In the more recent attack, greed (of the airline industry) and religious prejudice also played a role.

In 1941, it was obvious that Japan was determined to conquer all of Southeast Asia. It could not do so without an oil supply that the United States had cut off. Both sides were aware that war was likely. Anyone who knew history knew that the Japanese tradition favored sneak attacks at the beginning of a war. Yet there was little concern in this country. The "Japs" (as we called them then) were slanty-eyed, bandy-legged little "yellow bellies" with funny pagodas on their ships and airplanes made of bailing wire and glue. In a war, we would beat them in a few weeks. It was unthinkable that the Japanese could engineer a successful attack on Pearl Harbor.

More recently, despite Osama bin Laden's warnings, despite the successful attacks on the embassies in Africa, despite the attack on the destroyer USS *Cole* in Yemen, despite the first assault on the World Trade Center, despite the warnings from our own experts, no one took the threat seriously—not several administrations, not the CIA or the FBI, and not the Congress. Bin Laden was patently crazy. How could dark-skinned, backward people who went around in sheets carry off a major terrorist strike in this country? The FBI didn't hire agents who could read or speak Arabic. The airlines didn't take seriously the warnings of the report of the Gore commission on airline safety in 1996. Congress wouldn't appropriate more money for the FBI (which might have not made any difference, given that agency's incompetence).

Despite the first World Trade Center attack, despite the USS *Cole*, the FBI was unconcerned about a warning last August from a Minnesota flight school that an Arab in Minnesota was trying to learn how to fly a plane but seemed uninterested in learning to take off or land and that an airplane could easily become a bomb. Nothing to worry about, folks—the bureau had everything under control. I would like to know who the airline executives were that lobbied against the Gore commission's recommendation for stronger cockpit doors. I would like to know why the government failed to "take out" bin Laden, which was supposed to be the main reason for the Afghan war.

No, what happened on Sept. 11 was not the result of any mistakes the American government and the American people might have made. It was all the result of the evil on the other side. God bless America! The comparison of the present generation's experience and that of the Pearl Harbor generation is obscene. It is an attempt by the present generation, distinguishable in the past only by its ruthless greed, to find something special about itself, to assert a claim that it might become the "greatest generation."

January 25, 2002

U.S. comes up short in Afghanistan

Has the Afghan war been a failure—not a defeat certainly, but not a victory? The war was justified at the beginning as an act of self-defense, a necessary campaign to eliminate Osama bin Laden and his coterie of co-conspirators.

"We'll smoke him out," the president said. "And we'll get him."

We did smoke him out, but we didn't "get" him. The president now tells us that we will get him just the same. The problem is that we haven't got him yet. How can we claim a victory until we do?

Republican Clinton-haters have been triumphantly comparing President Bush's campaign in Afghanistan to that of the former president. Now, however, the only difference in the efforts of the two men seems to be that Bush managed to kill a lot more people. If the goal of a war is just—and halting bin Laden's terror was certainly a just goal—the failure to achieve that goal does not thereby become unjust. Moreover, we did deny bin Laden a protected base in Afghanistan, eliminated his bases, captured many of his low-level followers, and killed some of his immediate staff.

We also collected a lot of intelligence material (the usefulness of which remains to be seen) and perhaps disrupted some of his plans. We also knocked out the Taliban regime, for which few Afghans seem to be grieving. While achieving these limited successes, we killed thousands of people, many of them innocent civilians, and pushed a famine-prone land closer to mass starvation.

How does one reckon the balance of costs for such limited success? If we had been told at the beginning of the "war" that we would certainly have limited success, but that a lot of Afghans would die and that it was far from certain that we would capture the top leadership of al-Qaida (a statement which would have been the simple truth), there might have been second thoughts about the campaign.

Probably not, however. Americans wanted revenge. Killing a couple of thousand Afghans, innocent or not, would satisfy temporarily America's patriotic blood lust. A better case might be made for freeing the Afghan people from Taliban tyranny. Perhaps that would have justified the civilian casualties. Yet Bush has repudiated the task of "nation building" and left it to the United Nations. American troops will not remain for long. Furthermore, there are a lot of other tyrannical, women-hating regimes around the world. Should we knock them over? Should we rid the people of Saudi Arabia of their oppressors?

The prospects for the Afghans are not promising. The government in Kabul is a thin reed. The country is swarming with warlords, bandits, Taliban guerrillas, al-Qaida remnants, Iranian agents, Pakistan intelligence forces allied to bin Laden, and heroin smugglers. We have created new possibilities for the Afghans, but the most likely outcome of our brief but highly effective war against the Taliban is more chaos. Thus, the most candid judgment about the war is that it had some limited though problematic successes but did not deliver on its major promise.

Perhaps it should have been obvious from the start that there was not much likelihood that it could. Mullah Mohammed Omar (a secondary target of American rage) is alive and well and protected by some of our Pashtun allies. Bin Laden, his entourage and his immediate staff are most likely safely across the border and under the protection of rogue elements of the Pakistan army. Bush's victory is hollow.

The American public, now in its you-can-fool-all-the-people-some-of-the-time mode, will not at present accept such a judgment. But when the hyper-patriotism and the blood lust die down, the question will be raised of "how we missed bin Laden," just as a half century ago Americans began to wonder "how we lost China" and a quarter century ago "how we lost Iran."

What does the president do to sustain the war fever now that the Afghan campaign is winding down and bin Laden is still on the loose? His political guru, Karl Rove, is trying to package the November campaign as a plebiscite on the president as a war leader. To sustain this image and to cover up the failure to capture the chief enemy, some spectacular new demarche will be needed. Whom do we bomb next?

February 8, 2002

Sept. 11 was no Republican conspiracy

In the months after the Pearl Harbor attack the Republicans fashioned a theory to blame President Franklin Roosevelt, for whom they had a hatred that makes their descendants' hatred for President Bill Clinton look like deep affection. Roosevelt knew the attack was coming, they argued, and did nothing to alert the commanders in the Pacific. He wanted a disaster because he knew that the American people would need motivation to enter a war on England's side.

Most historians, acknowledging the bureaucratic incompetence that made the surprise attack the success it was, reject this conspiracy theory. They point out that what brought us into the European war was not the attack on Pearl Harbor but Hitler's subsequent declaration of war on the United States, one of the Führer's worst mistakes. If he had not declared war, then the United States would have had to concentrate on the Pacific, and England would have been in far worse danger. Many history books omit this critical truth.

Those Republicans who promote the theory blaming Roosevelt, even to this day, omit the fact that their hero, Douglas MacArthur, knowing of the attack in Hawaii, had his planes all neatly lined up at Clark Field for Japanese attackers 12 hours later.

Now, a similar conspiracy theory is emerging in left-wing e-mail postings. The people around Bush, they say, knew the attack was coming and let it happen because that would make Bush a popular wartime president. There were plenty of warnings, they say. The British, the Germans, the Russians all told us what might happen. The FBI in Minneapolis warned of Arabs wanting to learn to fly planes without bothering to know how to take off or land. The FBI was warned by the flight school that planes could be used as bombs. Using the same logic as the Pearl Harbor conspiracy theory, Washington must have known what would happen. Why didn't our leaders stop it?

I don't believe this stuff any more than I believed the Pearl Harbor conspiracy theories. Roosevelt was not about to sacrifice the Pacific fleet to get us into a war. Bush was not about to sacrifice several thousand lives to increase his ratings. One has to be really sick to believe such things. The people around Bush might be mean enough to steal an election, but they are not, any more than were Roosevelt's aides long ago, monsters. In both cases there were plenty of warnings and lots of bureaucratic incompetence. Stupidity explains a lot more than conspiracy.

That said, it is also true that the president and his staff and allies are using the World Trade Center disaster to push their right-wing agenda. To fight terrorists, the United States must transfer more of the national wealth to the rich, erode the Bill of Rights, permit the president to hide his documents, elect Republicans to Congress in the fall and not investigate the connections between the White House and the Enron stench. Anyone who questions aspects of the so-called war on terrorism is as bad as the terrorists themselves. Americans must support their president, right or wrong. Then go sing "God Bless America."

Bush's bellicose State of the Union speech is a perfect example of using terrorism as a technique for demanding support for his whole agenda. Unless North Korea, Iran and Iraq shape up, we'll go after them, too. Loud applause from Congress and from the American people still in the grip of war fever. Nuke 'em all.

When other countries expressed some concern about these threats, the president—on a tour to stir up more war fever—warned the rest of the world that it had better shape up, too, and decide whether it is on our side or on the other side.

The difficulty with this approach is that it can have only a short-term payoff, absent any more terrorist attacks (the prospect of which seems to delight the secretary of defense). If the struggle to reduce terrorism must be a long-term effort, and there's no reason to think it will not be, the country needs something more than injections of jingoistic fever. It needs more and better intelligence of the sort that would have taken seriously the Minneapolis warning, as well as a calm and rational population. Such a style, however, will not elect a Republican Congress in November.

March 22, 2002

We're no safer now than we were Sept. 10

The mix of self-pity and self-congratulation that marked the six-month anniversary of the World Trade Center catastrophe was both surrealistic and sick. In the midst of vows to move on to the "second phase" of the "war on terrorism" and the noisy celebrations of American patriotism (with talk of using nuclear weapons on the "axis of evil" sounding in the background), no one said what is self-evidently true: There has been only a marginal decline in the danger of more terrorism.

No one should be fooled by the elaborate system of harassment of air travelers at the airports around the country. Most of the pawing and groping, the peering at shoes and the breaking of fingernail files is farcical. The farce descends into madness when cretins want to strip-search a 79-year-old nun with a hip replacement and confiscate a Medal of Honor from an 80-year-old war hero (and former governor). None of this stuff is going to stop a determined hijacker who has checked baggage with a bomb in it and boarded the plane.

Like ration stamps during the war, airport "security" is for morale purposes. It is an effort to convince people that the government is doing something when in fact it really isn't doing anything. The one person who was detected was the alleged shoe bomber, who was spotted by an alert cabin attendant when he tried to put a match to his shoe.

In a few months or perhaps a year, when the government gets its act together, maybe there will be real security. Now air travelers are merely playing the odds. If Congress had resisted the efforts of the airline industry to sink the 1996 Gore report, there might be real airport security today.

The one marginal improvement to safety is the locked cockpit door. It guarantees that no one with a box cutter can take control of a plane and use it as a bomb (as the FBI was warned someone was preparing to do). The Gore report wanted that reform. None of the tragedies of Sept. 11 would have occurred if the airline industry hadn't resisted it. We are at least safe from that particular brand of terrorism. Everything else is smoke and mirrors.

The president told us on the six-month anniversary that the war on terrorism was entering its second phase. He neglected to say that the first phase did not succeed. Osama bin Laden and most of his top staff are still free (probably hiding under the protection of Pakistanis). The Afghan war has been mostly a failure. Indeed, it eliminated a base for al-Qaida and probably set its plans back, but those too mean only marginal improvement in the safety of Americans.

Bush, who likes being a wartime president, is apparently concentrating his efforts on "getting" Saddam Hussein now that he's failed to "get" bin Laden. Never mind that Saddam had nothing to do with the World Trade Center destruction and does not seem to be engaged in terrorism at the present.

Our precision bombs could surely eliminate Saddam's "weapons of mass destruction" if the CIA could figure out where the facilities that manufacture them are. They can't find bin Laden, however, and it doesn't seem likely they can find Saddam's weapons centers, either. They might want to subcontract the task to the Israelis.

The main reason for Sept. 11 was the failure of American intelligence agencies. There is no reason to believe that the FBI, which has yet to find the anthrax killer, would react any differently to the report from Minnesota about Arabs who wanted to learn how to fly planes but were not interested in takeoffs or landings. They are still the same stumblebums who let Russian spy Robert Hanssen run amok with their secret files.

About all the CIA seems able to do is to provide raw material for Tom Ridge's cute new color-coded alert system. Unless there is deep reform of these agencies (to say nothing of Immigration, which gave permission to the terrorists to change their visas six months after Sept. 11), nothing else really matters. The question remains whether such reform is possible.

Thus for all the flags, all the manic singing of "God Bless America," all the bellicose rhetoric of the president, all the hyper-patriotism, all the elaborate security precautions, all Attorney General John Ashcroft's destruction of civil liberties, the American people are not much safer than they were Sept. 10.

May 17, 2002

History's forgotten lessons

The ancient Greeks had a word for pride: "hubris." It means more than just pride, however. It connotes arrogance, blindness, self-deception, the kind of pride that the English had before their disastrous defeat by the Zulus in Africa in 1879; the kind of pride that led Winston Churchill to commit British (i.e., Australian and New Zealand) troops to the disastrous Gallipoli campaign in 1916; Hitler's invasion of Russia; MacArthur's crossing the 38th Parallel in the Korean War; Lyndon Johnson's continuation of the Vietnam War. In every case there were those who warned against the folly of the "best and the brightest" to whom no one listened.

We learn from the *New York Times* that the Bush administration has postponed its invasion of Iraq from September to sometime after the first of January—though the *Times* never told us before that the hubris behind the plan had chosen September as a target date. September would have been a better time for a war because it would have confirmed Bush's role as a "wartime" president before the November congressional election.

It would also appear that it is civilians who want the war, and the military is reluctant: civilians in the Defense Department, the vice president's office and the White House. The president, of course, has the impulse to finish what his father failed to finish.

The Defense Department figures that five divisions could easily clean out Saddam Hussein's government, even without any support from the Arab world or from Europe. The United States can do it all by itself and doesn't need anyone's help.

Just like the best and the brightest of the early 1960s casually assumed that the United States could easily clean up the Viet Cong.

No one apparently remembers how quickly Americans turn against land wars in Asia that involve drawn-out combat with heavy casualties. World War II had become very unpopular in the spring and summer of 1945 after the heavy losses in the battles at Okinawa and Iwo Jima. The public was ready to turn against it when the atom bomb ended the war. The Korean War swept the Republicans back into power after 30 years. Vietnam became a national disaster.

Knocking off Saddam has been sold to the American people as part of the amorphous and ill-defined "war on terrorism," though there is no evidence that he was involved in the World Trade Center catastrophe (not that he was much troubled by it). Attacking Iraq has been a goal of right-wing ideologues since, as they see it, our failure to destroy Saddam when we had a chance at the end of the Persian Gulf War. The "war on terrorism" provides an excuse.

Moreover, since the president has yet to "smoke out bin Laden" and "get him," Saddam could become a useful substitute. If he should escape, then we could "get" the pertinent ayatollah in Iran.

The American people endorse the idea. Killing Arabs is bound to be a good idea. The Democrats in Congress are reluctant to oppose it. One hopes everyone remembers this hubris when the body bags begin to return.

The situation is so much like that of 1965, when Lyndon Johnson decided to commit a quarter-million troops to Vietnam (against the advice of his mentor, Georgia's Sen. Richard B. Russell), that it would scare anyone who has any memory for recent history.

No one seems ready to ask the tough questions: What would such a war accomplish? What are the problems that the military leaders see? Can we really do anything we want anywhere in the world? What casualties might we expect? How strong would be the resistance of the Iraqis, who might not like Saddam all that much but who, like most Arabs, hate Americans? Why is everyone else in the world—especially those who are likely targets for his weapons of mass destruction—against the war? Should we take seriously the cockeyed argument that by knocking off Saddam we will force the Palestinians to make peace with Israel?

Before we blunder into another pointless land war in Asia, should we not have a serious national debate about the dangers and the possible payoffs? Or is it enough to cheer our president and sing "God Bless America"?

Hubris.

July 12, 2002

Ancient Arabs' jewel of a gift

If one could go back to Europe in, let us say, the 11th or 12th centuries and search for the most civilized place on the continent, where would one end up? If a German nun told us about the "ornament of the world," to which country would she be directing us? Where would we encounter the most advanced science, the most sophisticated poetry, the best mathematics, the best link with the wisdom of ancient Greece, the most beautiful art and architecture, the most religious tolerance?

France? Germany? Italy? England?

No way.

The "ornament of the world" was Al Andalus or Andalusia—Arabic Spain. It had an enormous impact on the rest of Europe for centuries, an effect that has been forgotten in most general histories of the Middle Ages. In a new book, called appropriately *The Ornament of Europe,* Professor Maria Rosa Menocal of Yale paints a vivid picture of this extraordinary era of about 300 years when the Umayyad Dynasty presided over a country in which even Jews and Christians wrote in Arabic script, used Hebrew or Mozarabic ("not arabic")—an early form of Castilian—and wore Arabic garments.

The Arab rulers of Spain respected, as the Qur'an demands, the religions of the book (Christianity and Judaism) and employed those who were not Muslim in their government service.

Where do you think we got Arabic numerals from?

Later a dynasty of fundamentalist Berbers from North Africa took over Andalusia and shattered the kingdom built around Cordoba, though the rich cultural mix persisted. Arab Spain split into many quasi-independent city states, and the Catholic kingdoms of the north were able to make progress in the "Reconquest." However, under such rulers as Ferdinand III (St. Ferdinand) and Alfonso X ("The Learned") who ruled from Toledo, both the rich cultural diversity and religious tolerance continued. Even today when one visits Toledo, one is astonished at the beauty of Andalusian art—and dismayed that there are no Jews in Toledo to use the beautiful synagogue.

It was only after Isabella of Castile and Ferdinand of Aragon finally occupied Grenada (wearing, it was said, Moorish garb) that the remarkable history of Andalusia came to an end. "Their Most Catholic Majesties" ordered both Moors and Jews out of a country in which their ancestors had lived for seven centuries and thus ended one of the most remarkable phenomena of European history.

It was not only a cruel decision, but also remarkably stupid, and Spain suffers from it to this day. One hears it said occasionally that the Christians in Spain killed Jews, but the Muslims did not. In fact, there were periods of Muslim mass murder in Andalusia, too, under the Berber dynasties. Tolerance in those days did not mean the same thing that it does today, but there was still a general atmosphere at many times in the 700 years of Arab Spain of a willingness to live and let live.

The story of Andalusia should inoculate us against the anti-Islamic and anti-Arabic prejudices we often hear—as from former education secretary William Bennett, who believes that Islam is inherently violent. The same argument could be made with equal unfairness against Mr. Bennett's Catholic faith up to recent times when many German Catholics participated willingly enough in the Holocaust.

There is a temptation to imagine Arabs as swarthy, illiterate, bearded people who live in desert tents, fire automatic weapons into the air, and blow themselves up to kill the innocent. Doubtless there are some such, too many indeed. But that ought not blind us to the diversity and richness of the Arab heritage and our debt to it. Our ancestors learned much from that heritage and passed it on to us.

The Andalusian Arabs were civilized when many of our ancestors were living in mud huts and painting themselves blue and when the Irish, who were trying to civilize again the remnants of the Roman empire, did not have roads or towns or ports and were often sacking their own monasteries.

And can you imagine multiplying Roman numerals, much less doing calculus with them?

August 9, 2002

Even at its best, war is never predictable

Some words of warning for Donald Rumsfeld, Paul Wolfowitz, all the civilian war hawks in the Defense Department and for the president who wants to clear his father's honor by going to war in Iraq:

Never, never, never believe any war will be smooth and easy, or that anyone who embarks on that strange voyage can measure the tides and hurricanes he will encounter. The statesman who yields to war fever must realize that once the signal is given, he is no longer the master of policy but the slave of unforeseeable and uncontrollable events, weak, incompetent or arrogant commanders, untrustworthy allies, hostile neutrals, malignant fortune, ugly surprises, awful miscalculations—all which take their seat at the Council Board.

You can put quotes around that paragraph. It was written by Winston Churchill in 1930, reflecting on the experience of the Great Boer War of

1899 to 1902, a war that the English thought would be a cakewalk. A "change in regime" was necessary in Natal and the Transvaal. The English also believed that their prestige and credibility were at stake. Incalculable wealth in diamonds and gold would belong to the winner. When the war came to an ambiguous end with perhaps 100,000 dead—many in the "concentration camps" established by the English for Boer women and children—it seemed much less glorious.

In 1950, General MacArthur promised that the "boys would be home by Christmas." The great powers who blundered into the August 1914 war also thought it would be over by Christmas. Hitler was confident he could capture Moscow and eliminate Russian resistance before winter. Lyndon Johnson's advisers often thought they saw light at the end of the tunnel.

War is always a great mistake. There are no just wars, but there are some necessary wars. The war against Hitler and the Japanese military was surely necessary, but terrible evil was done to German and Japanese civilians in the firebomb raids by British and American planes. The former were unsuccessful, the latter successful, but in retrospect, probably not necessary. Neither does the use of the atom bomb seem to have been necessary. In all three cases, however, those who made the decisions about these attacks believed that they were necessary. War blinds even the good guys to the evil they may be doing.

The Vietnam War was not necessary. However, after America's leaders had stumbled into the "Big Muddy," it seemed to develop a necessity all its own and created havoc from which our society has yet to recover. It is easy to compare Secretary Donald Rumsfeld to Secretary Robert McNamara and Paul Wolfowitz to McGeorge Bundy. The former two were successful businessmen turned war ministers and the latter two brilliant Cold War intellectuals. In both cases, with an attitude of serenity and insouciance that is astonishing, they launched this country (or plan to launch it) into an unnecessary war with little concern for the likely catastrophic consequences.

Suppose it will require only 250,000 American troops. It is not unreasonable to project a 5 percent casualty rate, perhaps 15,000 body bags. Tens of thousands—perhaps hundreds of thousands—of Iraqis will die. And Americans will worry no more about their deaths than we did about the deaths of Japanese and German civilians.

In the end, we will not have found Saddam any more than we have found bin Laden. Chemical and biological weapons will have fallen on Israel. Oil prices will have gone sky high. A shattering blow will have hit the fragile American economy. Inflation will shoot up. The International Criminal Court will have indicted many Americans (including perhaps the president). Iraq will be a mess. There will be more violence throughout the

Near East. Our relationships with our allies will have been sundered. The real war on terrorism will have been neglected. Iraq will be a mess, perhaps for years or even decades. The United States will be more of a police state than it has ever been.

One has the impression that experts have told the war hawks all these possibilities, just as the military leaders in the Pentagon have warned them against the war. Yet so arrogantly confident are they in American power and so impressed by the president's popularity ratings that they do not hear the warnings.

Unless someone can stop this relentless and manic rush to war, there will be bad times ahead, very bad times.

August 23, 2002

Why do we fear Saddam?

Why aren't the Israelis screaming about "weapons of mass destruction" in Iraq? Why aren't they demanding a "regime change"? Why aren't they shouting about "an axis of evil"? They must know that they would be the prime target for Saddam Hussein. Are they not afraid of him?

Perhaps they are able to contain their fear because they know that if he lobs one of his Scud missiles with something deadly aboard into Tel Aviv, they would wipe him and his country off the face of the Earth. They also know that, as crazy as he is, he knows that, too. Somewhere in all of the concern about Iraq, people have forgotten that Israel has atomic weapons and the ability to deliver them. Unless the Israel Defense Force is much less competent than one has any reason to believe, it probably has its targets already selected. Moreover, unless the Mossad is as incompetent as the CIA, it probably has a pretty good idea where Saddam is hiding out on any given night.

Why aren't the Iranians terrified of Saddam? They fought a long, bloody war with him not so long ago. Might he not wipe out Tehran just for the fun of it? And Syria should clearly be on his hit list. Its rival version of the Arab Socialist Renaissance Party (Baath) is a constant threat to Saddam's claim to Baathist orthodoxy. And Kuwait: Would he not invade it again? And would he not throw out the Saudi royal family and take over its oil? And has he forgotten that Egypt sent several (not very useful) divisions into Operation Desert Storm?

If all of these countries, clearly in range of Saddam's delivery systems, are not afraid of him, why is the United States? If they don't want to band together to get rid of him, why are we obliged to do it for them? Why must we risk tens of thousands of American lives and our fragile economy on a war that they apparently don't think necessary?

Or if it is necessary, could we subcontract it to Israel?

Michael O'Brien, a senior British Foreign Office type, remarked the other day that no one wants a war just so there can be a war. He has it wrong, however. The war-hawk civilian intellectuals in or near the administration—Dick Cheney, Donald Rumsfeld, Paul Wolfowitz, Richard Perle—do want a war just to prove that the United States is boss, even if the military leaders stoutly resist the idea. They began the present administration by deciding to push around Russia. Vladimir Vladimirevitch finessed them out of that scheme. So Iraq is the next best thing. The issue has become not why have a war, but why not have a war. It will tune us up to take on China.

Republican Rep. Dick Armey dissents. We should attack only when we're attacked, he says. The congressman is a typical Republican isolationist from an earlier era. He doesn't like the idea of silly foreign wars. What does he know? Yet, while the Democrats remain nervously silent (save for Sen. John Kerry), it is Republicans such as Armey and Bush One defense intellectuals such as Brent Scowcroft and Lawrence Eagleburger who astonishingly emerge as doves.

If Saddam is truly afraid of Israel (as he must be, because he didn't dump any poison gas on them during the last war), then surely he must be terribly afraid of the United States, for all his wild threats. He must realize that should he be involved in any terrorism in the United States, no American government could resist the demand to reply with nuclear weapons (however immoral such a response would be). Mess with America, and it'll wipe you out. Look what happened to Japan. It's not so much Mutual Assured Destruction, as with Russia during the Cold War. It's Assured Destruction for Saddam.

All of these considerations are unpleasant, not to say terrifying. The point, however, is that they raise the serious question that one rarely hears from the White House or from Capitol Hill about whether we have any solid reason for being afraid of Iraq. One hears that the president must make the case. Yet the real issue is whether there is in fact a case to be made.

Being a wartime president is great fun at first. Your popularity rating goes sky high. You can do no wrong. Unfortunately, that fun does not last. Ask Lyndon Johnson. Ask Harry Truman.

September 20, 2002

Hawks offer no proof to justify attack

If Saddam Hussein used his usual stalling techniques against a new wave of U.N. inspectors, would the United States be justified in going to war on the grounds that the U.N. had failed once again?

The "just war" theory is under attack within the Christian communities. There is no such thing as a just war, it is argued, because modern weapons are so horrific. All wars are therefore unjust, and the only alternative for Christians is passive resistance to those who attack them. Insofar as this position would deny humans the right of self-defense, it seems to lack common sense. If it were followed in the early 1940s, either Hitler or Stalin would have ruled the world, and most of us would be either dead or never born.

The pacifist argument does serve as a warning that even just wars create situations where terrible evil is done by the side that is legitimately defending itself. The Red Army, for example, raped 2 million German women in the final weeks of the war. The weakness of pacifism is that, if all wars are evil, then one cannot make a particular case against a specific war. One cannot argue that an American invasion of Iraq seems unnecessary because, by definition, all wars, even necessary wars, cannot be justified.

What causes, in addition to those required for any just war, might justify a preemptive strike against an enemy whom one suspects of preparing an attack against oneself?

The people who write about just wars normally list two conditions for a preemptive attack: the seriousness of the threat and its imminence. If the American Navy had encountered Admiral Yamamoto's fleet on its way to Hawaii, it would have been perfectly justified in attacking it. As the admiral himself said, the Japanese were determined to wipe out the American fleet so they could run wild in Southeast Asia (serious) and they were about to bomb Pearl Harbor in a matter of days (imminent).

In the present circumstances, if the U.N. inspections should fail (not an unexpected result), is the Iraqi threat to the United States serious and imminent? The gang of four war hawks around the president—Richard Cheney, Donald Rumsfeld, Paul Wolfowitz and Richard Perle—all insist that it is both. They are doubtless displeased that Secretary of State Colin

Powell was able to persuade the president to go the United Nations route and force Iraq to accept the return of inspectors. They have been saying all along that additional inspections will be a waste of time.

However, they offer no proof other than their own repeated assertions that an attack by Saddam is both imminent and serious. They have promised to "make the case" to Congress, to America's allies, to the U.N. and finally to the American people. They have in fact not produced such proof. One is entitled to suspect that none exists. They made up their minds long ago that Iraq was a threat that must be eliminated.

Iraq lacks the delivery systems to be a serious nuclear threat to the United States even if it develops atomic bombs. Its biological and chemical weapons have existed since before the Gulf War. That it has not turned them over to al-Qaida suggests that it will not. In both cases, attacks on the United States would, rightly or wrongly, lead to the elimination of Iraq. It does not then seem to be a serious threat to the United States. As for the imminence of such an attack, one wonders how the gang of four knows that it might happen in three years? If they have such evidence they should certainly reveal it to the American people.

Nor should one count them out because Powell has outmaneuvered them. They still have the president's ear, and in the past, he seemed to like what they were saying.

So without proof of the seriousness or the imminence of an Iraqi attack and because of the so-called war on terrorism, and despite the apparent American diplomatic victory at the U.N. in forcing inspectors back into Iraq, the United States may still stumble into a war that is evil and unjust and in which thousands and perhaps tens of thousands of people will die horrible deaths.

When good does evil to fight evil, it becomes indistinguishable from its enemy. God help us.

October 4, 2002

Following Bush over the edge

When Herta Daeubler-Gmelin, the justice minister in German Chancellor Gerhard Schroeder's cabinet, compared President Bush to Adolf Hitler because both men stir up fears of war at election time, she demonstrated how little history one needs to know to become justice minister in a cabinet made up of Socialists and "Greens."

Hitler never needed to create fears of war at election times because by the time he was ready to go to war, there were no elections in Germany. Granted, Bush's creation of the current war fever is a cynical attempt to win full Republican control of Congress (an attempt that will doubtless succeed). Schroeder was doing the same thing. Indeed, running against Bush was as cynical as Bush's running against Saddam Hussein. The Christian Democrat in Germany, incidentally, was no better than Schroeder. He ran against immigrants.

It would have been better, however, to compare the American president to Alexander the Great or Julius Caesar or Napoleon Bonaparte. Indeed, if the Bush Doctrine becomes the governing document for a new world order, the word "Bush" might become a common noun meaning emperor, as Caesar (Czar, Kaiser, etc.) became.

The Bush Doctrine formally installs the United States not only as a global power but as the only global power. No other nation in the world will be permitted to match America's military might. Any foreign power seen to be a potential adversary of the United States will be crushed whenever the United States thinks it's appropriate. Schroeder's Germans better not get too uppity. We beat them in two wars. We can do it again if we have to.

Bush, a man whose previous efforts never went much beyond presiding over a notably unsuccessful baseball team, has now proclaimed himself emperor of all the world. Not bad for a man who lost the presidential election by a half million popular votes.

One is astonished at how little attention the fantasies of the Bush Doctrine have received. Released after the orgy of the September anniversary, in the midst of the run-up to an Iraq war and at a time when Donald Rumsfeld is seeing al-Qaida agents swarming all around Iraq, the Bush Doctrine has hardly been noticed. No one has asked how many lives, American and others, might have to be lost, how many widows and orphans will be left in grief, how many cities destroyed to achieve this vision.

Nor has anyone wondered whether the goal of the Bush Doctrine can be achieved by American military and economic power all by itself. Even Alexander, Caesar and Napoleon had need of allies. There is no clear evidence in the Bush Doctrine that we need allies. We'll go it alone whenever and wherever we want.

Richard Perle, a powerful adviser to the Pentagon, is supposed to have said on the record that he hopes the United States has to go it alone in Iraq because that means we can use tactical nuclear weapons. Hooray for us!

Perhaps the American public is beginning to catch on. Polls show that more than half of Americans think President Bush is moving too quickly on Iraq. Yet one wonders if there is a sense in the country yet, so spooked by the Sept. 11 disaster, just how dangerous the present situation could be. Some Democratic politicians are making modest noises of dissent, but there is no sign that they are prepared to yell "stop before it's too late!"

In years to come, people will wonder, I think, how Americans could have tolerated the Bush administration's hysterical claims to imperial power and right, how they could have stood by in relative equanimity as the country plunged into folly.

During the War, Germans often said, "Today Germany, tomorrow the world!" The Bush Doctrine is a little different. It says we already own the world, so tomorrow or the next day we'll take out Iraq. And the day after that anyone else who seems to threaten us.

We live not so much in dangerous times as in times of mass hysteria, stoked by cynics who want to use the hysteria to claim all power for themselves.

November 29, 2002

New monster bureaucracy holds no promise

I sure am happy that we at last have a Department of Homeland Security. We've needed something like that for a long time. Most Americans will undoubtedly sleep better at night because they know that the creation of this department is the biggest change in the shape of the federal government since President Harry Truman thought up the Department of Defense back in the 1940s.

No one would dare complain that the Defense Department is the worst bureaucratic mess in our republic and that the attempt to combine the armed forces has been a crashing failure. Truman might have been able to pull off his merger if he were willing, more or less, to abolish the Navy. As it was, this last effort to solve a problem by a forced merger quickly degenerated into the futility of constant scheming and conflict among the services for more power and a bigger share of the budget. The result was a grotesque and inefficient process of military procurement, an enormous waste of money, and creeping paralysis. Truman would have been more successful if he had been able to carry off the combination of all three services into one "U.S. Military Establishment."

Obviously, President Bush wouldn't let something like that happen with his new plaything, would he? Yet isn't it somewhat curious that the party that has consistently opposed bureaucracy has created a new and monstrous bureaucracy? Isn't it odd that the president, for whom "Washington bureaucrat" has become a dirty word, has created a newer, larger and more muscle-bound bureaucracy than existed before the merger? What are his reasons for thinking that it will not go the same way as the Defense Department? How does he know that the bureaucracies that have been forced together in this shotgun plural marriage will not act like the Army, the Air Force, the Marines and the Navy? How will he prevent the same paralysis of bureaucratic infighting?

The answer is that he doesn't know because it is most unlikely that he or anyone else can prevent the merger from making the homeland more insecure rather than less (or perhaps, given the current disregard for civil liberties, it should be called the Fatherland Department). It is in the nature of bureaucrats to fight for turf and for money. The goal of winning these fights becomes more important than the formal goals of an agency, because winning the internecine battles for money and turf is seen as a matter of survival. A sociologist back in the last century called it the Iron Law of Oligarchy.

However, in the present mood in Washington, the creation of a new congeries of oligarchies and dubbing it "Homeland Security" is an easy substitute for actually improving security—for example, hunting down the involvement of Saudi royalty in financing terrorism.

Mergers rarely work—indeed, on the record, they almost never work. Consider for example BancOne or AOL Time-Warner. The former cost the new company all the wealth that BancOne (as it was called then, apparently because those in charge couldn't spell) had brought to the table. The latter destroyed the bubble wealth of AOL and devastated the wealth of the investors in the combined company. Corporate structures with their own style, their own mission, their own memories do not fit well together, whether the structures are government or business. In mergers, the result is almost always less than the sum of the parts. Every time you hear media celebration of this new monster, the words "Department of Homeland Security" spoken trippingly on the tongue, just think of AOL Time-Warner. The Bush administration is weakening rather than strengthening the effectiveness of the component parts of its new monster.

One must wonder why. Is it the fact that the merger will cost tens of thousands of government employees their civil service and collective bargaining rights? Is it the pork that has been sneaked into the legislation for insurance companies and drug companies? Those goals are understandable political payoffs.

But the pretense that the nation will be safer because this new, super bureaucracy is creeping down the Mall in Washington like the Blob from Outer Space is either dishonest or stupid. Or an excuse for not taking on the task of merging the FBI and CIA (and maybe the National Security Agency), which, as almost impossible as it may be, would truly improve our nation's security.

January 3, 2003

Bush on the warpath without proof

Early next month the war with Iraq apparently will begin. There's nothing like a good war to stir up patriotic fervor. Moreover, the so-called chicken hawks at the Defense Department have wanted to invade Iraq for years because they think that will bring an end to the conflict in Israel. The administration decided long ago that there would be a war. The so-called war on terrorism has provided a cover for starting it. The men around the president are persuaded that the American people will overwhelmingly support the war.

However, recent surveys call into question that assumption. Only 52 percent of Americans support a war, according to Gallup. Moreover, two-thirds of Americans insist that they want to see proof—either from the report of the United Nations inspectors or from American intelligence evidence—of the "weapons of mass destruction" that Iraq is alleged to possess.

Thus, it seems clear that the public is not convinced yet that a war is necessary. The administration has yet to provide clear and convincing proof that Iraq has these "weapons of mass destruction" and is prepared to use them. I wonder if our leaders really do have anything more than their absolute conviction that such weapons exist and that the president's popularity is so great that the public will go along with the war if he says it is necessary.

Is there any stronger evidence, and if there is, why haven't we seen it yet?

Yet last week's issue of *Time*—which celebrates the Bush-Cheney team as though it is Michael and Gabriel—provides data that runs against the notion that Americans are enthusiastic supporters of the administration. The president's approval rating has dropped to 55 percent. The country is split between those who say they trust the president (50 percent) and those who don't (48 percent). No one seems to have noticed that the 60 percent approval rating the media have celebrated all these months is about the same as President Bill Clinton's at the time of the Lewinsky scandal.

Moreover, 42 percent trust the vice president as opposed to 51 percent who have their doubts. It sounds very much like November 2000—too close to call. Maybe, in the absence of proof, the Supreme Court can be called in to resolve the doubt about attacking Iraq.

That's not much support for a war. If it turns out to be a short war and quick and "inexpensive" (which means a lot of Iraqi casualties but not many American ones), the public won't mind. But what if it's much longer, and the invading American divisions are badly chewed up, and the National Guard must be called into action, and the war drags on to the summer, and there's talk of a military draft? The country will be on the edge of another Vietnam.

Or what if the U.N. teams can't find very strong evidence of Iraqi weapons and throw up their hands in uncertainty? What proportion of Americans will nonetheless support a war, the proof of the necessity of which is problematic? More than a third, surely, but a lot less than half.

The administration seems bent on a gamble—a reckless gamble at best.

Saddam Hussein is a nasty, vile man. If he has atomic weapons ready to go, if he has large supplies of nerve gas and anthrax and smallpox germs and intends to use them soon, then there can be no serious objection to a war. One prays that it will be short so not too many lives—American and Iraqi—will be lost.

Messrs. Cheney, Rumsfeld, Wolfowitz, Perle, Safire and the *Wall Street Journal* are all convinced that the situation is urgent. We must strike at Iraq while there is still time. I do not question the sincerity of their convictions. Yet it does not seem unreasonable to ask—as do two out of three Americans—that they show us better proof than they already have.

And one wonders if the hapless leaders of the Democratic Party will continue to stand idle and silent as the country plunges into a war that, absent better evidence, might be senseless folly.

January 31, 2003

Is the impending war all about oil?

Cynics, leftists and populists all over the world believe it is.

The United States, it is said, wants to control Iraq because it has the second-largest oil reserves in the Middle East. One can make a good case for the argument. The United States is run by Texas oil millionaires whose friends and allies could make a lot of money if Iraq became a de facto

American colony. Moreover, such a victory would notably shift the calculus for world oil prices and upset the power of OPEC to plunge the world into periodic economic crises. Already unacceptably powerful (according to the argument), America would dominate the world's oil supply.

I doubt very much that these thoughts are absent from the minds of those in the White House and the Pentagon who want the war. How could they be? If it were not for oil, would the United States have much reason to care about the Middle East? Yet, it is not likely that the chicken hawks are quite that cynical. The war will only be indirectly about oil. It will be about weapons of mass destruction (which no one seems to have found yet), but with the oil possibilities on their minds if not on their lips.

In the absence of evidence that will convince the skeptical American people, there are other possible reasons for starting a war. First of all, it will convince the rest of the world that the Bush administration is as tough and strong as it says it is. It will make clear that the president's swaggering walk and pointed finger are proof that he is not a hollow man or just a Texas cowboy sheriff.

Moreover, it will provide the president with another opportunity to demonstrate his abilities as a wartime leader. Nothing helps a president's popularity with the people as much as patriotism in time of war.

Again, I'm not suggesting that the president and those around him are deliberately pursuing such goals. However, it is most unlikely that such thoughts are not on their minds.

Some of the other reasons for war are not secret. The chicken hawks are pro-Israel. One often hears from their media allies (the *Wall Street Journal*'s editorial page; William Safire in the *New York Times*) that the toppling of Saddam Hussein will solve the problems of Israel. They never explain why this would happen. The Palestinians have been resisting Israel one way or another for more than a half century. Can anyone seriously think that the end of Saddam would cause them to give up their fight? Quite the contrary, their suicide bombers would ratchet up their attacks to kill not only Israelis but Americans too.

It is also contended that a democratic regime in Iraq would open up the possibility for other democratic governments in the Arab world. One cannot imagine a more absurd notion. A quick survey of Arab countries suggests that there is no democracy and few civil liberties in any of them. It may well be that Western-style democracy is incompatible with Arab culture. Certainly, an American-style democracy imposed by force of arms in Iraq is not going to persuade Arabs that they should try to imitate such a regime.

Indeed, only Turkey provides an example of a relatively stable Western-style democracy in a predominantly Islamic nation, and Turkey is a frankly secularist country.

One assembles all these reasons for war, considers them together, and discovers that they are as thin as tissue paper. The only good reason for war would be that Iraq is an immediate threat to the United States. There may well be such a threat, but that remains to be demonstrated. The American leadership has at least convinced itself that the threat exists. Clearly, many Americans believe that the threat is real, although two-thirds remain skeptical.

Perhaps the government will at last show us some hard evidence.

I may well be mistaken—anyone on either side of the debate may be mistaken—yet it seems to me that a war at this time would be gravely wrong. Many of those young men and women we have seen bidding tearful farewells to their families will die—thousands, perhaps tens of thousands of them. Many Iraqis will die, too—perhaps hundreds of thousands. Our leaders will be condemned all over the world as war criminals, which they surely would seem to be.

All the reasons don't add up to war on Iraq.

February 7, 2003

If you feel a draft, watch out

The option of a military draft and compulsory national service has oozed out of the dark shadows in which it has hidden for a quarter of a century. The suggestion by Rep. Charles Rangel (D-N.Y.) that a draft is necessary so that war would not be fought mainly by minorities didn't win much support because it turns out that the overrepresentation of African Americans and Hispanics in the military is not all that large. Those who have supported compulsory national service have used his argument and the likelihood of war in Iraq as an excuse to push their agenda once again.

They argue that it is the duty of young people (men and women) to give some years of their life to the government. I don't know where this duty comes from, except maybe from the military traditions of ancient Sparta. The government does not own the lives of Americans of any age, unless they are convicted criminals. Compulsory national service would deprive the young of their freedom without due process of the law.

Many young Americans, perhaps more than ever, are willing to dedicate several years of service to some worthy cause. Why should this honorable impulse to volunteer be turned into an obligation? National service is a totalitarian idea that some ideologues support because it makes the country a neat, orderly place in which the government straightens out the rebellious young of the country. Nobel laureate Milton Friedman has argued for a long time that a draft is an unfair taxation of the young in favor of the older. The latter get the work and the bodies of young people at a much lower price than it would otherwise cost.

The availability of a plentiful supply of such young bodies is an open invitation to the leadership of the country to go to war. If there had not been a draft, our ill-advised involvement in Korea and Vietnam never would have occurred.

I fear that if our existing professional (volunteer) army is badly chewed up in the Iraqi desert, the present administration might call for a draft in the name of a patriotic victory in the war on terrorism.

Because many "right-thinking" Americans always have supported compulsory national service, the administration might possibly get its way.

I don't think it will come to this, though it is worth noting that the chicken hawks have not fought in wars and really do not know firsthand what war is like. If push comes to shove, they might not mind sending the drafted sons and daughters of others to die in the desert.

National service had its origins in 19th-century Europe, where massive reserve armies were thought necessary for national defense. When war threatened, the reserves were mobilized. Thus in the Franco-Prussian war of 1870, Prussia proved much more efficient in mobilizing its reserves and easily defeated the French. The idea was to get your soldiers away from their family and their work quickly, then hit the enemy with a quick and solid blow and win a victory in a single battle. The Germans routed the French at Sedan and won the war.

Then in 1914 France, Germany, Russia and Austria all mobilized quickly (because of the relative efficiency of their respective railroads). Once you have mobilized armies, there's not much you can do with them except start a war. In historical hindsight, there is little doubt that the mobilizations of the summer of 1914 made a foolish and unnecessary war inevitable.

Many European countries still require national military service, though it is not clear that the reserve military that it is supposed to produce means anything in modern war. It would be much better if there were some kind of international agreement to outlaw drafts. The cause of peace would benefit if the elderly people who run governments did not have at their disposal the bodies of young men and women they can use for cannon fodder.

The world would be a much better place if all countries had a small volunteer military, though it is tragic to see such people bid farewell to their families and go off to face the risk of disease and maiming and death in the desert because a president thinks that John Wayne is an appropriate model for world leadership.

There are too many in this country who proclaim the need for sacrifice when neither they nor their children are likely to be the sacrificial victims.

February 14, 2003

U.S. must prepare for war that might not go according to plan

These last two weeks Americans have suffered spasms of grief over the death of the crew of the space shuttle *Columbia*. Few understood—or cared—that the ultimate reason for their deaths is the same as that of the deaths of the crew of *Challenger*. As sociologist Diane Vaughan argued in her magisterial book on the earlier disaster, the Congress and president have tried consistently through the years to run a low-budget space program. Either the country should end the program or give it the money necessary for a program that is both successful and safe.

Yet there is an irony in the national grief over the deaths of seven brave astronauts against the background of preparation for a war in which thousands of brave Americans may suffer horrible deaths from poison gas or disease in the deserts of Iraq.

In its initial assessment of Saddam Hussein's weapons of mass destruction, the CIA said he was unlikely to use them unless he was attacked. Therefore, we prepare to attack him. If he does have the capacity to use such weapons, as our swashbuckling president argues, then he will surely use them against our forces in the desert. Why not? He has nothing to lose.

Almost certainly he will try to use these weapons against Israel, too. The Israelis will probably respond by using an atom bomb to obliterate

Baghdad. Such an attack will unleash all the furies of war in the Middle East.

Again, if he has nothing to lose, the Iraqi dictator may well do exactly what we are invading to avoid: He might turn over his anthrax and smallpox germs to al-Qaida. Thus, an invasion of Iraq may accomplish just those fearsome tragedies that it is designed to prevent. Saddam may well die, but he'll die convinced that history will hail him as the greatest Islamic leader since Saladin. Why don't the brilliant chicken-hawk thinkers in the administration take these terrible possibilities into account?

One thing seems certain: Americans will have many, many more people to mourn.

These disasters, please God, might not happen. But they might. What will those Americans do who mourned the *Columbia* tragedy yet were silent as young men and women were shipped off to horrible deaths?

Most likely they will stand around and sing "God Bless America"!

The United States will doubtless win the war. I hope that it wins in something closer to Secretary of Defense Donald Rumsfeld's six days than six weeks—not to say six months. A short war will mean fewer deaths, of both Americans and Iraqis. It might also mean that there will be no time for attacks on Tel Aviv.

Yet I have little confidence in the Pentagon's ability to win quickly and efficiently. The Army has been notoriously inefficient in such situations (consider the Apache helicopters in Kosovo). How long will it take the forces we are rushing in to Turkey to gather together their logistics, plan an attack, and then pour into northern Iraq? More likely they will just rush in, hoping with the help of the local Kurds to sweep away all resistance and to seize the precious oil fields of Mosul for the American oil companies before Saddam can set them on fire. Maybe they'll be lucky; maybe resistance will collapse quickly. Maybe. Yet such a slapdash campaign would invite a catastrophe if there are enough Iraqis prepared to fight.

If there is one lesson we can learn from military history, it's that the best-laid plans of even the most powerful armies and most brilliant generals quickly go awry when the battle begins. Napoleon had Waterloo all figured out. Yet he ended up running back to Paris.

I can't imagine the relatively small force we are sending into Iraq (three Army divisions, two Marine "expeditionary forces") turning tail and running. I hope that does not happen because it would cause so many more deaths. Yet war is always chaotic and unpredictable—not the easy, well-ordered, planned ballet that the president and the defense secretary and the chicken hawks seem to think. I wish they were less confident and more aware of everything that could go wrong.

February 21, 2003

No sympathy for American devil

Consider these words about war and the president:

War is in fact the true nurse of executive aggrandizement. In war a physical force is created, and it is the executive will to direct it. In war the public treasures are to be unlocked, and it is the executive hand which is to dispense them. In war the honor and emoluments of office are to be multiplied; and it is the executive patronage under which they are to be enjoyed. It is in war, finally, that laurels are to be gathered and it is the executive brow they are to encircle. The strongest passions and the most dangerous weakness of the human breast—ambition, avarice, vanity, the honorable or venal love of fame—are all in conspiracy against the desire and duty of peace.

Who wrote that rather baroque paragraph? A liberal democratic intellectual? A Protestant church person? Someone in the Vatican?

No. It was James Madison.

When he was president, Madison led us into a foolish war during which the English burned the White House. The flag still flying over Fort McHenry was a nice symbol, but not exactly a victory. The battle of New Orleans, which enabled some Americans to claim that we hadn't lost the war (which, of course, we had) came after the peace treaty was signed. Madison must have reflected that his earlier words were a chilling prophecy of what happens when a president is out of control.

At least Madison insisted on the passage in the Constitution that required that Congress must declare war—a passage that since Korea has become moot.

If one reads Bob Woodward's admiring book *Bush at War*, one can see Madison's point. A man of strong patriotism and deep religious faith, George W. Bush is not troubled by nuanced thought, a sense of the ambiguity of human events, or a need to build coalitions as his father did. He is innocent of the complex concept that, like his father and his predecessor, he is president not only of the United States but of much of the world and must protect his credibility with that constituency as well.

Instead, he says we can and will do it ourselves (whatever "it" might be), and we don't need anyone else. One leads by doing, and the others will follow. Too bad for them.

So he has people all over the world hating Americans and opposing the war, even in the countries whose leaders have embraced the American cause. Even in Ireland, where anti-Americanism was present only among the intellectuals until recently, the majority wants the government to ban American refueling stops at Shannon Airport, and members of the Catholic Worker attack American planes with axes and hammers.

"Our president," as Republicans like to call Bush (the term never applies to a Democratic president), having lost the election by a half-million votes, has succeeded brilliantly in turning the whole world anti-American. In fact, the Supreme Court delivered the United States into the hands of the hard-right, imperialist, fundamentalist, death-penalty wing of the Republican Party (the president's "base").

In the wake of the World Trade Center attack, the public bought the rhetoric of patriotic imperialism. Now it is changing its mind. Most Americans do not support a "go it alone" war. And the president's approval rating is down to 55 percent—lower than his predecessor at the time of the Monica Lewinsky scandal.

After September 2001, the United States enjoyed the sympathy and support of virtually everyone in the world. In a little over a year, the president has managed to waste all that sympathy. Not bad.

I don't mean French President Jacques Chirac and German Chancellor Gerhard Schroeder. They are merely cheap politicians who see votes to be won by pandering to the anti-Americanism of their own people. They are not important. The administration has offended by its insensitivity, its arrogance and its cement-headed imperialism the ordinary people of Europe—including our English allies and, heaven save us all, the Irish. And the pope!

Nice going, Mr. President!

March 14, 2003

War is not the Smart Option

The disasters that have afflicted American foreign policy in the last weeks should raise once again the question raised during the campaign three years ago: Is George W. Bush intelligent enough to be president of the United States? By a margin of a half million votes, the American people decided he was not. By a margin of one vote, the U.S. Supreme Court decided that he was.

The *Wall Street Journal* last week in an article about the Korean mess (written by three journalists) argued that the two sides are talking past one another. The key theme was that the North Korean government is frightened by the U.S. administration.

The fears, as it seems to them, are based on four events: the suspension of discussion during the first year of the Bush administration (while the president reviewed the Clinton administration's policy, just as he reviewed the terrorism policy till just before the World Trade Center attack); his gratuitous "axis of evil" category that included North Korea; his refusal to approve direct negotiations with North Korea; and finally, the warning of a possible "surgical strike" to take out North Korea's nuclear plants.

The "axis of evil" remark may have done it all by itself. You lump a country with Iraq, what do you expect that country to do except get ready to fight?

Now we are entering a war that most countries in the world—as well as most people—oppose. You lose almost all your allies, including perhaps Mexico and Canada. You cannot make a $20 billion bribe stick with the Turks (the world's most bribable people). You preside over the probable destruction of NATO and the Security Council by your rhetoric. Finally, you swagger into a news conference, and you talk about putting your hand on the Bible and swearing to protect the people of the United States. Saddam Hussein is a virtual ally of al-Qaida and is a direct threat to the American people, whom you've sworn to defend. Never mind that neither of these presumptions has been proved.

And all of this while the market and the economy tank because of war fear.

The *New York Times* quotes presidential staffers as saying that the president sees the world as a "biblical struggle of good vs. evil." The name of that is fanaticism.

The father built up coalitions. The son destroys them. It takes a lot of effort to destroy in less than a year coalitions that previous presidents spent a half century and more putting together. This is not a very smart man, but one who is surrounded by very smart people who have managed by their arrogance in a couple of years to drive off almost all of our friends and allies and lead us into a foolish and frivolous war.

Suppose that all goes well and the war is won in a couple of weeks. Suppose that the people of Iraq do eagerly welcome their American liberators.

Suppose even that some weapons of mass destruction are found and destroyed. It would still have been a bad war, a war fought out of fear and rage with disregard for the simple principles of morality. Many men and women on both sides will be dead because of Bush's personal conviction of his own moral goodness. It is all justified in the name of "freedom," which seems to mean that the United States is free to do just about anything it wants.

I make no case for the 12-year failure of the Security Council or the verbal gyrations of Hans Blix. Yet the only reasons for starting the war now seem to be that our troops are in place and that the president has grown impatient with Saddam.

Are these sufficient reasons for the death and destruction, the broken bodies and the broken hearts that our pious, if not all that smart, president and his team of chicken hawks are about to cause?

I don't think so.

If this country was truly the great country it pretends to be and indeed has on occasion been, it would be great enough to show some self-restraint before it began to drop its bombs.

God bless America? God save America? Or God forgive America?

March 21, 2003

Pope doesn't tell us what to think

A while back, the *New York Times* sent one of its reporters who writes fiction about the Catholic Church out to interview Catholics about the conflict they feel when they make up their minds whether to side with the pope or the president over the war. (This was the same woman who assured the world on the front page of the *New York Times* that "healthy priests" began to jump ship in the 1970s.)

She knew there was going to be conflict among Catholics over the pope and the president because, as she told her readers, Catholics tend to be "conservative." If you're a fiction writer on things Catholic for the *New York Times*, you don't have to check with its survey unit, which could have told you that on most political issues Catholics tilt in the liberal direction.

Sure enough, she found what she was looking for: Catholics anguished about whether they should go along with the pope against the president.

They were used to obeying the pope, but they were American patriots who, like the president, were fearful of what Saddam Hussein might do with his weapons of mass destruction. If you're sent out on assignment to find conflicted Catholics, you'll certainly be able to find them. What's it like to be a person whose instincts are conservative when the pope who tells Catholics what to think insists they should oppose the war?

Great story. It confirms what many Americans know about Catholics: They really can't think for themselves! Might it be that Catholics who disagree with the pope on many issues are quite capable of making up their own minds on the war? To settle the issue, they might ask the survey people to publish cross-tabulations of attitudes toward the war by religion, something the *Times* rarely does, perhaps because to do so would be to admit that religion is important in American life. I expect that such a tabulation would show that Catholics tend to be against the war, not because of the pope but because they tend to be Democrats, and this war is a Republican war: 70 percent of the Republicans support it as opposed to 30 percent of the Democrats.

The pope is also in trouble with the Republican punditocracy, which has been lecturing him recently on why the war against Iraq is indeed a just war.

The *Wall Street Journal* also warned the pope that he ought to rein in the Vatican publications and the Curia cardinals who are clearly anti-American.

Maybe they are. Like most Europeans, the Curia has been anti-American for a long time. His Holiness minimally has been impatient with American foreign policy. Might one say that is his right? Does not a moral and spiritual leader have the obligation to speak up against evil when he sees it? Does he not have an obligation to apply the just war doctrine to the events he observes? His opinions on the subject deserve attention and respect from Catholics—and everyone else.

However, he is not telling Catholics what they should think, only what he thinks. He is not obliging us in conscience to accept his reading of the situation. One should not have to say that; yet so strong is the current surge of anti-Catholicism in America, one has to repeat it over and over again—and not expect to be heard. The people in the major media know that Catholics have to agree with the pope.

Those of us who have grave doubts about the war will quote the pope often, if only to challenge the fundamentalist piety of the Bush administration, if only to suggest that God is not always on the Republican side. Maybe, just maybe, the pope knows a little bit more than George W. Bush about war and peace.

Some of the Republican pundits shade their criticism of the pope with allusions to the moral problems in the Catholic priesthood. Those who write letters pull no punches. Usually in obscene terms they suggest that the pope should both shut his mouth and do something about clerical sexual abuse.

That argument merely shows how morally and intellectually bankrupt many Republicans are these days. Bush's war has corrupted them.

March 28, 2003

Final Four beats the war

War is not a spectator sport! For Lent I've given up watching the war on TV. The media obsession with the war is immoral. It hides the killing. Even if my beloved Arizona Wildcats lose to the hated Fighting Irish, I will watch basketball instead of the war.

I will watch the news every evening—on the BBC, whose reporters are more objective and its anchors less pompous. I'll listen to the morning news on the radio (six minutes) and tune in National Public Radio when I'm driving.

Otherwise, I will avoid the war coverage, which is a fraud and a fake and a phony. It doesn't cover the war at all. The nightly explosions in Baghdad make striking pictures, but they don't show people dying, which is what is actually happening. Viewing American armored vehicles racing through the desert is exciting, but it shows nothing of the real battles in which people die on both sides, but mostly Iraqis. Iraqi soldiers surrendering might make one proud to be an American, but one rarely sees Iraqi bodies in grotesque shapes on the desert.

TV coverage of the war is even less realistic than a basketball game. In the latter, you actually see players beating up on one another in choreographed violence that violates the genius of the game. In the war, you see planes taking off from aircraft carriers, but you don't see men and women dying when the flyers "deliver their ordnance." TV coverage inoculates those who watch to the horrors that are actually happening. One can watch it and sleep the sleep of the just and the untroubled—unless one has a vivid imagination.

I hope and pray that the American victory is quick and complete. That way, fewer people will die. In a war between the half-truth and the lie, I'm on the side of the half-truth. I also hope and pray that our renewed friends in Turkey don't engage in what is historically one of their favorite pastimes—genocide of the Kurds (having rid themselves of all the Armenians).

By not obsessing about the details of the victory, I miss all the talking heads who in their brief moments of public attention are often in error and never in doubt, and the narcissistic reporters who are mostly cheerleaders for the United States. I won't have to listen to Defense Secretary Donald Rumsfeld, who may all by himself have alienated most of the world. I will miss Vice President Dick Cheney's sneer, a loss that's an unmitigated blessing. I will not have to endure M. Le President du France Jacques Chirac's daily charges that the war is illegal—though I will continue to drink Rhone wine.

Besides, the cheerleaders on March Madness are more attractive.

I also miss the anti-war protesters who are punishing the ordinary people on their daily rounds and not the Bush administration in the slightest. Perhaps some in the administration remember that during the Vietnam War, after every major protest, support for the war went up. (The president would not remember, since he was AWOL much of the time.)

How can we permit the Big Dance while the country is at war? We did the NCAA all through the Vietnam War; why not now? I'll lose some interest when my Wildcats make their exit.

Some folks seem to think that there is almost an obligation in conscience to glue themselves to the TV monitor because "our boys" are dying over there. That's fine for the poor folks whose loved ones are fighting this silly and dangerous war, but for the rest of us, it would be an unhealthy obsession, especially since a lot more of the Iraqis are dying. However, that doesn't matter because they're Arabs and talk funny and blew up the World Trade Center.

War is about killing people, as Rumsfeld keeps telling us. It's not a spectator sport. The greed of the networks has turned it into a spectator sport, and that is a lot more than just a venial sin.

April 4, 2003

Lessons unlearned haunt U.S.

During the Vietnam War, Pete Seeger wrote "Waist Deep in the Big Muddy," a morose song that claimed that Lyndon Johnson had mired the

United States in the "Big Muddy," a dark swamp from which there was no escape.[1] Because the U.S. military never seems to learn from its mistakes, it would appear that we are once again deep in the Big Muddy.

The strength of American military might exists in its technology, firepower and air power—none of which is much good against guerrilla warriors who are ready to die. The war in Vietnam was lost finally because our military leadership was never able to cope with the Viet Cong. Is there any reason to think that the leadership of today is better able to cope with the Fedayeen Saddam?

The much-abused CIA warned about the Fedayeen. The geniuses at Defense dismissed the CIA long ago when it refused to report that Iraq was involved in the World Trade Center attack.

I do not blame the troops for getting themselves into the Big Muddy, nor even their officers. I blame the civilian leadership (just as in the time of the Vietnam War) for putting American fighting men and women in what seems to be an impossible position. I blame especially the civilian "defense intellectuals" who thought this whole crazy war up. I blame the "chicken hawks": Wolfowitz, Perle, Cheney, Kristol and especially Donald Rumsfeld, who is emerging as the Robert McNamara of the early 21st century. McNamara, some readers will remember, was the brilliant corporate executive who as secretary of defense led the American military into the Big Muddy. A published story now claims that at the start of the planning for his foolish, dangerous war, Rumsfeld thought it could be won in three days with 30,000 troops. Now the generals (like Barry McCaffrey) who fought in the first Iraq war are saying that the 90,000 troops inside Iraq are dangerously few compared with what is needed.

Rumsfeld is telling the world that we will not engage in street war in Baghdad, but rather surround the city and lay siege to it until there's an internal revolution—a cockeyed notion if there ever was one. In both cases, many Americans would die and thousands and thousands of Iraqis. The Brookings Institution has suggested that 5,000 Americans might die and 20,000 might be wounded. It estimates that Iraqi military casualties might exceed 100,000, and civilian casualties might be much higher.

What happens when you want to liberate a country that does not want to be liberated? What happens when the "only superpower" is humiliated by a handful of fanatics in flowing desert robes?

Even in details, this venture into the Big Muddy is like the last one. Reporters from the front lines describe serious problems. Central Command headquarters is optimistic in its daily briefings. The Pentagon blames

---

[1] Copyright by T.R.O. 1967.

journalists for exaggerating the problems. The president, who now apparently thinks he's Abraham Lincoln (as did Lyndon Johnson), solemnly warns that we will stay the course in a war that will be long and difficult. One wonders why he didn't warn about pro–Saddam Hussein guerrillas before the war. Or even if he knew about them.

So one hears responsible people in nice restaurants returning to the theme of their predecessors 35 years ago: "Let's kill them all!" Yeah, and then let's go after the French, too.

The American plan was to "decapitate" Iraq in the first air attack, then to "shock and awe" it with the biggest air strike in history, then to destroy Saddam's command and control systems, then to accept the surrender of the Iraqi army and deal with those in the leadership who wanted to break away from the Baathist Party's dominance, then finally to accept the acclaim of the liberated Iraqi people.

Don't look now, but none of those things has happened. Who thought they would? The chicken hawks, obviously.

The United States will doubtless win the war eventually (unlike the Vietnam conflict).

The question is at what price in lost influence, credibility and human lives.

April 18, 2003

Victory doesn't justify war

A quick and easy war does not mean that the war was necessary or just. The American attacks on Mexico in 1846 and on Spain in 1898 were quick and easy (although casualties were heavy in the eight-year war against the Filipinos). Few historians today would doubt that both were in fact exercises in American imperialism. Similarly, the quick and apparently easy victory in Iraq does not mean that the war was either necessary or just. Or that casualties after the war is finished may not be, like the fiasco in the Philippines, much worse than those during the war.

The American military is clearly the most awesome war machine in human history. Our soldiers and Marines fought bravely and compassionately. It is less clear why they should have fought in the first place—much less die because of sniper shots or car bombs. To rid the world of Saddam

Hussein? Was that worth all the lives that were lost, including Iraqi lives? Because Iraq had weapons of mass destruction? Perhaps, but we don't seem to have found them. Because they might use those weapons on us? Patently, when they had every reason to do so, they did not. To give the chicken-hawk "defense intellectuals" in the Pentagon a new toy to play with?

Clearly, the competence of the American military has scared lots of people. Putin, Chirac and Schroeder are making nice again. They wanted us to win, they say, only they still don't think the war was necessary. The North Koreans are pleading for a non-aggression pact in which we will promise never to attack them. The Syrians are trembling in their boots. Even Ariel Sharon is now saying that he's ready to give up some of the West Bank settlements—the major obstacle to peace in Palestine.

Because people will never like an imperial power that can do so much so quickly, maybe it's a good thing that they are afraid of us. It's hard to believe that so many Arabs (though not in this country) wanted Saddam to win. It's harder still to believe that so many "left-liberals" in Europe would have been delighted with an American defeat or at least a much more costly victory. Rome ruled a long time on fear. Perhaps the United States can too.

Why do they hate us? Because the Bush Doctrine says that since we are the only superpower, we will do whatever we want no matter what anyone else thinks. Speak loudly and carry the First Marines and the Third Infantry. Moreover, even in Ireland, where the hatred for us is quieter than elsewhere, they will tell you they are infuriated every time they see President Bush and Donald Rumsfeld on TV. I respond that the American people did not elect Bush, and that at least the Irish are spared a steady diet of John Ashcroft.

Bush does not seem to understand that he is not only the president of the United States, he is president of the free world. In his public posture he must remember that his base is not just the Southern fundamentalists who would vote for him no matter what, but millions of people around the world who are disposed to look to the United States for leadership. He has lost them, it is to be feared, and will never get them back.

He seems to be saying in effect that he doesn't much care about that. He is not interested in being the president of the free world. Yet every U.S. president since FDR has played that role—some with remarkable grace and wisdom. It is not an option for an American president. He cannot give up the role without causing chaos. I wonder if Bush is intellectually capable of grasping that in fact it is an essential part of the burden of his office. He certainly does not seem to understand it, and none of those around him, especially the satraps who want to build a new American empire, are about to tell him.

On the other hand, the rest of his global constituency does not understand how devastating the World Trade Center attack has been to Americans. The American administration merely has to say "war on terrorism" and the people cheer for whatever the president wants to do. I doubt that anyone can turn the United States from the destructive path on which it now seems bent. Not even Tony Blair.

May 2, 2003

U.S. miscalculates in Iraq

Watching the Shiite Muslims marching through Karbala and Baghdad last week brought back uncomfortable memories. It was Iran in 1979 and 1980; Jimmy Carter was president, and the insufferable Walter Cronkite was counting off the number of days Americans were being held prisoner in the U.S. embassy in Tehran.

If one were to believe the Bush administration and the "defense intellectuals," the United States would soon establish a democratic Iraq. But the marching and shouting Shiites wanted America to go home and let them establish their own Iraq: an Islamic state like Iran.

This wasn't the way it was supposed to be at all. The Iraqi people were supposed to be celebrating their liberation—especially the Shiites, who had been oppressed during Saddam Hussein's brutal reign. Now the leaders of the religious majority were demonstrating against us, without any hint of gratitude for their liberation.

U.S. Defense Secretary Donald Rumsfeld told us that there would be no Islamic republic. Iraq would emerge as a democratic society. Yet democracy, if it means anything at all, means majority rule (except in American presidential elections). The Shiites are 60 percent of Iraq. If they get to vote, their mullahs will take over the country. Then they will impose an Islamic republic, and life will become very difficult for the 40 percent of Iraqis who are not Shiites. The choice seems to be either no democracy or another Iran.

An important Iranian cleric issued a "fatwa"—a mandate for the Shiites to take control of the country and get rid of the Americans.

If any officials in the administration were aware of this development (which should have been a self-evident possibility), they certainly didn't tell the American people. President Bush celebrates victory and doesn't seem to grasp that the majority religion of Iraq is not grateful to us for liberation and wants us to go home so that it can quickly impose an authoritarian rule that would be only marginally better than that of the Baath Party. Will the American occupation forces and military government have to fight off an Iraqi branch of the Hezbollah, the Iranian-supported terrorist suicide bombers who periodically blow themselves up in Israel?

It begins to look like Deputy Defense Secretary Paul Wolfowitz's dream of Iraq as a democratic ally in the Middle East was a pipe dream—and a dangerous one at that.

Somewhere in the government, someone must have known that—probably someone in the CIA or the State Department. The strong possibility of such a development ought to have been obvious to anyone who knows anything about Islam. Yet no one seems to have informed the president or the American people. In effect, those who did not warn us, lied to us—just as did the vice president, who assured us that the Iraqis had developed a nuclear bomb (or had almost developed it).

Most of the national media, especially the news networks, seemed serenely unaware of the Shiite problem in southern Iraq. Their talking-head experts informed the country that the Shiites were there but never suggested that they might almost immediately begin their own theocratic revolution. They were supposed to dance in the streets and throw flowers on the American tanks. Instead, nervous American troops have to gun them down.

The victory celebrations are at best premature. They deceive Americans into believing that most problems in Iraq have been solved. More lies. There are a lot of ayatollahs between Baghdad and the Persian Gulf, and they are very dangerous people. It would appear that once again the U.S. government has made a major mistake because it simply cannot factor the religious dimension into its calculations. The mistake is particularly odd in an administration that seems to believe so strongly in divine guidance. Apparently, there are other leaders in the world who also believe that they have a direct line to God—men who, astonishingly, believe that we are infidels, although in fact we are a nation of pious, God-fearing evangelicals who, like the president, read the Bible every day.

One wonders if the time will come when Cheney, Rumsfeld, Wolfowitz, Richard Perle and William Kristol will feel uncomfortably like Baron von Frankenstein.

May 16, 2003

Europeans don't understand us

Brian Cowan, the foreign minister of Ireland, had wise words about the United States at a recent meeting of European foreign ministers. The *Irish Times* reported that "Mr. Cowan said Europeans must understand that the terrorist attack of Sept. 11, 2001, had changed the U.S. perception of the world, making security the issue which dominated all Washington's foreign policy decisions. Many in the Bush administration and in conservative think tanks no longer believed that a more integrated Europe was in Washington's interest."

"He said that many Europeans now question Washington's commitment to the multilateral institutions which it helped to establish after the second World War," the report continued.

That is the best brief summary of contemporary America that has come along in the last two years. Europeans do not understand the depth of fear and anger and desire for revenge that mark contemporary American life. Americans are terrified that they will be attacked again. This fear is in part responsible for the collapse of the airline industry and for the stagnation of the American economy. Europeans might well argue that Americans should move beyond their anger. However, they have not done so and that is a fact that most European leaders must deal with—hopefully, without moralistic lectures about how Americans should behave.

This malaise has been reinforced by the sensationalism of the American media and the deceptions of the Bush administration. The notion of invading Iraq existed in the minds of the "defense intellectuals" before the World Trade Center attack. The administration used the "war on terrorism" as an excuse for the war against Iraq. It hinted that Iraq was somehow tied in with al-Qaida and involved in the World Trade Center destruction. Indeed, perhaps a quarter of the American people believe that to be the case, though there is no substantial evidence for it. There were hints that Iraq already had an atom bomb. The president repeatedly asserted that Iraq had "weapons of mass destruction" and that it was capable of lending them to terrorists. An attack on Iraq was not so much a "preemptive war" but, in a time of terror "after Sept. 11," a legitimate and indeed necessary act of self-defense.

Under the circumstances, many Americans believed that the failure of our allies of the past to stand by us in self-defense was an act of betrayal. Saddam Hussein wants to kill us and our children, they said in effect, and you people, for whom we have done so much over the last 50 years, are prepared to let him do it. We can no longer compromise with you. This was just what the defense intellectuals wanted. It provided them with an excuse to push harder for their policy of ending the postwar system of alliances: What good is mutual security when it means security for you but not for us? M. Chirac and Herr Schroeder played right into their hands.

I opposed the war because I knew that an invasion of Iraq was on the agenda even before President Bush's dubious election and because there was no evidence that Saddam had any intention of turning over whatever weapons he had to religious fanatics who might use them on him. I understand why many Americans thought that our long-term European allies were useless—an attitude that the Bush administration did nothing to dispel. The European leadership operated in reckless disregard of the temperament of the American people. For the sake of a few short-run gains in histrionic image, they antagonized even those Americans who opposed the war and provided aid and comfort to those in the administration who thought allies were worthless anyway. The European leaders arrogantly (with the apparent exception of Cowan and his government) felt there was no need to factor into their calculations a sense of the tremulous state of American public opinion, to understand that frightened people are vulnerable to a demagogue of the sort who will fly out to aircraft carriers dressed like a jet jockey although he had disappeared from active duty during his last year of military service.

May 23, 2003

Bush answers on 9/11 overdue

After the Bay of Pigs disaster when the CIA tried to invade Cuba, President John F. Kennedy took personal responsibility and ordered an independent investigation. In fact, the invasion had been planned during the Eisenhower administration, and JFK could easily have blamed the mess on his predecessor.

After the Pearl Harbor attack, President Franklin D. Roosevelt established an investigative commission chaired by Supreme Court Justice Owen D. Roberts, a Republican who had been the prosecutor for the notorious Teapot Dome scandal.

Patently, President Bush is not going to assume responsibility for the World Trade Center catastrophe. His political allies blame former President Bill Clinton (as they are blaming him three years later for the current recession). Moreover, Bush continues to stonewall attempts to set up an independent investigation of what went wrong and continues to sit on the 900-page report prepared by a bipartisan congressional committee.

The White House excuse for this cover-up is that discussion about what went wrong in the months before the destruction of the World Trade Center would interfere with the "war on terrorism." There are several things wrong with this argument. First, if there is not something to hide, why not release the report? Second, FDR and JFK had real wars to fight—the former against imperial Japan, the latter a cold war against world communism. Third, the "war on terrorism" is a metaphor (just like the "war on drugs," the "war on AIDS," the "war on hunger," the "war on poverty") for a struggle against international criminals. It is a useful political label for a president who wants to be re-elected as a wartime leader and to land on an aircraft carrier dressed in flight gear (even though he was in effect AWOL for at least a year during the Vietnam War). The metaphor conceals what is different in the struggle against Islamic fundamentalism when compared to the war against imperial Japan. Admitting the mistakes the administration made in July and August 2001 will not give aid and comfort to anyone, and certainly not to al-Qaida.

Instead, the president continues to respond to terror with his cowboy rhetoric: We will get Osama bin Laden. We will get the Mullah Omar. We will get the terrorists who blew the hole in the USS *Cole*. We will get the anthrax killer. We will get Saddam Hussein and his sons. Most recently, we will get the killers who attacked the compounds in Saudi Arabia.

The last will be quite a trick since the killers were suicide bombers, and Bush will have to bring them back from the dead to haul them into court.

No one seems to notice that we have not found bin Laden or the mullah. The *Cole* terrorists escaped from a jail in Yemen—undoubtedly with the help of some elements in the Yemeni government (although Attorney General John Ashcroft, with the usual display of sanctimony, has indicted them). We have not found—or perhaps not arrested—the anthrax killer. Saddam is hiding somewhere, probably in a bunker in Baghdad with his sons. Thirty of his top aides are still on the loose.

The people Bush proposed to smoke out and "get" are still free. More-over, some of the CIA officials who "dropped the ball" in the summer of 2001 have been promoted. Yet the media, who were so eager to pry into the private life of President Clinton, seem disinclined to uncover the real story of what happened during that summer and whether the same people who dropped the ball then are still dropping it.

Nor have they paid any attention to the president's claim out there on the aircraft carrier *Abraham Lincoln* that al-Qaida was on the run. After the explosions in Saudi Arabia and Morocco and the threats in Kenya, it would appear that al-Qaida is not on the run at all. It would also appear that if one continues to believe Bush's rhetoric, one is accepting as true statements that might be less than true. Finally, it is high time that someone in this country remembers FDR and JFK and wants to know what is really hap-pening. What's the president trying to hide?

June 27, 2003

Bush was just plain wrong on Iraq

Humans tend to see what we want to see. If facts seem to challenge our preconceptions, we reject them. Thus, practically everyone in Chicago believes Sammy Sosa's explanation of the corked bat. I personally think White Sox fans put the bat in the wrong place, where Sammy picked it up by mistake. Sox fans would do anything to ruin the Cubs' season and to divert attention from their own miserable showing. Right?

Moreover, our attitude on the Martha Stewart case is shaped by our opinions about women who muscle their way to the top in the corporate world. My suspicions about her indictment are also based on the propen-sity of federal attorneys to promote their own careers by going after "big fish" with technical indictments. (Stewart "obstructed justice" by denying she had engaged in insider trading. Failure to confess guilt immediately is apparently a crime in itself.)

Thus, I think it is unfair to say that the Bush administration deliberately deceived the American people about Iraqi weapons of mass destruction. The deception was not deliberate because the president, the vice president and the secretary of defense believed with their heart and soul that Saddam Hussein was a serious threat to the United States. Indeed, the "intellectu-als" around Dick Cheney and Donald Rumsfeld advocated "taking out"

Saddam even before the Supreme Court selected Bush to be president. The World Trade Center attack provided the rage among the American people to sell such an invasion.

The intelligence reports, like all such reports, were uncertain, problematic, ambiguous. The hawks in the administration saw what they wanted to see and concluded that they were right: Saddam had weapons of mass destruction, which he was ready to use; he was cooperating with al-Qaida; he had or would soon have a nuclear bomb. The hawks knew all these things were true and had known it for some time. There were plenty of hints in the intelligence data to support what they already knew.

Remember me and the White Sox? Didn't they send a thug to torment Sammy at Camden Yards?

So the hawks ignored the weakness of the data and argued that we had to get Saddam before he got us. Preemptive war was all right because Saddam was ready, willing and able to work mass destruction on the United States. Now that most of the intelligence that confirmed their faith seems questionable, they are unable to back down and say that maybe they were wrong.

Similarly, they are unable for reasons of faith to admit that they were wrong about Iraqi reaction to our invasion. The Iraqis would dance in the streets and throw flowers at our tanks. Instead, they loot, they shoot at us, and they riot against us. The hawks can't admit that they were wrong on this subject, either.

So I do not believe that the deception was deliberate. They did not intend to lie to the American people. Rather, they wanted to prove to the American people that they were right, with little respect for the poor quality of their data.

The point is that, however sincere they were, they did deceive. They were just plain wrong. The president was just plain wrong. People who make such terrible mistakes should not be retained in office. In large corporations, officials who make similar errors in judgment are discarded (usually with a fat purse in their pocket). The whole chicken-hawk cabal should be swept out of office. In American politics, this is usually accomplished by congressional investigation. However, given the Bush administration's propensity to stonewall and cover up and the pro-administration bias of much of the media, full-scale investigation is unlikely. Despite token movements in that direction, the mantra "national security" will be invoked to prevent investigation. Just now the federal government can do almost anything it wants.

It must be emphasized that while lies are immoral, bad judgment at the senior level of government—being so utterly wrong—is intolerable and dangerous in a nuclear world.

July 11, 2003

U.S. could use some Irish hospitality

GALWAY—Out on Inishmore, the largest of the three Aran Islands, the waitress who took our order at the biggest fish restaurant where all the buses stop was a young—and frightened—Chinese woman. The new invasion of Ireland has spread to those three steps away from Europe, as poet Seamus Heaney has called the Islands.

It used to be that the housekeepers in the hotels of Europe during the summer were bright, cheerful young Irish women. Then things changed as the Celtic tiger began to roar. The housekeepers in the Irish hotels were Spanish, not women from Kerry. Now the housekeepers, both men and women, are Chinese. They are very efficient, smile politely, say good morning just the way the Irish used to. Perhaps, however, like all previous invasions of this lovely and soggy island, they are merely in the process of becoming Irish, as did the Celts and the Danes and the Normans and the "old" (i.e., Catholic) English and even the so-called Anglo-Irish. As G. K. Chesterton remarked, some countries have conquered other countries while Ireland has won over whole peoples.

It's difficult to judge the Irish reaction to the current Asian invasion. They will comment that you see them everywhere, which is true, and remark that it will prove an interesting development. Doubtless there is some anti-Asian sentiment in the pubs at night, but it has not slipped into public discourse. A country that has shipped its surplus population to all the continents cannot consistently complain when it is asked to absorb immigrants—though prejudice never considers consistency.

Moreover, with the addition of new countries to the European Union there will be other waves of immigrants—Polish, Slovak, Hungarian, Slovene—that cannot be rejected. While the EU has given member countries a period of grace before they must be open to all citizens of Europe, the Irish government has declined to accept such a postponement. Any European is welcome. Ireland is thus true to its own heritage and to its Catholic tradition. The big test may come when Romania is admitted. Romanians are the one group of current "illegals" that for some reason the Irish can't stand.

Imagine, then, what they think of the treatment of immigrants in the United States. The Irish papers report dispassionately the story of Ms.

Bridget Reuter, who has been married to an American citizen for 33 years and in January 2001 was granted permanent residency in the United States. Late last year she traveled to Ireland for a niece's wedding in Clare. Immigration officials at Shannon Airport rejected her attempt to return to the United States on the grounds that she should have sought an "advanced parole" for her trip to Ireland since her new status had yet to be "formally adjusted," more than two years later. The Office of Homeland Security threatens to bar her return to the United States for 10 years. She has an ailing husband, a son and two grandsons waiting for her in Lubbock, Texas. Apparently they'll have a long wait.

Immigration regulations have been obscure and punitive for a long time. However, in the era of such cement heads as Tom Ridge and John Ashcroft, they have become worse. Patently, Ms. Reuter may be a threat to the United States. She may have links to al-Qaida and may be an agent of Saddam Hussein or Osama bin Laden. Keep her out!

Does one have to say that these rules would be appropriate for Nazis but hardly for a country that claims to stand for freedom? Or does one have to add that the Irish, who are unhappy with the United States because of the Iraq war, think that we are not the land of the brave but the land of hypocrisy?

One might try to explain to them that the rules are applied dispassionately to everyone—whether an Arab wife and mother and grandmother separated from her family, or an Irish wife and mother and grandmother separated from her family. We don't discriminate against Arabs. Our discrimination is fair and equitable. We discriminate against everyone.

God bless America!

July 18, 2003

Stressed Americans ripe for GOP con

Republicans are the party of the rich, so it seems appropriate that when they are in power they take care of the rich. The irony is that not all Republicans are rich. So the Republican spin merchants must explain their economic decisions in terms that their "base"—religious fundamentalists, poor white Southerners, alienated workers, hyper-patriots—can accept. Heaven forfend—you should excuse the expression—that the base might understand that money is being taken from them and turned over to the oil billionaires. Even the "base," dimwitted that it is, might not like the reverse Robin Hood tactics of the administration: Take from the poor and give to the rich.

Hence, Republicans must portray the various tax cuts as benefits to all Americans and explain that the most recent one will provide an economic incentive that will create more jobs. You must not let the "base" know that two-thirds of the money will go to the top 10 percent of the country, and that the top 1 percent will receive on the average $200,000 of paybacks. It is most unlikely that the rich and the super-rich will engage in the kind of consumption that would force business to increase its capital spending. More jobs might appear if the money were spread around among the rest of the population. Soak the rich, as the late Huey P. Long of Louisiana once proclaimed, and spread it out thin.

Similarly, the House version of the Medicare reform bill is admittedly the first step in the long-term goal of privatizing Medicare. However, it is presented in all seriousness as a bill to decrease prescription costs for the elderly. Thus, the GOP can go into the presidential campaign insisting that it has done something for the elderly, when in fact it hasn't done much, except increase profits for drug companies and insurance companies. Someone ought to ask senators and representatives whether they are willing to give up their own federal health insurance, which is much more generous than Medicare, and join the rest of the population in the risks of astronomic prescription-drug bills.

Finally, plans to eliminate overtime pay are presented as a scheme to deprive union workers of their exorbitant wages (like $40 an hour, if carpenters work on Sunday) and provide more jobs for non-union workers, which means—though they don't say it—immigrant workers who come cheaper than Americans.

How can they get away with such sleight of hand? How can they deceive so many about their goals when the winners from such legislation or proposed legislation will be the rich and the powerful?

How could they convince so many that the war in Iraq and the subsequent quagmire were justified by "weapons of mass destruction" when these weapons did not exist and the evidence that they did was largely cooked? On President Truman's desk the sign said, "the buck stops here." On President Bush's desk the sign apparently says, "the buck stops at the CIA."

The answer, I think, is that Americans are still so obsessed with the surprise and pain of the World Trade Center attack that they will believe just about anything the country's leaders say. Hence, those leaders can stonewall the commission investigating the World Trade Center attack, and they can prevent a thorough investigation of the Iraq war. Americans want to believe that the Bush administration is telling the truth.

It is fooling most of the people most of the time. It hopes to fool enough of the people long enough for re-election. And the media, which screamed in outrage when President Bill Clinton lied about his sex life, are not screaming about the fabrications of the Bush administration about taxes, Medicare, work hours, the attack on Sept. 11, and the Iraqi war. Obviously, dishonesty about sex is a worse threat to the republic than dishonesty about war and taxes.

The administration obviously intends to tough it out, just as Nixon did. Maybe it will work. However, at the end of the eight years, the country will be in a terrible economic mess, its civil liberties in tatters, hated by the rest of the world—and probably still fighting a foolish war in Iraq.

July 25, 2003

Trapped in a quagmire, again

The trouble with war is the unintended consequences. Consider August 1914. No one wanted a long war in which 15 million to 20 million people would die. The wars in Europe after the end of Napoleon's empire were all quickie conflicts. Two armies came together and fought a single battle. The winner of the battle was the winner of the war. Some territories were exchanged, and everyone went home. The classic example was the Franco-Prussian war of 1870. Emperor Napoleon III took on the Prussians at Sedan, was soundly defeated and surrendered. The Prussians went home with Alsace and Lorraine, the emperor abdicated, and that was that, except for the sanguinary uprising of the Paris commune.

In 1914, the Austrians wanted to teach the Serbs a lesson. The Russians wanted to protect their fellow Slavs. The Germans assumed they would roll through France just as they had in 1870. The Russians assumed they would overwhelm the Germans by sheer weight of numbers.

They were all wrong. The Serbs kept fighting for four more years. The Germans virtually destroyed the Russian army at the battle of the Masurian Lakes, a prelude to the collapse of the Russian empire in 1917. The Germans almost made it to Paris.

Or consider our War between the States. The hotheads in Charleston figured they'd teach the Yankees a lesson by taking Fort Sumter. President Lincoln figured he could defeat the South in three months with his 75,000 volunteers. After the first battle of Bull Run (or Manassas Junction, if you wish), the two sides locked themselves into an orgy of destruction that would last another four years. Obviously the Confederacy won. The South is running the country now, isn't it?

Human nature seems doomed to underestimate the consequences of war, to take for granted that it will be easy and short when in fact it often is not.

It is now reasonably clear that the American government had inadequate intelligence not only about the weapons of mass destruction in Iraq but about what would happen after the war was won. Although there were warnings about the number of troops necessary for occupation, the costs of the occupation and the reactions of the Iraqi people, these warnings were dismissed. The brilliant "neo-cons" in the Defense Department did not foresee the looting, the sabotage, the hostility to Americans. They did not anticipate the power of Shiite clerics. They did not expect that the remnants of the Saddam Hussein regime would be able to mount a guerrilla war. They did not expect the Iraqis to cheer when American soldiers were killed. Apparently, they had never heard about the guerrilla war that ancestors of the Iraqis had fought against the British in the 1920s. In those days the Arabs were glad to be rid of the Turks, whom the British had driven out, but they didn't feel enough gratitude to enter quietly into the British empire. Yet men like Paul Wolfowitz thought the Iraqis, Arabs and Muslims would let the hated Americans set up a democratic—and pro-Israel—state.

This intelligence mistake cannot be blamed on the CIA or on 10 Downing Street.

So now the United States has trapped itself in a quagmire in Iraq, and the end game is not clear. When Arabs in Lebanon blew up a Marine barracks, President Ronald Reagan withdrew our forces. But Texans don't run away, so that option is not available. We might finally decide to turn the whole game over to the United Nations, but that would involve national humiliation.

So we will be trapped in the quagmire indefinitely as the president's approval rating plummets. What will the administration do? My guess is that it will turn mean—though that will only make matters worse. The soldiers from the 3rd Division who complained to ABC News are under threat of punishment. The ABC reporter is dismissed as a homosexual Canadian. These punitive actions are likely to be only the beginning. The ultimate unintended consequence could be a police state.

August 29, 2003

U.S. sinking in Iraq quagmire

Faced with persistent sabotage and an increase in guerrilla violence, the Bush administration faces unpalatable options in Iraq, especially as Iraq approaches the beginning of the year before the election. Real imperial powers ought not to be distracted by elections.

It can send more American troops, either National Guard or Reserve units, or new units drawn from recruits or eventually perhaps from a draft. This choice is unpalatable because it would be an admission that the administration had made serious mistakes in its calculations about how many troops were needed. Moreover, it would give the lie to the president's claim on the aircraft carrier that the war is over.

It can invite the United Nations to send in troops. However, the other Security Council countries are not likely to approve such action unless the United States eats humble pie, admits that it was mistaken in its confidence, and permits the U.N. to take charge of Iraq. It is virtually unthinkable that the president could accept that humiliation in an election year.

It can withdraw from Iraq. If the army ever manages to capture Saddam Hussein, it can claim victory and say in effect to the Iraqis, we know you don't want us here. We don't want to be here either. Rebuild your country yourselves. Fight the swarming Saudi berserkers yourselves. We're out of here. But such a strategy—probably the wisest—would also be an admission of failure.

It can continue the present strategy, at the cost of $1 billion a week, hoping that the United States can muddle through and that, as was said in Vietnam, there seems to be light at the end of the tunnel. Eventually, the Iraqis may settle down and the neighboring countries can stop the flow of Saudi and Palestinian crazies. In another six months things might be a lot better. However, at the present rate, they may be a lot worse. American soldiers may still die every day and truck bombs may explode every other week. The military would be tied down in a seemingly never-ending war. This paradigm is so similar to Vietnam as to be frightening.

Yet, the administration might well decide that if the "sacrifices" in Iraq can be portrayed as necessary to win the "war on terrorism," Bush may keep his éclat as an able wartime president and win the election despite being trapped in the Big Muddy. He might be successful in situations that doomed both Harry Truman and Lyndon Johnson.

One recalls what Sen. George Aiken said of Vietnam: The best strategy would be to claim victory and go home. The present administration has proven itself very skilled at spinning reality so that truth becomes invisible. Does anyone remember "compassionate" conservatism? Or "no nation building"? Or more recently, the president's claim that his energy bill would solve the problem of the nation's erratic electric grid? Everyone knows that Alaskan petroleum is just what the grid needs! The spinmasters could fool the majority of the American people into believing that defeat was really victory. Having been clever enough to steal an election, the administration may well be able to pull off an imaginary victory in Iraq. What's the point in being a Teflon president unless you can do that? So far, most Americans still dismiss criticism of the administration's Iraq policy as "politics."

Finally, God, who apparently advised Bush to invade Iraq, might well intervene with a miracle because everyone knows that God is on our side, isn't He?

The American public grows skeptical of prolonged wars rather quickly. But this is a special time in the nation's history. The savage jolt to American self-confidence and self-esteem caused by the World Trade Center attack has played into the hands of the spinners. They got us into the war by playing games with the truth. They may also be able to spin a cover-up that will persuade the public that the Iraq situation is not as bad as it seems. Can they get away with it? Maybe they can also pretend that unemployment is not serious.

I wouldn't bet against them.

September 12, 2003

U.S. no safer than two years ago

After the remembrances of the World Trade Center disaster this week, it is proper to ask whether you're safer than you were two years ago. Any sensible response would say that, despite the much-publicized war on terrorism, you're not much safer and maybe a little less safe. A major improvement is that there is now a bulletproof metal door protecting each cockpit on American planes. That protection was first suggested by the Gore commission in 1996. The airline industry, fearful of the extra expense, persuaded Congress to reject the recommendation. If the four planes taken over by the terrorists two years ago had such doors, all the people killed in the World Trade Center explosions would still be alive. For reasons that escape me, the media have been reluctant to blame the airlines and Congress for their folly.

The security farce at the nation's airports succeeds only in persuading travelers that they are safe when they board an airplane. If you harass and insult enough people, everyone will feel safer in the air. It's a shell game, a card trick. You are not safe from heat-seeking missiles fired from the ground or from bombs in baggage and mail and express parcels that have not been screened. Nor has there been enough screening of planes from other countries. Thus, if a Canadian plane is off course and headed for an important target, will the government scramble jets to shoot it down? Or a French or a German plane?

Ground missiles could be deflected by protective systems used by the Air Force, but such protection, proposed in a bill by Sen. Dianne Feinstein (D-Calif.), would cost $10 billion—money that Congress and the administration doubtless feel could be more wisely used in the Iraq sinkhole. Finally, destructive weapons could be smuggled in on ships or in railroad trains or even on riverboat barges.

Despite all the happy talk about the new Department of Homeland Security, this bureaucratic monstrosity is a shackled giant that, like the rest of the administration, confuses spin with substance. Secretary Tom Ridge recently assured us that he was creating 5,000 more air marshals. The small print revealed that he would train 5,000 officers from other departments so that they could be used on planes if necessary. However, there will be no more marshals on planes next week than there were a couple of weeks ago, before his announcements.

The military has knocked over the Taliban regime in Afghanistan. Arrests and killings have dealt a setback to al-Qaida. However, the Taliban is resurgent there and is still killing American soldiers. Moreover, despite promises to the contrary from the president, our intelligence services have not found the Mullah Omar or Osama bin Laden or Saddam Hussein or the anthrax killer.

Most important, terrorism will persist until the Palestinian conflict is settled, but the administration's belated and lackadaisical "road map for peace" has failed.

Finally, the Iraq war, which is supposed to be part of the war on terrorism, has created more terrorists. The "neo-conservative" intellectuals around the vice president and the secretary of defense argued that al-Qaida had infiltrated Iraq. The Bush administration has convinced 70 percent of the American people that Saddam Hussein was personally involved in the World Trade Center bombing, even though there is not a shred of evidence to support this allegation. However, there are now hundreds, perhaps thousands of new terrorists—whether al-Qaida or not—emerging in Iraq because of the war. How long will it be before some of them come to America? When the president claims that the war in Iraq is essential to the war on terrorism, he deceives. The war, which may well be endless, has not made Americans safer, but rather put them in greater danger.

The government has therefore done very little to deal with the threat of international terrorism other than to insist on those metal doors on airplane cockpits. The rest has been spin. The country is not safer now than it was two years ago, despite all the money that has been spent. National security ought to be a major issue in the next election. The claim of the Bush administration that it has dealt effectively with the threat ought to be exposed to the full light of day, where the spin doctors can no longer hide the truth.

September 19, 2003

Big lie on Iraq comes full circle

Joseph Goebbels, Hitler's propaganda chief (director of communications, in the current parlance), once said that if you are going to lie, you should tell a big lie. That may be good advice, but the question remains: What happens when people begin to doubt the big lie? Herr Goebbels never lived to find out. Some members of the Bush administration may be in the process of discovering that, given time, the big lie turns on itself.

The president has insisted that Iraq is the central front in the war on terrorism, a continuation of the administration's effort to link Iraq to the attack on the World Trade Center. While almost three-quarters of the public believe that Saddam Hussein was personally involved in the attack, the polls after the president's recent speech show that less than half believe that Iraq is the "central front" of the war on terrorism. Moreover, the majority believe that the war has increased the risk of terrorism. A shift is occurring in the middle, which is neither clearly pro-Bush nor clearly anti-Bush. The big lie is coming apart.

There is not and never has been any evidence that Iraq was involved in the 9/11 attack. None. The implication of such involvement was an attempt to deceive, a successful attempt at the big lie.

I'm not sure that the president knows it is a lie, however.

Also, the weapons of mass destruction story was never true. It now appears that Saddam panicked in 1995 when his sons-in-law defected to Jordan and revealed the truth about his weapons development. He immediately ordered the destruction of all the evidence. The U.N. team before the war would have no more found any weapons than the Americans after the war.

Again, I'm not sure that the president knew the weapons argument was false. Perhaps some of his advisers believed it, or, as the Irish say, half-believed it. However, the American people now seem to suspect that they haven't been told the truth.

Why, then, did the United States invade Iraq if the reasons given for the war were so problematic? It would seem that the answer was the same as the reason for climbing Mt. Everest: Iraq was there. The administration recited the "war on terrorism" mantra as a pretext for doing something that its intellectuals had wanted to do for years. No one in the administration expected that such a war would lead to more dangers of terrorism rather than less. The mantra has been used as an excuse for many things, from the Patriot Act to drilling for oil in Alaska. It won the 2002 election for the Republicans. It is supposed to win the presidential election next year. Will the big lie work? Perhaps, though it would seem that some are growing skeptical about its constant repetition.

Moreover, the corollary mantra, which says that Americans must make sacrifices to win the war on terrorism, is also in trouble. Who makes the sacrifices? The rich Americans celebrating their tax "refunds"? The Republican leadership who have few if any sons and daughters in harm's way? Giant corporations like Dick Cheney's Halliburton or Bechtel? No, the sacrifices will be made mostly by the sons and daughters of the poor and the working class who must fight the war. Jessica Lynch joined the army so she could get money for a college education. Her roommate, Lori Piestewa, who was killed in action, joined because she was a Native American single mother who needed the money to raise her two children.

There will be sacrifices made by schoolchildren who depend on state and local money, which has disappeared into the "war effort"; the elderly who will not benefit from prescription drug reform; the working men whose overtime pay the president wishes to cut; the chronically unemployed whose jobs have disappeared; and the future generations who will have to work to pay off the president's huge debt.

"War on terrorism" is a metaphor. It is not an actual war, like the World War or the Vietnamese or Korean wars. It is rather a struggle against fanatical Islamic terrorists, exacerbated if not caused by the conflict in Palestine. When one turns a metaphor into a national policy, one not only misunderstands what is going on, one begins to slide toward the big lie. One invades Iraq because one needs a war.

October 3, 2003

Bush's missing exit strategy draws down support on Iraq

A democracy cannot engage in imperialism unless it does so on the cheap. Most of the great imperial nations—Rome, Persia, China, Mexico, Mongolia, Britain in its earliest days—did not have to cope with critical media, pushy legislators, muttering troops, restless people. If a modern superpower is not willing to limit its "go-it-alone" imperialism, then it must be prepared to win its unilateral victories quickly, inexpensively and with few casualties. It also must send the boys home immediately after the war is over. The light at the end of the tunnel, the exit strategy, must be explicit from the very beginning. Otherwise, popular support will quickly wane.

The United States through the years from NATO to Kosovo proved extremely skillful at building coalitions. The elder President Bush was especially polished in this art. Without coalitions, the United States can occasionally pull off small-time victories such as those in Grenada or Kosovo. The basic insight into American foreign policy, framed by President Bush and Vice President Dick Cheney and the so-called neo-conservative intellectuals around them, was that as the only superpower in the world, the United States, however good it might have been at multilateral coalitions, didn't have to bother with such stuff anymore. The administration announced what it was going to do, called that consultation, and then went ahead and did what it wanted to do.

What about the taxpayers, the Congress, the families of service men and women, the editorial writers and the columnists? The answer was that the

U.S. military could move with such speed and efficiency that the imperialist war would be over before the critics had the time to complain. At one time, Secretary of Defense Donald Rumsfeld is supposed to have said that the United States could win a war in Iraq with 30,000 troops. When the Army chief of staff dissented, he was dismissed impatiently, the way a father dismisses a troublesome child.

Looking back on the war in Iraq, Rumsfeld may well have been right. A Marine division and an Army division swept away Saddam Hussein's ridiculous army with little difficulty. All the president's men assumed that the time after the war would be a pushover, a cakewalk. Now they find that they need more time, more money and more troops—at least another year, at least two more divisions, and at least $87 billion. Moreover, in the absence of more troops from other countries, the Army will have to mobilize several more National Guard and Reserve brigades.

No one should expect the leaders of other major countries—most of whom dislike Bush intensely—to react with any great enthusiasm to his speech at the United Nations, in which he lectured them on their obligations to assist in Iraq. The president was caught in a bind of his own making. He could not give even a hint that perhaps he made a mistake and thus win support from our former allies, because that would weaken his support with his political base: heavily Southern and evangelical.

Nonetheless, support for the war in Iraq, the president's personal popularity and satisfaction with the state of the country all continued to sink like a rock. The chickens of a quick-and-easy unilateralist war, which the president sold as part of the war on terrorism, have come home to roost. The absence of the fabled weapons of mass destruction has not helped much.

French President Jacques Chirac (who is more popular among the Iraqis than Bush), however, has given the president a marvelous exit strategy, which would notably help the latter's presidential chances. Turn it all over to the Iraqis within a year. If the president were agile enough to do that and claim victory in the process, his re-election chances would go up. He might fool a lot of people, though it's not clear that his "base" would accept such a strategy. A "victorious" exit celebrated as a success in the war on terrorism before the middle of next August would give him a good shot at winning the election, no matter what mess remained in Iraq. However, a president who has urged the people to "stay the course" might not be able to pull that off—not with the media as critical as they now (at last) are.

The lesson of all of this is that a superpower in a reasonably democratic society can afford imperialism only if there is rock-solid evidence that it will be on the cheap.

October 31, 2003

It's not supposed to be servitude

Several of the Democratic presidential candidates have proposed plans for national service, usually so far down on their platforms that no one ever hears about them. It's an old idea that has been around for a long time, whose time has not come and ought never to come.

The assumption behind it is that young men and women should be forced to spend some time in their lives (six months to two years, in most forms of this proposal) in the service of their country, and perhaps be subject to later "call up." In this view, the government has the right to demand such service and to pass laws that will constrain them to it. In some forms such service would give the president the right to "call up" a certain number of them for special service when needed, just as he can now call up the National Guard and the Reserves.

The problem with this line of reasoning, which astonishingly appeals to many of those who call themselves "liberals," is that while people of every age may well have some moral obligation to serve their country, there is no obligation to serve the government of the country. The slippery equation of the country with the government is a dangerous intrusion into the freedom of citizens. If the young are the special targets of such service, then it is a form of regressive taxation against them in favor of older people. It is also a form of imprisonment without due process. Because you're young, we have the right to call on you to serve the country in ways that interfere with your education, your life plans, your freedom of choice.

If young men and women wish to volunteer for either public service like the Peace Corps or private services like those affiliated with most religious denominations, then more power to them. If they don't want to do that, no one has the right to coerce them to do so. Moreover, the notion of volunteer service as a requirement for graduation is an oxymoron. If you have to do it, then it's not voluntary. It is laughable that high schools that usually do not teach young people to think for themselves or to write a decent paragraph of the English language assume that they have the right to engage in "character formation" outside the school environment.

The school ought to be content to provide opportunities for service but not force young men and women to engage in the opportunities, just as the government should make available opportunities but not constrain anyone to sign up for anything. Moreover, since the government is notoriously inept at running anything that involves thousands of men and women, the more of these opportunities that are private the better.

To reward volunteers for their service seems to defeat the altruistic theme of being a volunteer. On the other hand, one could argue that if there were some educational reward, young women like Jessica Lynch would not be forced to risk their lives in foolish wars so they could go to college.

Volunteer service looks good on one's resume, but a good resume should not be the primary motive for volunteer service, or it stops being volunteer. More generally, the government should not try to bribe young men and women to volunteer for anything.

The national service obsession, which has been around for a long time, is a manifestation of the (Calvinist) liberal temptation to do good. If that kind of liberal determines that something would be good for someone else to do, then it's perfectly all right to force the person to do it. It is good for the young to serve their country (which means their government), therefore we will force them to do it. In my tradition (here represented classically by Aquinas), virtue is acquired by the repetition of free acts. To be honest, however, many in my tradition have devoted their lives to imposing virtue on everyone.

Finally, the national service temptation could easily be transformed into a draft if the government decided, for example, that it needs 10 more divisions right away. The military was good for me, older lunkheads frequently argue; it made a man out of me. Their memories are doubtless highly selective. What is the contemporary military or national service likely to do for women, save to give them practice in resisting rape?

November 7, 2003

Out of Iraq before the election

All but the most intransigent radical critics of the president agree that the United States must "stay the course." Even if the war was unnecessary, even if it was based on flawed (perhaps deceptive) intelligence, even if the current mess was the result of foolish—not to say nonexistent—

planning, it would be wrong simply to walk away from chaos that we created. We cannot abandon the people. We cannot risk our credibility as the only superpower in the world. We cannot make fools of ourselves. We must not become the laughingstock of the world.

That paragraph summarizes the conventional wisdom of 1968. It was the wisdom of "the best and the brightest" around President Lyndon Johnson, and it became the wisdom of Richard Nixon and Henry Kissinger for the next four years (while the number of American casualties doubled).

No two historical situations are exactly the same. Vietnam and Iraq are not the same places. The two wars are not precisely the same. Fair enough. However, in both cases the United States entered a war with the best intentions, monumental ignorance, and no exit strategy. The government never asked how and when it might be time to leave. So the two wars slogged on, as Secretary Donald Rumsfeld would say, with no end in sight. We must stay the course, even if we don't know how long the course will be.

Might one say, in all due modesty, that this is crazy?

Could we not say to the Iraqis: Hey, you don't want us as an occupying power, and we don't want to be here any more than you want us to be here. So you have six months to get your act in order, and then we're out of here.

It will be said that this is a radical design for the end game. Maybe it is, but I predict that by, say, April or May, it will be the Republican paradigm, the final stages of the administration's "mission accomplished" in Iraq. As Sen. Warren Austin advised President Johnson, it is time to proclaim victory in Vietnam and get out. Johnson didn't listen. For him, winning the 1968 election wasn't worth the humiliation of an ignominious retreat.

For President Bush, winning the 2004 election will be worth the humiliation of an ignominious retreat. Mindful of his father's loss in 1992, there is nothing more important than winning the election. I would not deplore a decision to get out several months before the election as cowardly or divisive. On the contrary, I would praise it as wise, no matter what the president's motivations might be. It would have been surpassingly wise if Johnson had pulled the plug in 1968, however much credibility was lost. How many lives is "credibility" worth?

Sometime after the New Year, Karl Rove, the president's political guru, will whisper the truth in the great man's ear: We won't win the election unless we are out of Iraq. We have to be out of there by Labor Day or we'll be accused of running out on our allies to win the election. If we do it during the summer, or even better, at the end of spring, we can declare it a victory.

That would not be a difficult promise to keep. The administration has proved that it can spin almost any decision—like disguising the tax cut as a benefit to the middle class. The leadership in France and Germany might chortle with glee at our "humiliation," but how many votes can they deliver?

What about American voters? Would they be deceived by a spin that declares that a defeat is victory? The president's "base," Southern evangelicals, might have a hard time swallowing it. Their hyper-patriotism might be offended by the fact that we had lost another war. Yet they would buy almost anything to sustain their stranglehold on the country. As for the Democrats, how can they criticize the administration for exiting a war they say it shouldn't have entered in the first place? Most Democrats won't vote for him anyway.

And the always-shifting middle, which was once taken in by Bush: Will it be taken in again? I wouldn't bet against it, especially if there is a modest decrease in unemployment and Saddam Hussein is somehow found. The formula for a Bush victory is simple: Cut and run.

December 26, 2003

Bush hasn't justified war

Was the capture of Saddam Hussein a major victory for the United States? It was certainly a victory in the extended Iraq war. It was a victory for President Bush over the man who plotted to kill his father. It was a victory for the U.S. military and its intelligence service—especially for the lieutenant and the corporal who figured out how to find him. It was a victory for the Republican Party's plan to keep a stranglehold on American politics. But was it, as the president told us, a victory in the "war on terrorism"?

Despite the media hoopla and the White House spin doctors, it was not. The administration legitimized the invasion of Iraq as part of the "war on terrorism" and deceived the American people into believing that Saddam was involved in the Sept. 11 attack and that he had "weapons of mass destruction." No one, except possibly Vice President Dick Cheney and the *Wall Street Journal*, believed that Saddam was involved in the attack on the World Trade Center. The weapons of mass destruction have disappeared.

The president asks a TV interviewer what difference the mass destruction question makes, now that we have eliminated Saddam from power.

Note how slippery the administration line has been. The purpose of the war now is to get rid of an evil man who had done horrible things to his own people, even if he wasn't a real threat to us. Would those Americans who are willing to settle for that rationale have bought it at the beginning of the war? Such is the slipperiness of the administration's dishonesty that it can get away with a change in motives for the war. Do those who buy this shifting of the deck of cards want to send American troops into North Korea or Iran or a half-dozen African countries to rid the world of similar evil men?

The truth is that Cheney and Defense Secretary Donald Rumsfeld and their "neo-conservative" intellectuals wanted a quick little war with Iraq to display America's strength as the world's only superpower even before the 2000 election. The attack on the World Trade Center provided an excellent excuse to unveil America's unilateral, preemptive foreign policy. Has the war made the United States any more secure from al-Qaida?

It would seem that it has not. Quite the contrary, it has stirred up a whole new phalanx of terrorists in Iraq with which we did not formerly have to contend.

It is reasonably well known that Osama bin Laden instructed his forces to have nothing to do with Saddam because Saddam was a secularist and a socialist and not a good Muslim. A man who imagined himself as the holy Caliph of a new Islamic empire could hardly tolerate Saddam as one of his subjects.

The Iraq war, prolonged by unspeakably bad planning for the postwar period, has distracted the United States from the battle with terrorists. If the military force sent to Iraq and the immense efforts to capture Saddam had been diverted to pursuing bin Laden, Americans would be much safer today.

The ultimate failure of the Bush administration is that it permitted itself to be so consumed by its need to take on Iraq that it lost interest in hunting down bin Laden. Its ultimate dishonesty is the (effective) deception of the American people about Iraq.

So, brave and good American men and women continue to die in Iraq, as do good Iraqi men and women. The military tells us that the Army will have to remain for two more years. The war was not only unnecessary, it was unjust by any and all of the traditional canons of an unjust war.

Gen. Curtis LeMay, who led the firebomb raids on Japan (far more destructive than the atom bombs), once remarked that if the United States should lose the war, he would be tried as a war criminal. The United States won the war, and no Americans were tried as war criminals. The victors are never tried.

The Bush administration is planning a trial for Saddam. The Europeans are insisting that it must be a "fair" trial, whatever that might be for such a man. No one in the Bush administration will be tried for the unjust and unnecessary Iraq war—at least not by a court on Earth.

January 30, 2004

The case against the Iraq war

Although Howard Dean may be toast politically, he was absolutely right when he said the safety of Americans did not improve when Saddam Hussein was captured. In fact, American casualties have increased since the capture. Saddam, it turns out, was never a threat to the United States. He might have become one in the future, but he was not at the time the war began. Nor, despite the redoubtable insistence of Vice President Dick Cheney, was Saddam ever allied with al-Qaida.

David Kay, the American official who headed the search for weapons of mass destruction, says that there are none. Secretary of State Colin Powell, who will certainly be dumped next year if President Bush is re-elected, says virtually the same thing. Kenneth Pollack, author of *The Threatening Storm: The Case for Invading Iraq*, in an article in the current issue of the *Atlantic Monthly*, admits that the case was inadequate and that American intelligence, especially under pressure from the administration, failed badly. He concludes: "Fairly or not, no foreigner trusts U.S. intelligence to get it right anymore or trusts the Bush administration to tell the truth."

In the same magazine, James Fallows argues that the failures in postwar Iraq were not the result of the absence of planning, but of U.S. leaders ignoring the excellent planning that had been done. When the National Intelligence Council ran a two-day exercise on postwar Iraq, for example, the office of the secretary of defense forbade Pentagon representatives to attend. Fallows concludes: "When the decisions of the past 18 months are assessed and judged, the administration will be found wanting for its carelessness. Because of the warnings it chose to ignore, it squandered American prestige, fortune and lives."

Finally, Peter Maas, in a long article in the *New York Times*, describes the guerrilla war in Iraq and makes it clear that it is problematic that America can win such a war. We did not do a very good job with the Native Americans in the Plains. We lost 4,000 American lives and killed perhaps 200,000 Filipinos in the little-known "pacification" after the Spanish-American War. We failed miserably in Vietnam at the cost of 58,000 American lives and hundreds of thousands of Vietnamese lives. There is no particular reason to think we will escape from Iraq with any more dignity than in our final, hasty days in Saigon.

We will leave behind not a democratic Iraq but another Shiite theocracy—not quite as rigid, perhaps, as the one in Iran—and the prospect of continuing conflict among Iraq's diverse tribes. Those who knew something about the Middle East warned that such an end game was likely. Arab culture does not seem to be compatible with what Americans define as democracy.

The war, it is clear by now, was unnecessary, ill-conceived, unjust and doomed to humiliating and costly failure. It was, as Fallows says, "careless." Most everyone in the world knows this truth except half of the American people, whose patriotism and fear of terrorism are superior to their perceptiveness.

Two questions remain: Did the administration deceive itself? Were the grim and solemn warnings of last year's State of the Union address what the leaders really believed? If the former, how could the leaders have been so wrong? If the latter, why did they try to deceive the rest of us?

The second question is whether, if the situation were really as bad as they said it was, would a preemptive war have been just? I find it hard to say no to this question because they would have had us believe that Saddam was almost ready to attack and that we had to act immediately in our own defense. However, they deceived us and perhaps themselves too.

The war is not now the big election issue that Howard Dean tried to make it. It does not follow, however, that it will not be a big issue at the end of next summer. Bush might have sidetracked the war as an issue by admitting in the State of the Union speech that there were some errors in judgment and mistakes. It is not in his nature or the nature of those around him to take such a risk.

February 13, 2004

Bush playing us for fools on WMD

The argument goes something like this: We didn't deceive you about the weapons of mass destruction in Iraq. The CIA deceived us. Therefore we will investigate, but the investigation will be not be finished till after the election. The weapons of mass destruction should not be an issue in the election. Neither should the billions of dollars for Iraq that will be in next year's budget.

Pretty slick. On the basis of past performance, it will probably work. The administration has delayed and stonewalled the commission investigating the World Trade Center attack, and no one seems to question what it's trying to cover up. Now the administration blames the "intelligence community" for failure to provide accurate information about Iraq and ducks responsibility for its own deception of the American people. No one gets the chance to ask whether Vice President Dick Cheney and his staff chewed out CIA analysts because of their failures to find the kind of evidence that the administration wanted.

In fact, it was pretty clear all along that the evidence was weak. Secretary of State Colin Powell's presentation at the United Nations (which was billed as a rerun of Adlai Stevenson's display of photos of Russian missiles in Cuba) was not persuasive. The best he could provide were hints and clues—hardly enough to start a war in which many young Americans and thousands of Iraqis would die.

As many of us knew all along from reading and hearing the neo-conservative intellectuals who do foreign-policy thinking for the administration and as former Treasury Secretary Paul O'Neill has confirmed, the administration from the beginning wanted to invade Iraq for a number of possibly good reasons. Bernard Lewis (an Islamic scholar who is a kind of guru to the neo-cons) thought that a democratic state in Iraq would tip the balance toward "modernization" in the Arab world. It would take pressure off Israel. Saddam Hussein was a very nasty man who might eventually develop nuclear weapons. Anyone who reads the *Wall Street Journal* or William Safire's column in the *New York Times* was familiar with these arguments. Unfortunately for those who supported such a war, the idea would not have been acceptable to the American people.

The Sept. 11 attack on the World Trade Center changed the climate of opinion in this country. The American people, it was assumed, would support an invasion of Iraq if the idea could be developed that Saddam was somehow allied with the attack. Hence, it was important to assemble evidence that an attack from him might be imminent.

The CIA, which is being blamed for the bad intelligence, was reluctant to make too much of its own clues, but it gave the administration the best it could provide, which wasn't very good to begin with and now is perceived as worthless. Perhaps there was "yellow cake" uranium being imported from Niger. Perhaps those aluminum cylinders were for shells of nerve gas. Perhaps there was a nuclear weapons program in that suspicious-looking factory. There had to be missile launchers somewhere. President Bush presented this "intelligence" in somber tones in his State of the Union speech a year ago. Thereupon the United States invaded Iraq with the solid support of the citizenry, the media and the Congress. (Sen. John Kerry must wish every day that he had been more skeptical.)

Now that the WMD argument has failed, the administration falls back on its original arguments. The men around the president must assume that the American people are too dumb to catch on to this ploy and to their attempt to take WMD off the table for election campaigns. Having fooled most of the people most of the time, they might well be right.

Yet the latest Gallup Poll makes one wonder. Half the people now believe that the Iraq war wasn't worth it; 43 percent believe the president deliberately deceived them about the war; and Kerry has a 53 percent to 46 percent lead over the president in Gallup's election poll. Maybe you can't fool all the people all the time.

February 27, 2004

Iraq more than Bush bargained for

In 1914 the German General Staff had a perfect plan for winning a war with France. It was called the Schlieffen Plan. It forecast that Germany could mobilize its entire reserve army on the efficient national railway system, move through Belgium, and capture Paris in 34 days. Indeed, it specified where the army should be on the way to Paris at each day of the month following mobilization. Schlieffen and his successors on the General Staff assumed that modern wars would be fought in one big battle, winner take all, as in the Battle of Sedan in the Franco-Prussian War of 1870.

The plan was a brilliant example of detailed Teutonic efficiency. In effect, it dismissed the importance of French resistance. The lessons of the Franco-Prussian War left little doubt that the French army was not to be taken seriously. The challenge for Germany was simply the skillful movement of its troops across the countryside for the big battle, which it would surely win.

The Schlieffen Plan almost worked. Field Marshal Gen. Helmut Graf von Moltke deviated a bit from it in the closing days or it might have worked. However, Gen. Ferdinand Foch managed to pull together a fighting force that just barely stopped the German advance at the first battle of the Marne. Neither side won that battle. The allies counterattacked and drove the invaders back, but the German army stopped the counterattack. Long years of trench war and bloody, useless battles began.

Early in 1915 Field Marshal Erich von Falkenhayn (who replaced the disgraced von Moltke) went to German Chancellor Theobald Bethman-Holweg and said the war could not now be won and that Germany should seek terms for peace. The chancellor said that such negotiations would humiliate the kaiser. And so the war went on—for the next 30 years, really—and tens of millions died, and the whole system and structure of Europe collapsed, to be revived only at the very end of the 20th century.

The best laid plans of mice and men . . . And of generals and secretaries of defense . . . No one has ever wanted a long war. Those who start wars assume that they will win quickly and easily. But war has a dynamism of its own that captures those who launch it and drives them where they never wanted to go. As someone has said of the 1939 renewal of the Great War, the half-truth fought the lie.

Very few Americans have noticed the irony and the humiliation of the Bush administration's seeking the help of the United Nations to pull our chestnuts out of the fire in Iraq. A year ago our swaggering, smirking president and our cocksure secretary of defense, Donald Rumsfeld, embraced a unilateralist foreign policy. The United States was the only superpower. It could do whatever it wanted. It did not need the U.N., it did not need NATO, it did not need any of our former allies. We would clean up the mess in Iraq all by ourselves before Saddam Hussein created a mushroom cloud. Now the administration pleads with Kofi Annan to make a deal for us about Iraqi elections—elections that will surely not produce the democratic Iraq we promised.

The U.N. might not be all that much, but it is the only international organization the world has, which the Bush administration now seems to admit. Among its many defects is the pretense of Franklin Roosevelt that France is a great power, which it was not in 1870 or 1914 or 1939. Yet every American president from 1945 on somehow managed to work with the U.N. to achieve this country's foreign-policy goals. Bush, under the influence of the "neo-con" intellectuals, decided that such effort was unnecessary. Rumsfeld designed a plan that would "take out" Saddam quickly and almost painlessly. Now it turns out that the United States needs the help of the U.N. to extricate us from the quagmire we have created for ourselves. Alas, there is no Marshal von Falkenhayn around to tell the president that it's time to get out.

April 2, 2004

America should heed Clarke's warnings

Richard Clarke's *Against All Enemies* is one very scary book. Unlike most people who have an opinion on it, I've read the book.

It is understandable that the administration has become hysterical in its attacks on Clarke. If his account is accurate, then the president is a man of limited talents, capable of absorbing only simple proposals, and surrounded by advisers from Cloud Cuckooland. Yet for all the viciousness of the assault, no one has explained why a registered Republican civil servant who has served in five administrations, three of them Republican, would write such a book unless he was genuinely worried about the state of the country. As for it being a partisan political book, it would have been published last November, a year before the election, if a security check on it was not deemed necessary. Clarke's story fits with that of Paul O'Neill, the former secretary of the treasury, who describes the same kind of White House. One can only hope that enough Americans take seriously the possibility that Clarke is telling the truth before al-Qaida blows up some American commuter trains.

Even more scary is the implication of the book that Americans are not much safer than they were in August 2001. The two agencies with primary responsibility for security—the CIA and the FBI—are apparently paralyzed by bureaucratic concerns about their turf. The former in particular seems worse than useless, and its computer system doesn't work very well, if at all. The Department of Homeland Security has no control over either agency and has become, as many predicted it would, a cumbersome monstrosity. Clarke suggests that the billions of dollars pumped into the Iraq war could have been spent notably improving the domestic war against terrorism or setting up a single police agency to deal specifically with domestic terrorism.

Apparently, Condoleezza Rice had never heard of al-Qaida when she came to the White House. Her major concern seemed to be that there were too many employees in the counter-terrorism group. The administration was not interested in such notions as the war on terrorism, which it had inherited from the previous administration. Rather, it worried about China and a missile defense system.

However, the real creatures from Cloud Cuckooland are Donald Rumsfeld and Paul Wolfowitz, who had equated the war on terrorism with a war on Iraq before and after the Sept. 11 attack. Wolfowitz insisted that the first World Trade Center attack could not have been the work of rag-tag Islamic radicals but must have been sponsored by a state—Iraq, of course. At the one and only meeting on terrorism, Wolfowitz played the anti-Semitic card against Clarke for suggesting that, like Hitler, Osama bin Laden might do exactly what he said he would do. It was offensive, he said, to compare an unimportant person to the instigator of the Holocaust. After the attack, he insisted that it had to be the Iraqis who were responsible.

Even before they came to office, Rumsfeld and Wolfowitz wanted to take over Iraq. Their response to the World Trade Center catastrophe was that now they could take over Iraq as part of the war on terrorism, though there was no proof that Iraq had ever engaged in terrorism against the United States or that it planned to.

Thus, in the name of protecting the United States, they led us into a foolish, ill-conceived war that diverted money from genuine homeland security and fulfilled bin Laden's prediction that the United States would invade an oil-rich, Islamic country. Instead of reducing terrorism, the war and the horrendous mess afterward generated more terrorism, such as the attack on the trains in Barcelona. The hundreds killed in that attack are blood on the administration's hands.

Previous presidents have been inept. Woodrow Wilson gave away the store at Versailles after a bad case of the Spanish flu had laid him low. Jimmy Carter's staff were from adjoining sectors of Cuckooland. Yet it is terrifying that in these terrible times such men are not only losing the war on terrorism but running on the platform that they've virtually won it.

April 23, 2004

Is military draft in the works?

There's a sign on the horizon, no bigger than a man's hand, that there's a military draft in the works. The Defense Department has announced that Selective Service is making preparations for another draft, "in case one is needed." The *New York Times* in an inane editorial pleads with the president to articulate a goal for the war, stating that if it "was clear and comprehensive and people understood how to reach it, then Mr. Bush could . . . even bolster the desperately straitened military with a draft if Americans understood the need to sacrifice."

If the editorial writers of the *New York Times* are talking about a new draft that would send young men and women to die in the deserts of Iraq fighting crazy religious fanatics, then the idea is certainly being whispered about in the upper echelons of American society. A draft would not be proposed before the election—if it were, Bush would be wiped out in a landslide. But a wise person would not bet against the draft being proposed next January.

What in the world is the *Times* talking about? Why should Americans sacrifice for the Iraq war? Not by the wildest stretch of the imagination can one seriously argue that the war in Iraq is to defend vital American interests. We found that there were no weapons of mass destruction there and no connection with al-Qaida or the Sept. 11 attack. The only issue seems to be whether we can impose democracy on Iraqis who don't seem seriously to want it or to prevent a civil war that will happen anyway as soon as our army leaves. Americans are supposed to accept the need to sacrifice their unwilling sons and daughters to fight for such absurd goals?

There are many authoritarian liberals who have a kind of illicit romance with the draft. Young people owe their country a part of their lives, even their lives itself (not their own sons and daughters' lives, of course). Military service is good for you, some veterans insist. It will make a man out of a drifting late adolescent. What it will do for a young woman remains to be seen—probably teach her how to live in a world where rape is commonplace.

Building up the army with a draft will serve only the needs of the Bush administration to "win" a war. Gen. Eric Shinseki, then-chief of staff of the Army, said that 200,000 would be needed to pacify Iraq. Donald Rumsfeld made fun of him in public. Now the Defense Department seems to be engaged in remote planning for a draft army that will be much larger.

How many men and women, it must be asked, will be required to pacify Iraq and to turn it into a freedom-loving democracy? How long will it take, how many lives must be sacrificed to protect the honor and the legacy of Bush and Cheney and Rumsfeld and their crowd of imperialists?

Doubtless it will be argued in favor of a draft that we all must make sacrifices for a war on terrorism. It might be better if one sent men and women in their 40s to fight in a foolish, unjust, immoral, criminal war. It would be good for them. They'd have to lose weight and get back in good physical condition.

Bush has made "the war on terrorism" a mantra to cover everything his administration has done. But the Iraq war has nothing to do with the war on terrorism, as we now know. It was a plan of Cheney and Rumsfeld and their coterie of "neo-conservative" intellectuals (like Paul Wolfowitz) long before they came to power. It was supposed to make the United States a major power in the Middle East; to provide a democratic alternative to the typical Arab autocracy; to give the United States control of major oil fields; to take pressure off Israel; and to establish that the United States was a superpower that could go anywhere in the world and do anything it wanted. The "war on terrorism" was only a pretext to implement this plan, as accounts of the early White House reaction to the Sept. 11 attack seem to indicate.

Does one have to say that none of these goals has been achieved or can be achieved?

I wonder why Sen. John Kerry sounds so much like Hubert Humphrey in his support of the continuation of the war. I hope at least he makes opposition to a new draft a major issue in the election.

April 30, 2004

How we got into this unjust war

While Bob Woodward's *Plan of Attack* confirms earlier books by former Treasury Secretary Paul O'Neill and former White House terrorism expert Richard Clarke, it is more effective because it is more even-handed and permits the various actors in the drama to speak for themselves.

Some conclusions I draw from the book:

- Once President Bush was elected and put together his team, a war with Iraq was locked in. Men like Vice President Dick Cheney and Defense Secretary Donald Rumsfeld had made up their minds that invasion was essential. Deputy Defense Secretary Paul Wolfowitz had written the plan for invasion in 1996. The only countervailing force was Secretary of State Colin Powell. He was frozen out, however, by the others, in part because the president felt intimidated by him.
- CIA Director George Tenet provided "evidence" about weapons of mass destruction to support the war, which he described to the president as slam-dunk proof but which was in fact very weak. Woodward himself says that a story he co-authored about dissent within the American intelligence agencies should have appeared on Page 1 of the

Washington Post instead of Page 17. Apparently, Bush and Cheney still believe that weapons will be found, and so will the link to al-Qaida. They are, I think, the only ones who believe in either global folk tale.

- The administration sold the public—and perhaps the president sold himself—on the Iraq invasion as part of the "war on terrorism." That was a rationalization for the war perhaps, but it was never the real reason. It was a deception, perhaps even a lie, from beginning to end. The real reason is that "all the president's men" wanted the war.

- The slogan "war on terrorism" (or "war on terror") was false from the very beginning. Yet it has been a powerful political mantra for the administration to win support for almost anything it has wanted to do. The struggle against terrorists is not a war in any sense that the word has normally meant. It has the same value as, for example, the "war on drugs."

- The president's personality and religious faith—in combination— make it impossible for him to have serious second thoughts or even to admit any ambiguity. If a decision is "right," then it is right no matter what. Many Americans, perhaps a slight majority, think this is "strong" leadership. My feeling is that it edges toward religious fanaticism and is not altogether different from the "rightness" of Osama bin Laden's faith. If there is a mistake, it is not the president's mistake. It's God's mistake because God told him he had made the right decision.

- A president serves the nation better if he admits, at least to himself, how problematic all political decisions are. President John F. Kennedy, for example, took full responsibility for the Bay of Pigs fiasco, even though he inherited the project from his predecessor. During the Cuban Missile Crisis, Kennedy's stubborn resistance to those who wanted war prevented a nuclear holocaust. A president who has no self-doubt, no ability to question his own mistakes, is a very dangerous man.

Finally, besides some outlines of responsibilities, there was very little in the plan of attack that took seriously the problems of postwar Iraq—problems that last week caused Rumsfeld at least to admit some uncertainty. There is not the slightest indication that anyone knew about or considered seriously the difficulties Britain encountered in Mesopotamia (as it was then called) in the early 1920s—or the cruelty necessary for Britain's victory.

The war is a stupid, unjust and criminal war. It is a quagmire from which no immediate escape seems possible. Many more Americans are going to die so that American "democracy and freedom" can be imposed on the Iraqis—whether they want them or not. Many more Iraqis will die, too. Americans who support the war share in its criminality.

May 14, 2004

Bush has no excuse in abuse scandal

The current shock and outrage at the White House and the Pentagon are as phony as a $17 bill. The president might not have known what was happening specifically at Abu Ghraib but had to know in general how the CIA and military intelligence were "softening up" prisoners for interrogation. Could he have been so stupid as to think that captured al-Qaida leaders had a change of heart and freely revealed their secrets?

A couple of months ago, *Atlantic Monthly* published a chilling article on new methods of interrogation that soften up prisoners by mental torment. Perfected by the British in Northern Ireland, such interrogations do not need electrodes or truth serum or clubs or torture machines to break the human body. Rather, they use more sophisticated techniques of psychological assault: sleep deprivation, humiliation, temperature manipulation, sensory deprivation (hence, hoods over the head), erratic feeding and endless cacophony to break the human spirit. A person can be broken by such assaults without a single mark on the body. The article raised the question of whether in the struggle with terrorists such tactics might be tolerable.

Abu Ghraib added to the mix the use of women for sexual humiliation and someone with a digital camera. There are several interrogation centers around the world like Abu Ghraib. Any credible investigation should look at all of them.

It is unthinkable that the top brass in the government were not aware that the CIA was playing such games with captives in many detention centers. It is also unthinkable that congressional leaders and senior journalists did not know about this interrogation of captives in the search for weapons of mass destruction. If the president did not know, then he was guilty of what we used to call in the seminary "vincible" ignorance. He should have known, and there is no excuse for him not knowing. One can bet on it: The low-level grunts will be blamed, and the CIA and the MI brass will go unscathed. Also, poor Don Rumsfeld might have to take the fall to cover for the president.

Is there any chance of winning the war in Iraq? Ought not we support the troops by insisting that they be brought home? Should not the United States specify the day—Jan. 1, Feb. 1, whenever—that we're out of there? Is there any other way it can end? All right, there will be national humiliation like the helicopters taking off from the roof of the embassy in Saigon. But that's going to happen anyway.

The Iraqis don't like us and don't want us around. In the copyrighted Gallup survey of Iraqi attitudes, 58 percent of the respondents said that U.S. troops had behaved badly even before the Abu Ghraib pictures appeared—81 percent in Baghdad. Seventy-one percent of them see the Americans as occupiers, not liberators; 40 percent think that attacks on the Americans are justified; and only one-third of the Arabs think they are better off under the Americans than under Saddam (87 percent of the Kurds do).

Chairman Mao said that guerrillas swim in the sea of the people. Patently, the sea is big enough in Iraq to support a prolonged "insurgency." The enemy now is not the "few thugs and foreign agitators" whom the president denounces, but the Iraqi people. They don't want us in their country, they don't like us, they want us out. They indeed want democracy (the Gallup data show), but not at our hands.

Our troops are not to blame for Iraqi hostility. Rather, the Bush administration, which sent them into the war untrained and unequipped to be an occupying army, much less a counter-insurgency force, is responsible. The troops do not speak the language, do not understand the culture and religion, and cannot distinguish the harmless Iraqi from someone who wants to kill them. It is unfair and cruel to force young soldiers—and even worse, older Reservists and National Guard members—to struggle in such an impossible situation.

The president is the responsible person in this country; the buck stops at his desk, as Harry Truman said once and forever. He may scapegoat others, he may duck and weave, but he either knew what was going on or should have known. Those Americans who will vote to re-elect him will support the man responsible for Abu Ghraib.

May 28, 2004

How war in Iraq derails real war on terrorism

"Colombo Bay" sounds like it might be a novel by Joseph Conrad. It is instead a story by Richard Pollak about his voyage from Hong Kong to New York on a container ship named the *Colombo Bay*, which indeed stopped at the capital of Sri Lanka. The *Colombo Bay* also reveals just how badly the real war on terrorism has been compromised by the Iraq war.

We've all seen railroad flatcars loaded with freight-truck containers. These are carried to ports and loaded on thousands of container ships, which carry them around the world. The *Colombo Bay* carries more than 3,000 such containers, and it is not the largest of the container ships.

These vast ships are the tramp steamers of our era. They travel from port to port at speeds of 22 knots, unloading some containers and picking up other containers. Their turnaround times are much less leisurely than in Conrad's era, although the similarity to his stories is striking. Container ships have become the lifeblood of global trade and have added a trillion dollars to the U.S. annual business inventory. We couldn't do without them.

But think of the possibility for terrorists in those 3,000 containers on the *Colombo Bay*. When it docked off New York, the crew discovered that the seal had been broken on a container that carried missile warheads manufactured in Germany and shipped by rail to a French port for transit to the Raytheon Corp. The French authorities had broken the seal to inspect the contents and (with characteristic French efficiency) had placed a makeshift lock on the container and made no annotations on the shipping papers.

The Coast Guard spent two days clearing the container. Pollak comments that the Coast Guard's equipment is obsolescent (helicopters 20 years old) and its computers a generation behind—and unable to communicate with the computers of the FBI, CIA and INS. Terrorists would have seen that a proper seal was on one of their containers.

Pollak adds that in 2003, Sen. Ernest Hollings, author of the Maritime Transportation Security Act, requested $1 billion for the Coast Guard for port security as an amendment to the $87 billion appropriation for the war in Iraq. The amendment was rejected. It was a classic example of how the administration's distraction with Iraq interfered with a critical component of homeland security—which is not the same thing as President Bush's Frankenstein monster Department of Homeland Security.

The president talks about homeland security, but, under the malign influence of the vice president and the "neo-con" intellectuals, he has made the war in Iraq a substitute for the real war on terrorism. Almost three years after the World Trade Center attack, O'Hare Airport does not have the equipment necessary to inspect checked luggage because the Transportation Safety Administration does not have the money to pay for the equipment.

But $25 billion more is going to his criminal war. The public still gives the president high marks on his success in the war on terrorism, mostly because people are judging by the war in Afghanistan and the early success in Iraq. However, our airports and our seaports are still not safe. How many more years will it take?

And how many years to straighten out the messes at the FBI and the CIA? A recent estimate was six years. When will that start?

Thus, despite all the talk about security during the years since the destruction of the World Trade Center, very little has been done to improve the security of our republic, other than talk. The majority of Americans expect another attack. They are wise to do so.

Because the terrorists will almost certainly try something before the presidential election, the container ships and airport checked baggage are perfect targets—and not much better defended than was Logan Airport in September 2001. Think of a "dirty" bomb exploding in New York or Long Beach Harbor.

If all the time and money and energy expended on finding weapons of mass destruction and capturing Saddam Hussein had been spent on protecting this country by measures besides harassing air travelers, the country would be much safer.

June 4, 2004

This time, Europe's hatred justified

COLOGNE, Germany—There were American flags all over the house I visited the other day in the suburbs of this lovely city. Two of the children of the house—two German kids on the edge of what we would call young adulthood—had studied in the United States and learned to love the country. What about the Iraq war? I asked their father, a social-science colleague. They are able to make the distinction, he replied, between the war, of which they strongly disapprove, and the United States, which they admire.

In other words, between the country and its present leadership. It is not a distinction that everyone in Europe is ready to make. Hating America is the anti-Semitism of the European intelligentsia. It always has been. Unfortunately, the Bush administration has poured fuel on the flames of that hatred.

Why hate America?

There are many reasons. We are rich and powerful—and sometimes obnoxiously loud. The United States saved Europe in two hot wars and one cold war. It provided the umbrella of military protection that enabled Western Europe to achieve the prosperity it now takes for granted. Cologne has come a long way from the ruins that Heinrich Boll described in his early novels. Without the Marshall Plan, the Berlin airlift and the Seventh Army, that re-emergence could never have happened. Gratitude for American help? Rather, resentment and envy. No good deed goes unpunished.

Moreover, from its first tentative steps, American policy supported the development of what is now the European Union. For that, Europeans, so proud that their borders now include most of the continent, will never be able to forgive us. Like I say, no good deed goes unpunished. It is great fun to bite the hand that has fed you.

Now hatred for America is so strong that in countries like Germany and Spain political losers can become winners simply by running against George W. Bush. President Jacques Chirac, a corrupt and incompetent man, rises to new heights of popularity because he filibusters against the invasion of Iraq. One hears that he believed that would be his legacy. He stood up to the United States and saved Saddam Hussein, an ally of France. It would also appear that Saddam believed that the United States would not invade because France and Russia would save him. He had not read the writings of the neo-conservative intellectuals who had infiltrated the Bush administration and were determined to invade Iraq, and indeed preferred a unilateral invasion.

It is galling that, in retrospect, Chirac and German Chancellor Gerhard Schroeder and Russian President Vladimir Putin were right. Saddam was a bad man whom the world had to watch closely. But he did not have those weapons of mass destruction and had not participated in the World Trade Center attack. Indeed, Deputy Defense Secretary Paul Wolfowitz, the prince of darkness of the neo-conservatives, admitted that the weapons were a bureaucratic pretext for a war that was desirable for other reasons (like "reshaping" the Middle East).

This time European hatred of America was absolutely correct, though most do not make the distinction of my friends here in Cologne between the Bush administration, which was not elected by the majority of Americans, and the good spirit of our country. This time the country is not being punished for its good deeds but for a very bad deed: a criminally unjust war.

It is useful to see how the war is covered by the European media, such as the BBC and *Irish Times* (which I read every day). Their "slant" is a useful correction to that provided (until very recently) by American media. However, there is also an evident satisfaction—one might almost say celebration—of the humiliation and corruption of American power in Iraq.

A retired American diplomat who had served in Ireland recently blamed the *Irish Times* for the World Trade Center attack. It is true the newspaper has historically been critical of the U.S. government, but no more critical than of the Irish government. Yet it delights now in every new American failure.

Hopefully, when the United States breaks out of its present obsessions, there will be enough people like my young Koelners who realize what it really stands for.

June 11, 2004

Is U.S. like Germany of the '30s?

BERLIN—I can understand, my German friend said, why Germans voted for Hitler in 1933—though he did not receive a majority of the vote. The Weimar Republic was weak and incompetent. The Great Depression had ruined the nation's war-devastated economy. People were bitter because they thought their leaders had betrayed them in the war. They wanted revenge for the humiliation of Versailles. Hitler promised strong leadership and a new beginning. But why did they continue to support that group of crazy drug addicts, thugs, killers and madmen?

The historical question remains. I leave aside the question of the guilt of the whole German people (a judgment beyond my competence because I am not God) and ask what explanations might account for what happened. Hitler turned the German economy around in short order. He was crazy, of course, a demagogic mystic sensitive to aspirations of the German spirit. He appealed skillfully to the dark side of the German heritage. Anti-Semitism was strong in Germany, as it was in most European countries, but not violent until Hitler manipulated it. He stirred up the memories of historic German military accomplishments and identified himself with Frederick the Great—thus placating the Prussian ethos of the German army. He promised glory to a nation still smarting from the disaster of 1918. Germany was emerging from the ashes, strong and triumphant once again. He also took control of the police apparatus. The military might have been able to dump him till 1937. After that he was firmly in power. The path lay open to holocaust.

Can this model be useful to understand how contemporary America is engaged in a criminally unjust war that has turned much of the world against it, a war in which torture and murder have become routine? Has the combination of the World Trade Center attack and a president who believes his instructions come from God unleashed the dark side of the American heritage?

What is this dark side? I would suggest that it is the mix of Calvinist religious righteousness and "my-country-right-or-wrong" patriotism that dominated our treatment of blacks and American Indians for most of the country's history. It revealed itself in the American history of imperialism in Mexico and after the Spanish-American War in the Philippines. The "manifest destiny" of America was to do whatever it wanted to do, because it was strong and virtuous and chosen by God.

Today many Americans celebrate a "strong" leader who, like Woodrow Wilson, never wavers, never apologizes, never admits a mistake, never changes his mind, a leader with a firm "Christian" faith in his own righteousness. These Americans are delighted that he ignores the rest of the world and punishes the World Trade Center terrorism in Iraq. Mr. Bush is our kind of guy.

He is not another Hitler. Yet there is a certain parallelism. They have in common a demagogic appeal to the worst side of a country's heritage in a crisis. Bush is doubtless sincere in his vision of what is best for America. So too was Hitler. The crew around the president—Donald Rumsfeld, John Ashcroft, Karl Rove, the "neo-cons" like Paul Wolfowitz—are not as crazy perhaps as Himmler and Goering and Goebbels. Yet like them, they are practitioners of the Big Lie—weapons of mass destruction, Iraq democracy, only a few "bad apples."

Hitler's war was quantitatively different from the Iraq war, but qualitatively both were foolish, self-destructive and criminally unjust. This is a time of great peril in American history because a phony patriotism and an America-worshipping religion threaten the authentic American genius of tolerance and respect for other people.

The "real" America is still remembered here in Berlin for the enormous contributions of the Marshall Plan and the Berlin airlift—America at its best. It is time to return to that generosity and grace.

The strongest criticism that the administration levels at Sen. John Kerry is that he changes his mind. In fact, instead of a president who claims an infallibility that exceeds that of the pope, America would be much better off with a president who, like John F. Kennedy, is honest enough to admit mistakes and secure enough to change his mind.

June 18, 2004

When containment meant progress

BERLIN—I came here for prayer, reflection and nostalgia. At this place on June 26, 1963, John F. Kennedy gave his famous "Let them come to Berlin" speech. On a warm Sunday afternoon, a flea market in the Rathaus (city hall) Platz vies with the memories of four decades ago. Yet images from old films come back. The president is speaking to a crowd in front of the city hall of West Berlin. I can almost hear his conclusion, "Ich bin ein Berliner!" and the ecstatic cheers of the Berliners.

The sponsor of the conference I attended here, an insightful and successful businessman, said of those four words: "They are the most important words spoken in the German language in the 20th century." (And that should suffice for the begrudgers who say that the word "ein" was a grammatical mistake.)

You don't ask someone to explain poetry, so I didn't ask my friend what he meant. It seemed clear enough anyway. Kennedy's identification with the people of Berlin, surrounded as they were by the wall, meant that they were no longer former enemies. They were friends whom we would always stand by, no matter how many tank confrontations there might be at Checkpoint Charlie, no matter how many fulminations from Nikita Khrushchev. The United States would never sell out the people of Berlin.

The head of the East German communist government promised that the wall would last for 100, maybe 500 years. For several decades, that seemed to be a distinct possibility. In fact, it lasted less than 30 years. Then suddenly and almost without warning it was gone. America had stayed the course in Berlin and in the rest of Europe.

Berliners claim that they will never forget Jack Kennedy, who had only a few months to live after his speech here. A young woman at our conference told us how proud her mother was that as a child she had seen Kennedy ride by in an open car. The speech has become one of the masterpieces of American political rhetoric. (Watch a TV clip of it some day and absorb the passion and power of his refrain, "Let them come to Berlin!") Even the hard-left Berliners are cautious in their criticism of America. Berliners might not like the Iraq war, but they know how much they owe America. We never sold them out.

It is fashionable these days to patronize the Cold War—a fight, as it seems, between two evil giants struggling for hegemony. In fact, protecting Berlin and the rest of the West was never essential to the American self-interest. They needed us; we did not need them. Yet we made promises and by and large kept them. "Staying the course" in those days meant something different from what it has come to mean today. It meant toughness and patience, a line firmly drawn but guarded with restraint—as in the Cuban Missile Crisis. America led and cajoled its allies rather than running roughshod over them. When we lost our restraint, as in Vietnam, we helped no one.

The strategy, often called "containment," did not satisfy many Americans. Some said it was too weak. Others said it was too tough. John Foster Dulles spoke about rollback. There never was any. Ronald Reagan spoke of the "evil empire" but negotiated with it. Every president since Harry Truman practiced containment because there wasn't any choice. Finally it worked, better than we had expected and sooner than we had hoped. Now there is a United Europe from Gibraltar to the Vistula, and Berlin is a city once again.

Unfortunately, under the influence of so-called neo-conservatives, the United States now does whatever it wants whenever it wants and doesn't need the help of its old allies. "Staying the course" means that we continue in our follies no matter what the cost and how futile the loss of life.

Pondering this history a few miles from Checkpoint Charlie, I reflect that in such an incredibly small place, with tanks on either side, trigger fingers on the guns, the present incumbent of the White House, acting on instructions from God, might have "stayed the course" by pushing through the Russian tanks and heading for Moscow.

And a lot of us would be dead, and many of us would never have been born.

June 25, 2004

Bush could learn from Reagan

In the recent celebration of the "legacy" of Ronald Reagan, one often heard that he made us proud of America again. We were once more a city shining on a hill. Such doubts do not occur in most countries. The English, the French, the Dutch, the Spanish, the Poles—none of them worry about whether they are the light of the world. There are some exceptions. The Germans are beginning to ask if it is acceptable again to be German. The Irish are not happy unless they are unhappy about Ireland, especially as it becomes more prosperous.

Why this need to be cheered up about America? The constant criticism of this country through its long history by Europeans is part of the explanation. Moreover, we periodically become uneasy because we are afraid that we have not lived up to our goal of being a "new order under heaven," the light shining on the hill.

Are we a light to the world?

In some ways we are. My research has shown that Americans are the most generous people in the world in both their money (percent of income) and their time. Volunteer rates in this country are the highest in the world, and the motives by which Americans explain their volunteering are the most altruistic in the world. Americans are also among the most religious people in the world. Nor is that religion devoted entirely to self-righteous and hypocritical efforts to impose virtue on others. My research also shows that the generosity and volunteer activities are substantially religious in their motivations.

The American immigration dream still works. While we may not like immigrants as faceless groups, we are, compared with Europeans, remarkably tolerant of immigrants as individuals. We are properly disgusted that France will not permit young Muslim women to wear their scarves to school. The refusal of the Bush administration to scapegoat Muslims is greatly to its credit. The wide varieties of colors, religions and customs that can be found on streets such as Atlantic Avenue in New York and Devon Avenue in Chicago are taken for granted. Tolerance of diversity (not quite the same as approval) flourishes in this country, as the increase in acceptance of homosexuals in the last decade demonstrates.

America is nowhere near perfect in any of these manifestations of light from the mountain. Sometimes the light is dim or blacked out. We crusaded against slavery and for civil rights, but also against drinking, dancing and card-playing. We still often succumb to the "manifest destiny" temptation to cloak imperialism behind good intentions. The same good intentions that led to the Marshall Plan and American protection of Europe and Asia from communism incline us to try to set the world aright in places such as Vietnam or Iraq, to make Southeast Asia and the Middle East, as President Woodrow Wilson would have put it, "safe for democracy."

The greed of corporate leaders does not provide much light to the world, nor does the propensity of executives to squeeze profits out of the pensions and health-care benefits of their employees. Finally, the light fades because of our past history of racism and its continued presence on our hill. If Reagan persuaded us to be proud of our virtues, he did not lead us to be clear-eyed about our faults.

Yet there was one important incident in his years as president that received little notice during the festival that marked his death. In 1983, he sent a contingent of Marines into Lebanon to "monitor" peace in that country's endless civil war. Muslim terrorists drove a truck bomb into the Marine barracks, killing hundreds. The president promptly withdrew the Marines and took full responsibility for the mistake. If someone is to face court martial, he told his aides, it should be me and not the officers in charge.

Reagan admitted a mistake, blamed no one but himself, and then, in words that would be used by supporters of the Bush administration, "cut and ran." As the supporters of the president try to identify his deeds with those of Reagan, they should use the Lebanon affair as a paradigm to examine their own behavior. Their contention that the torture of prisoners is the work of just a few rotten apples is a blatant escape from admitting presidential responsibility for whatever happens on his watch.

July 9, 2004

Americans deserve look at U.S. emergency defense plans

Last Monday they laid the cornerstone for the "Freedom Tower" where the World Trade Center used to be. "Freedom" is the mantra, the battle cry, the shibboleth of the "war on terrorism." Many Americans think that if they invoke this magic word often enough—without too much concern for its content—they have established their bona fides as patriots. They don't realize that terrorists cannot destroy freedom, but fear can. The real threats to freedom come not from Islamic terrorists, but from the American government. It whispers that we must sacrifice freedom so that freedom will be secure. If Americans yield to the fear of fear itself, then the terrorists have already won.

The decisions of the Supreme Court last week regarding detainees in Guantanamo and American citizens held without access to counsel or courts are an authentic, if modest, victory for freedom. They halt—please,

God, not temporarily—the creeping fascism that has threatened this country since the World Trade Center attack.

"Fascism" is not an exaggeration. It is, among other things, a political philosophy that says that the leader is above the law, that a commander in chief in a time of war has unlimited power in the name of national security. This is a claim that has been made seriously by lawyers in the White House, the Pentagon and the Justice Department in recent years.

Some documents have been released, some have been leaked, some are still hidden lest Congress find them in an election year. They argue more or less explicitly that in time of war the president as commander in chief can suspend the Bill of Rights, hold men it has designated as enemy aliens indefinitely without trial or legal counsel, imprison American citizens in the same circumstances, authorize moderate or even intense torture for intelligence purposes, and suspend the treaty-authorized Geneva Conventions. Indeed, one memo seems to suggest that there is no limit to what the president can order in wartime. Commander in chief has morphed into generalissimo, caudillo, el jefe.

Anyone who does not think that such a philosophy is incipient fascism doesn't know what fascism is.

It is argued in the president's defense that he has not authorized most of these violations of human rights. Doubtless he hasn't read the long and ponderous legal memos. Yet he has authorized detention without trial or counsel. So he must have relied on some of these memos. Moreover, the stone wall the White House has built to hide more documents about torture seems to hint that efforts to rewrite the Constitution may have been more extensive than we now know.

Many Americans (such as Rush Limbaugh) defend these theories, but recent surveys show that most Americans reject them. Although there is powerful residual support for a "strong" president in wartime and profound ignorance of the Bill of Rights, there seems to be a gut instinct among Americans that these abridgements of freedom are wrong.

Some liberals suggest that the administration is capable of canceling the November election on the grounds of national security if it looks as if Bush would lose. I doubt this. Yet I don't doubt that somewhere in the bowels of Justice or the Pentagon or Defense, one might find a note or two hinting at the possibility of such behavior. The election will go ahead regardless of the polls—though perhaps another terrorist attack might put it in jeopardy.

It is known that some time ago (before the World Trade Center attack), Defense Secretary Donald Rumsfeld and Vice President Dick Cheney had drafted proposals for what should happen if most of the members of Congress were killed in an attack. Surely there should be plans for such an eventuality. Yet, given the contempt for the Constitution that seems to exist among some administration lawyers, those plans should be made public and discussed to make sure that a surviving president—any surviving president—cannot suspend the Constitution and impose a new form of government on the country.

Under any circumstances the disaster blueprint should be made public. However, the lack of regard for the Bill of Rights in the Justice Department under Attorney General John Ashcroft and the suggestion by White House Counsel Alberto Gonzales that the Geneva Conventions are "quaint" make it imperative that Americans know before this election what plans the administration has to reconstitute the country after a disaster.

July 23, 2004

Leaders need dissenting voices

Some commentators attribute the failure of American and British intelligence services on Iraq to "group think"—the power of a group's cohesive culture to blind its members to data that would challenge its conclusion. The term "group think" originated in a brilliant book written by the psychologist Irving Janis in 1972. It describes how competent, intelligent, dedicated humans can accept a group consensus despite powerful evidence that it is in error. The importance of group unity constrains them to agree with something that they might not have accepted in another context. The classic example in Janis's study is the attack on Pearl Harbor in December 1941. The American commanders were able and intelligent men, but they "knew," as everyone else did, that the Japanese would never dare to attack Pearl Harbor.

The *New York Times*, which has apologized editorially for believing the Iraq evidence, used the group-think theory as an explanation of what happened. That might be half the story, but another theory from sociology in the era after the war must be applied, that of William H. Whyte's *The Organization Man* (1956). In this theory, loyalty to an organization and the demand that one keep one's bosses happy constrain a person to tell the bosses what they want to hear. The CIA and the British intelligence services, like all human organizations, permit relatively little dissent. If you disagree constantly with what the leaders "know" is true, your career will be in serious trouble.

The most interesting case discussed by Janis is the Cuban Missile Crisis. A consensus existed that the United States should attack the Russian sites and invade Cuba. However, Attorney General Robert Kennedy said that they were not going to make his brother the Gen. Tojo (the Japanese premier at Pearl Harbor time) of the 1960s. Later, the president kept asking what happens when the first Russian soldier dies. A nuclear war was avoided because of "no men"—men who violated the consensus and said "no," one of them a president.

The only way to avoid disastrous mistakes by intelligence agencies is to legitimate and encourage adversarial voices—men and women who argue vigorously that a policy decision is wrong (as did the tiny and unheard State Department intelligence unit to whom even Secretary Colin Powell did not listen). Indeed, these men and women must be ex officio obligated to present the opposite case, so that their careers will not suffer because they did their job. Someone in every agency has to be a Robert Kennedy. That's a difficult, perhaps impossible, role to play when you know that the bosses all the way up to the Oval Office want to go in a certain direction. There need not be any formal pressure, though Vice President Dick Cheney's frequent visits to the CIA certainly were pressure—as were Secretary of Defense Donald Rumsfeld's instructions to his people to stay away from the CIA.

There was no pretense that the Bush administration was judiciously weighing the pros and cons of a war. Everyone knew the White House was looking for justification. Sure enough, it got it!

An administration needs inside its inner circle a dissenting voice, someone who insists repeatedly: "You shouldn't do that!" But in an administration that values loyalty as much as the present one does, that voice will not be heard. The president wanted "regime change," and the CIA gave him reasons for it—a "slam dunk," as CIA Director George Tenet called it.

Some Bush supporters are arguing that the Senate committee cleared Bush of deceiving the American people. Such a claim is nonsense. He may not have deliberately lied. Nonetheless, he passed on to the American people reasons for war that were weak. He may not have been aware that they were weak, but he should have been. The buck stops at his desk. To blame the loyal CIA for providing him inadequate information is to shrug off the responsibility that comes with leadership. Britain's Tony Blair had the grace to assume responsibility. In the present White House, the president is never responsible for anything that goes wrong. Whether he deliberately deceived us does not matter. The fact is, he did deceive us. He should have known better.

July 30, 2004

9/11 action? Not before Nov. 2

It seems that there is a new rule in American politics: Nothing is done during an election year, lest it affect the outcome of the election. This law was spoken by the speaker of the House of Representatives last week when he solemnly announced that members were going to take a very close look at the report of the 9/11 commission and not rush into anything during an election year. So the representatives went on vacation, and the senators with them. After all, members of Congress work very hard and are entitled to free time. Recklessly driving up the national debt isn't easy work. Besides, because only 38 at most of the 435 seats in the House are "in play" this year, no one has to worry about losing his or her job.

When there was some public outcry, Congress replied that the relevant committees would return after a couple of weeks to begin working on legislation. Given the record of Congress in getting anything done, it is safe to bet that there will be no legislation before the election.

And no one will raise the question of why Congress failed to enact the recommendation of the Gore commission in 1995 that the cockpit doors on airplanes be bulletproof and locked—which would have saved 3,000 lives on Sept. 11.

The president said he would study the report very carefully. That is an interesting comment because he stonewalled the idea of the commission for a couple of years on the grounds that it would distract from the war on terrorism, until he was forced into it by the families of the victims. Moreover, he tried to appoint the ineffable Henry Kissinger as commission chairman. It is therefore the president's own fault that the report—with its criticisms of his actions both before Sept. 11 and his foreign policy since—appeared during an election year. The commission was restrained in its comments because it wanted unanimity during an election year. Republican members of the commission doubtless hoped that people would not read it too carefully.

At this writing, the president is busy trying to turn the report into a political asset. Since he does not read books, he has not read the pages following 363, which are an implicit but stinging indictment of the terrorism policies of his administration.

Then there is the Senate committee that studied the failures of the American intelligence services before the Iraq war—failures that in ordinary times would have humiliated a president, but not these days. Again in the name of unanimity, the committee postponed the completion of its investigation until—guess when?—after the election.

It is also said that the grand jury investigation into who in the White House "outed" a CIA officer (to punish her husband for reporting that there was no "yellow cake" uranium shipped from Niger to Iraq) will continue until after the election.

Heaven forfend that the issues of who messed up on Sept. 11 and in preparation for the Iraq war should affect the outcome of the election. Heaven equally forbid that these matters be debated during the campaign. Heaven protect the American people from thinking there are issues besides abortion and gay marriage, and whether people will "warm up" to John Kerry. Nor should anyone dare to ask why it required almost three years since the World Trade Center attack to produce a detailed report of the failures of our intelligence agencies and a blueprint to reform them. Nor should there be a debate about a foreign policy that has alienated the world, nor about why the dead in Iraq are now about a third of those who died in the 9/11 disaster. No one should ask about how much safer Americans really are today. Not during an election year.

There is a conspiracy of silence to protect the Bush administration from the voters' judgment about its mistakes. Such pretense supports the president's insistence that he has not made any mistakes and is not responsible in any way. It is all the fault of the CIA and the FBI—and, of course, the Bill Clinton administration.

American elections used to be about responsibility and accountability. Now it would seem those subjects are taboo. A president is neither responsible nor accountable—not till after the election!

August 13, 2004

Homeland security's heavy hand

The week before last, after a blue moon and in the middle of the dog days (when the dog star rises with the sun), the Bush administration cried wolf. Tom Ridge, czar of Homeland Security, scared the living daylights out of the country on a dog-day Sunday afternoon by listing financial institutions that had been targeted by al-Qaida. He praised the president for his leadership on homeland security: a nice boost for the sagging re-election campaign. Troops in full armor and carrying automatic weapons appeared around the targets. It was a grim Sunday evening in America.

The next day the stock market—allegedly the target of the plotting—pushed the Dow average higher. Perhaps the blue moon, dog-day omens were not good for crying wolf again. It also emerged that the material about the targets had been gathered four years ago, though it "may" have been updated as recently as January. The head of MI6, the British intelligence agency, raised questions about frightening people when there was no evidence of immediate threat. He also wondered whether the release of so much information might endanger ongoing intelligence operations.

Clearly, the discovery of al-Qaida computers was a major breakthrough, even if the computers tell more about its past than about the present. However, the Bush administration has cooked up a couple of weeks of fear. Whether it has cried wolf once too often remains to be seen. Meanwhile, Homeland Security doesn't seem to have the time or the money to make the nation's ports secure.

It does have the time, however, to practice cruelty. It discovered 292 refugees from the volcano eruption on the island of Montserrat in 1995 (many of them descendants of the Irish slaves Cromwell had exiled to the Indies). This year Homeland Security canceled their "temporary protected status." Either they must go back to Montserrat, which is unsafe, or to England or to anywhere. But they must leave the new families they have formed and their new jobs and new homes and depart the United States. What kind of men and women take pleasure in such cruelty?

I encountered recently the harsh face of Homeland Security and the Patriot Act in the Harbor Country of western Michigan. The victim snatched away by Ridge's goons is Ibrahim Parlak, the proprietor of the Cafe Gulistan restaurant in Harbert. My friend and colleague Roger Ebert (who introduced me to the wonders of the cafe) insists that Parlak, granted permanent residence and political asylum many years ago, runs the best restaurant in this part of the world.

Parlak is a gentle, soft-spoken man, lovingly kind to his 7-year-old daughter and warmly friendly to all his clients. His story since he came to America—after time in a Turkish jail—is a perfect type of the American dream: a poor immigrant working hard, making a success of himself and becoming a true American. His big mistake was applying for U.S. citizenship. That gave the vile people at Homeland Security a chance to reconsider—after more than a decade—this grant of political asylum.

We cannot afford in this country to lose such an admirable potential citizen.

Parlak is not a violent man and never recommended violence in his time as a Kurdish nationalist, much less is an "aggravated felon." However, given the hatred of the Turks for all Kurdish nationalists, if he is sent back to Turkey he may very well die.

I trust those who have his fate in their hands understand that the Kurds are the solid allies of the United States in Iraq and are strongly pro-American. As centuries-long victims of oppression by Iraqis, Iranians and Turks, they are loyal to their friends, and the United States is their friend. The charges against Parlak seem not only wild but innocent of understanding of the Kurds or the situation in that part of the world. Perhaps someone could tell Ridge that the Kurds are our allies.

The alternative to deportation and death is apparently permanent detention—which means until the goons in Homeland Security are swept out of office.

August 27, 2004

Bush's lies cause untold pain

I was perhaps 14 years old. I was praying late in the afternoon in our old basement church. At the front of the church, beneath the Blessed Mother's altar and our parish service flag with its many blue stars and, in 1942, a couple of gold stars, a woman was praying fervently. She was perhaps 12 years older than I was, fashionably dressed, and apparently distraught.

"Dear Lord," she cried out suddenly, "why didn't you take me instead of him?"

By that time in my life I had become an incorrigible if precocious news consumer, reading newspapers every day and listening to the news broadcasts on our Philco radio. I knew all about strategy and tactics (or thought I did) and followed the war on maps. Casualties were a part of war. Men died, and that was a shame, but they had died in a good cause. I was not aware of the pain of loss so many mothers, daughters, wives, lovers and sweethearts would suffer. Later I would hear a news commentator reflect on the line "only one of our planes was lost" about the tragedy of the loss of a single life and the agony of those who had loved that pilot.

War, I realized then, is not a game but horrible madness: 20 million Russians dead, 600,000 Germans killed in air raids that did not shorten the war by a single day. Classmates and friends killed in Korea, children of classmates and friends dead in Vietnam—each death a loss from which many others would never recover. Even those who were on the right side, as we were in the World War, did terrible things and caused enormous human pain. The woman in St. Angela Church, from whose grief I had quickly and silently fled, had told me what war was all about.

The brief obituaries of almost a thousand young men and women dead in Iraq tear at my heart: the promise of lives obliterated and a wake of pain left behind, some of it to blight the survivors for the rest of their lives. And what of the grief of the Iraqi survivors we watch without much sympathy as they scream at us on the TV screen? They are only Arabs, no more important in our calculations than the Indians wiped out by cowboys or the cavalry in old-fashioned Westerns.

One sees bumper stickers that read, "No one died when Clinton lied." Harsh words. Yet the Iraq war is the result of deceptions in which the president and his administration have indulged and indeed continue to indulge. Planned before the attack on the World Trade Center, it is not part of the so-called war on terrorism. Iraq was not involved in the attack and was not seriously linked with al-Qaida. There were no weapons of mass destruction. There is little hope of a peaceful and democratic Iraq. The Iraqis hate us (as the Gallup Polls there indicate). There will not be a shift of the balance of power in the Middle East. The ouster of Saddam Hussein eventually might cost thousands of American and tens of thousands of Iraqi lives.

Some defenders of the president argue that he did not deliberately deceive the American people. Yet he and the vice president and the "neo-con intellectuals" continue to repeat the falsehoods, modifying them ever so slightly so they will enjoy some superficial plausibility: We may still find the weapons of mass destruction; there were some "connections" between Iraq and al-Qaida.

If you tell a big enough lie and tell it often enough, some people will believe you. Never admit your mistakes, never assume responsibility for the consequences of these mistakes. Keep repeating the same old deceptions—often with a show of anger—and enough people will believe you to re-elect you. The war proves that you are a strong leader, a man who can make the tough decisions, a man not greatly concerned about "sensitivity."

If ever there were high crimes and misdemeanors, the lies about the war in Iraq fit that category. We are an odd people. We impeach a president because he lied about his private sex life, which killed no one and harmed no one beyond his family. Yet we support and may well re-elect a "strong" president whose lies are responsible for so many flag-draped caskets, so many poignant obituaries and so much grief. How many women are sobbing in church these days because of Bush's lies?

September 10, 2004

Voters have no choice on Iraq

It would appear that the Vietnam War is an issue in the current election, but the Iraq war is not. Sen. John Kerry's service in Vietnam is subject to debate, though the lack of service of the president and the vice president apparently is not. But the ongoing war in Iraq has been ruled out of bounds.

The senator asserts that he would have voted for the war resolution even if he had known that there were no weapons of mass destruction, and the president brags about his own success in the war. That means half of the American people who think the war was a mistake have little to choose between the two men.

In fact, the war has been a catastrophe—and not the catastrophic success that the president, in a curious turn of phrase, calls it. It was ill conceived, badly executed and disastrously followed up. The neo-conservative intellectuals who had determined on the war before the World Trade Center attack had argued that the seizure of Iraq would change the balance of power in the Middle East, end the crisis in Palestine, and frighten off the terrorists. Indeed, immediately after the attack on the WTC, Donald Rumsfeld and Paul Wolfowitz tried to use it as an excuse for an Iraq invasion. The former was convinced that the war could be won with a relatively small number of troops. The commanders who wanted twice the number were shouted down and dismissed.

The American people were told that Saddam Hussein had weapons of mass destruction and would use them on us soon unless we took action. The dissenting intelligence was suppressed and ignored; we were told the Iraqi people would welcome us with open arms and throw flowers at our tanks.

No one among the brilliant intellectuals (Wolfowitz, etc.) seems to have known enough about the history of Iraq to have predicted that the various factions would immediately start fighting one another. No one understood that if the United States destroyed order, security, industry, fuel, water and food supplies, the Iraqis, ill at ease with a foreign occupying power, would quickly grow restless and rise up against us—which they did a year ago. Both the Shiites and the Sunnis want us out of their country.

They don't trust Americans to respond to the chaos they created, and on the basis of the facts of the situation, they have no reason to.

"Hey, we got rid of Saddam Hussein for them, didn't we?" pro-war Americans shout. "Aren't they grateful for that?" Indeed they are, but they are not grateful for the chaos in their country. Most Iraqis were better off under Saddam. They had jobs, food, water, electricity, stability and order in the streets. They blame the chaos on the United States—and with good reason. They wish we would go home and mind our own business—a not unreasonable demand.

Now, American troops are at risk whenever they leave their bases. Some sections of the country (the Sunni west) and some cities (the Shiite ones, like Najaf) are off-limits to the troops. When they ride in much of the country, they are targets for roadside bombs (like the one that killed seven Marines last week) and rocket-fired grenades. Foreigners risk kidnapping and decapitation. There is no power in the country to prevent such murders. The United States destroyed the power and has not replaced it.

More than 1,000 Americans are dead and close to 10,000 wounded. There is no exit strategy, no escape route. We must stay there, the president tells us, until a stable Iraq is established. But he doesn't say how this will happen, and the weak performance of our puppet government there suggests that it won't be able to do the job.

Bush's suggestion that the "insurgents" are mostly Arab troublemakers who have sneaked into Iraq is laughable. He has created in Iraq a nation of terrorists who will come back to haunt us. He has maneuvered the United States into the Big Muddy and has no idea how to get us out without a serious loss of prestige. That, if anyone remembers, was Henry Kissinger's argument for continuing the Vietnam War four more years.

Unless Kerry can come up with a better plan now, he will not deserve to win the election.

September 17, 2004

Terror "war" doesn't meet definition

Is there really a clash of civilizations? Or are we entering the Third World War? Or the Fourth World War? Such are the models and metaphors being proposed to cope with the horror of the mass murders at

Beslan in Russia. The American Right (as in the *Wall Street Journal*) proposes the first. Russian leadership proposes the second. The Vatican's Cardinal Renato Martino proposes the third. The last also agrees with Homeland Security Director Tom Ridge and Attorney General John Ashcroft that nations must give up many of their liberties to engage in these conflicts.

Each model is both an exaggeration and a dangerous (self-)deception. Arab armies are not moving on Tours, the Turks are not closing in on Vienna, the Crusaders are not attacking Jerusalem. Neither side is forcing conversions on the other side. Nor are massive armies moving back and forth across Europe with tens of millions of casualties, as in the two real world wars. Cities are not being destroyed in hideous air attacks. Women are not being raped by the millions. The Cold War, nasty and unpleasant as it was, did not involve any of these horrors, despite Cardinal Renato Martino.

What, in fact, is happening? Small bands of religious fanatics are killing relatively small numbers of innocent people—small compared with the casualties of the Great War. These are terrible events, but Islam is not engaged in open conflict with the West. Many Islamic leaders denounce the killings. Most Muslims do not approve of the killings. Islam is not the enemy, only a very small number of very dangerous Muslims.

Most Muslims don't like America. However, it is not, as President Bush inanely says, that they want to destroy our freedom (Ashcroft will do that, given enough time). The reason, as the Muslims see it, is our oppression of the Palestinians and more recently the Iraqis. Our great "war" leader has been too busy with other things to deal with the Palestinian mess. Yet there is no more critical challenge in the struggle against terrorists.

Indeed, the metaphor "war on terrorism" is exaggerated and misleading. In fact, it is a struggle against fanatical terrorists. If the word "war" is used to describe the horrific American Civil War *and* the current struggle against terrorists (to say nothing of the "war on drugs," the "war on pollution," etc.), then the word has lost all meaning. Moreover, "terrorism" is an abstraction, while terrorists are specific people and specific organizations. "War on terrorism" is useful only to persuade the American people that Bush is a wartime president and to justify the foolish and now dangerous war in Iraq.

The United States enjoyed extraordinary goodwill all over the world in the months after the World Trade Center attack. That would have been the time to fashion an international alliance against terrorists and to bring the best strategic minds together to plan the struggle.

Russia would certainly welcome such an alliance now, but it is too late. Indeed, the United States is blamed because it has negotiated with

Chechnya's leaders. The State Department, in the finest spirit of Bush's unilateralism, says that it will talk to whomever it wishes.

However, the president assures us that the invasion of Iraq is part of his successful war on terrorism and that the country is safer because of the invasion. He does not address the question whether some of the hundreds of billions of dollars invested in Iraq might have better been spent on assuring the safety of our ports (only 2 percent of the containers coming to America are screened) and our commuter trains and buses. These kinds of targets are simply waiting for al-Qaida to attack. The war in Iraq, therefore, destroyed any chance for a major universal alliance against terrorists, created thousands more terrorists, and diverted money from authentic homeland security.

Language shapes thought. The abuse of language leads to abuse of thought. Many of the presuppositions of American policy are the result of sloppy thinking. However, exaggerated and deceptive language is very useful in the political game, especially if you want to present yourself as a strong leader in time of war.

September 24, 2004

A dove in good company

I get a lot of hate mail from conservative Catholics who are furious at my criticism of the Iraq war. You have no right to use your office, I am told, to criticize our fine Christian president. You are a disgrace to the priesthood. I may leave the Catholic Church because of you. Why don't you quit the priesthood now and stop harming the church? You are even worse than the priests who abuse little boys.

Those are some of the printable messages. At least half of the hate letters are obscene.

I am also told that I don't support the troops. I do indeed support the troops, with the plea that the government get them out of the quagmire in which they're bogged (as the administration's recent intelligence report makes clear).

Anyone who reads a column has the right to attack the writer. I don't mind the hate—or even the obscenity of some of the haters. I would be disappointed if my columns, designed to make people think, did not stir up some animosity. Moreover, the favorable mail exceeds the hate mail, though sometimes just barely.

Yet I am curious that the writers think that a priest does not have the right—and indeed the obligation—to express a moral teaching. If a priest believes a war is immoral, he should say so. Moreover, in my criticism of the Iraq war, I have a priest of considerably more importance than I in the same camp—and potentially much more troublesome.

The pope.

His Holiness and his colleagues in the Vatican have opposed the war since the very beginning. John L. Allen in his superb book on the Vatican—*All the Pope's Men*—devotes 65 pages to detailing, day by day, the Vatican's position on the war. Allen comments that this mobilization of the Vatican apparatus around opposition to the war is unique in modern history. The papacy does not accept the theory of unilateral preventive war. It does not agree with the Bush administration's foreign policy. It did not think that all possible grounds for a peaceful solution were exhausted before the American attack and, like most of Europe, it did not believe that there was sufficient evidence of weapons of mass destruction—and it turns out that they and not the Bush administration were right. It urged that nothing happen until the completion of the U.N. arms inspection—and it turns out that here again the pope was right and the president was wrong.

"War," the pope said on Jan. 13, 2003, "cannot be decided upon, even when it is a matter of ensuring common good, except as the very last option and in accordance with very strict conditions, without ignoring the consequences for the civilian population both during and after military operations."

The teaching on the Iraq war is not "authoritative." Yet, ought not Catholic conservatives, who virtually worship the pope, at least listen to him respectfully on this subject?

Why don't American Catholics react to the pope's warning about the war? Mostly, I suspect, because they don't know about it. The national media pay little attention to the pope save when they bash him for something. The rhetoric of the Vatican is often so complicated that it is not entirely clear what is being said. The Catholic media (official diocesan papers), with some exceptions, are afraid to offend their super-patriotic leadership. Some parish priests may be reluctant to quote the pope on the Iraq war for fear that their people will be angry.

A constant concern in the pope's comments is fear of the death of innocent civilians. Iraqi deaths don't count, quite literally. The Defense Department refuses to count them. Some estimate that Iraqi casualties are as high as 30,000. If the war goes on long enough, Americans may kill as many Iraqis as did Saddam Hussein. Today, every time people die in Iraq,

Americans are blamed because if they had not come, these people would still be alive.

Yet, most Americans are unconcerned about the death of Iraqi civilians. They wear towels on their heads and walk around in their pajamas. They speak a funny language and believe in a funny religion. They scream at us with hate. Why should Americans worry about them? They're barely human.

October 1, 2004

Terror won't take 4 years off

Suppose that, in fulfillment of the predictions of Homeland Security Secretary Tom Ridge and Attorney General John Ashcroft, terrorists wanted to demonstrate their power before the election, to make their own little contribution to the re-election of George W. Bush. What might they do?

They might hide anti-aircraft rockets near five major American airports and fire them at the same time. Although the technology is available to intercept such rockets, no effort has been made to install it.

Or they might place explosives into the cargo sacks that go unscreened on commercial aircraft and time them to go off at the same time. Although the technology exists to screen such sacks, no effort has been made so far to install it. Like the anti-rocket equipment, there is no money for such protection because of tax cuts and funds for Iraq.

Thus, despite the constant harassment and torment of passengers at the screening stations, air travel is only marginally safer than it was three years ago.

But the president says we're safer and he is "strong in the war on terror" and we must believe him.

Or terrorists could load explosives into the hundreds of container ships that enter American ports every day. These could be timed to go off at the same time—a custom that terrorists seem to like.

An amendment was introduced in Congress a year ago to improve security in American seaports, but it was voted down because more money was needed for Iraq.

But the president says we're safer and he is "strong in the war on terror" and we must believe him.

Or they could leave backpacks on a couple of scores of commuter trains around the country and replicate the destruction in Madrid. So far, no one has seemed to lift a finger to prevent such attacks. The same thing could be done on buses. A dozen suicide bombers could blow themselves up on commuter buses in a dozen American cities. So far, no one has done anything to protect buses. The costs of such protection, we are told, would be prohibitive.

But the president says we're safer and he is "strong in the war on terror" and we must believe him.

It has been three years since the World Trade Center attack, and now the new CIA director says it will take five more years before the CIA is in a position to respond effectively to terrorism. One wonders what the CIA has been doing, if anything, during the last three years.

But the president says we're safer and he is "strong in the war on terror" and we must believe him.

Thus, three years after the surprise attack in New York City, the American people are almost as vulnerable to another attack.

But the president says we're safer and he is "strong in the war on terror" and we must believe him.

Patently the people still believe that, although the president has messed up every other issue, he should be re-elected because he is a "strong" leader in the war on terror.

Those whom the gods would destroy, they first make mad.

Those who will vote Bush back into the White House this time—without his having to steal the election—will have only themselves to blame when terror strikes again and again and again in the next several years. The streets of America could easily become as unsafe as the streets of Israel, in substantial part for what America has done to the streets of Iraq.

If one looks at second terms in the White House since 1948, they have almost always been unpleasant experiences for the country. The Korean War smote Harry Truman in 1950. Lyndon Johnson was undone by Vietnam after 1964. Richard Nixon was forced out of the White House after 1972. Ronald Reagan's faculties notably deteriorated after 1984. Bill Clinton was impeached. In the last half century, then, only Dwight Eisenhower experienced a relatively benign second term. Having sowed the wind in his first four years in office, Bush is likely to reap the whirlwind. Alas, so will the American people.

Americans have never dumped a wartime president, no matter how stupid or incompetent he may have been. They won't dump the present incumbent either.

And God help us all.

October 8, 2004

Exiting Iraq is the only solution

The day of the first presidential debate, television served up pictures of the 38 children who died in an explosion in Iraq and their grieving mothers. The blood of those children is on George W. Bush's hands for starting this ill-advised war, and on the hands of all of those who continue to support the war, including John Kerry. The "insurgents" killed the children, but the failure of the Bush administration to provide security in Iraq also killed them.

It is absurd to say that the world is safer now that Saddam Hussein is in custody. In fact, there are thousands of terrorists today who did not exist before the invasion of Iraq. Certainly Iraq is not safer. The only solution is to admit we made a terrible mistake—as we did in Vietnam—and withdraw our troops. This will be a humiliating defeat, but then, so was Vietnam, and the nation survived. The elder George Bush is said to have advised his son to develop an Iraq exit plan before the invasion. He did not, and those children died because he did not.

Not knowing any history, Americans seem doomed to repeat their mistakes. A major lesson of history is that one cannot put down an insurgency when the people of a country are sympathetic to it. The British learned that in the American Revolution. They learned it again in Ireland and India. But there is no memory of the casualties among Americans (more than 2,000) and Filipinos (tens of thousands) in the Philippine insurgency after the Spanish-American War, a nasty imperialistic campaign.

In Korea we learned that the United States cannot fight a long land war in Asia without losing the support of its own people. In Vietnam, just 20 years later, we learned that lesson again, and the lesson that you can't defeat with a puppet government a dedicated guerrilla army to which the people are sympathetic.

In Iraq we are making all the mistakes: land war in Asia, puppet government, insurgents enjoying considerable sympathy, and no exit strategy. How could the administration have been so stupid! The president is not smart enough to know any history. Vice President Dick Cheney and Defense Secretary Donald Rumsfeld presumably are smart enough, but apparently they don't read history. They both tried after the World Trade

Center attack to start the Iraq war then. The neo-conservative clique around them, which is in fact making policy, reads books—even history books—but it had other agendas.

Sen. Kerry proposes to have all the troops home in four years! How many more Iraqi children will die in four years? How many more American families will lose sons, fathers, husbands, brothers, sisters, wives, daughters and sisters in four years?

The president says it sends the wrong message to put a time limit on withdrawal. He doesn't seem to be able to articulate what the right message is. Perhaps columnist Robert Novak is correct when he hints that after he wins the election, the president will cut and run.

I hope Kerry wins because he may change his mind once in office (nothing wrong with changing your mind) and because he will at least clean out the vipers' tangle of neo-conservatives who talked the president into the war. Moreover, Kerry is not likely to reinstitute the draft or to get us into another "regime change" war in North Korea and Iran. I remain doubtful, however, that American voters will turn out a wartime president, even one as incompetent as Bush is.

There are arguments against withdrawal from Iraq. We will lose prestige and credibility around the world? The thunderous silence after Bush's United Nations speech shows just how much credibility the United States currently possesses. The Iraqis will fight a civil war? They already are. Turkey and Iran will be drawn in? They're welcome to it. The radical Islamists (mostly Saudis) will claim a great victory? They sure will, and we gave it to them when we decided to invade Iraq. We will lose the Iraqi oil? Ah, so that's why there's a war?

If you support the war; if, with the president and Kerry, you want to "stay the course," the next time you see the bodies of children strewn about a street in Iraq, ask yourself if their blood is not on your hands.

October 29, 2004

For God's sake, vote him out

There are two proportionate reasons for rejecting President Bush's bid for re-election. Both the United States and the world are a mess. Mr. Bush is responsible for both messes. The first president ever to claim de facto infallibility, Mr. Bush tells us that he follows his instincts in decision-making after praying over the decision and talking to God. He admits no mistakes—how could anyone who has a direct link to God make a mistake! In his next administration he will receive more divine inspirations that will make both the country and the world even more messy.

Consider the American economy. He has turned the biggest budget surplus in history into the biggest deficit because he wanted to give more money to the "haves and have mores," as he called them. He has presided over the largest job losses since the Great Depression. He has stood idly by while hundreds of thousands of American jobs have flown overseas. His reform of health care has made it more expensive and more difficult for the elderly. He declines to rein in the greed of the drug companies and thus drives many Americans to Canada—of all places—to buy the medicines needed to stay alive. He has cast doubt on the future of Social Security. He has been on the bridge during the current absurd panic over flu vaccine; the deaths of those elderly and children who are not able to obtain flu shots are on his hands. What if one of those who die is your parent or spouse or child? He has not lifted a finger to help the many Americans whose pensions are being eaten up by greedy employers. Oil prices are climbing rapidly, and the stock market is tanking.

We want four more years of this stuff?

Fecklessly he started the ill-advised and ill-prepared war in Iraq in which some Americans have to come close to mutiny to protect themselves from orders to bring contaminated fuel in badly equipped trucks to units that won't accept it. He misled the American people about the weapons in Iraq and the involvement of Iraq in the World Trade Center attack. He is disgusted, he tells us, by the kidnappings and the beheadings, the car bombs and roadside bombs, the ambushes and murder of civilians, but the bad decisions he and his cabinet made were mandated by God and could not have been mistakes. Pat Robertson tells us, however, that Mr. Bush told him that God had disclosed that the casualties in Iraq would be light. Maybe that was God's mistake!

Do we want him to continue with these God-driven policies for four more years? Eleven hundred dead Americans already. How many more thousands will have to die before God will tell Mr. Bush to get out of Iraq? How many tens of thousands more Iraqis will have to die?

The world is a mess because the United States is the natural leader of the free world and the American president the natural president of the free world. He blew the capital of support and sympathy that flowed to the United States after the World Trade Center attack by his "Bush Doctrine," which turned him into the bully of the free world. Next year the Poles will leave Iraq because the Polish people don't like the war. The Poles—our strongest allies in Mr. Rumsfeld's "New Europe"—are fed up with us! Four more years of divine inspiration and what will be left of America's power and prestige? We will still be a giant but, like Gulliver, a tattered giant chained to the ground by our president's madcap inspirations.

The pope is infallible only in certain limited circumstances and on specific matters. Unlike the pope, Mr. Bush apparently sets no limits on the policy decisions that will be made by conversations with God. We want four more years of those decisions?

The president, like every human, is entitled to his own relationship with God. He is entitled to use that relationship to make decisions, to justify them later, and to stick to them no matter what happens. Many Americans will accept such decisions because they believe he is a "godly" man. Not everyone else has to tolerate four more years of his divine right to govern.

Even if the election is close, Mr. Bush will win it. His lawyers are ready to go back into court and the supine Supreme Court will give the country four more years of divine-right rule.

Do we really want that?

November 12, 2004

How many more Iraqis must die for our revenge?

The election is over and so we can forget about the Iraq war. It is no longer a political issue and hence matters to no one. The American electorate has followed the tradition of standing by a wartime president and thus endorsing the president's war. It was once his war. Now the election has made it our war. The issue is closed.

A recent report suggested that if one compares the number of deaths that usually occur in Iraq per year with the number since Bush's invasion, the cost of the war in dead Iraqis may be more than a hundred thousand human beings. Now Iraqi deaths don't count because they look funny and talk funny and have a funny religion. Besides they're Arabs, and we have a score to settle with Arabs because of their attack on the World Trade Center. Yet if we are able to sustain the number of deaths that have happened as a consequence of the invasion, we will soon have accounted for as many as Saddam Hussein did. That's a lot of dead Arabs—and a lot of bereaved spouses, parents, children, other relatives and friends. How many will we have to kill before we're satisfied with our revenge?

Someone might say that when leaders of a country have caused so many deaths they might just deserve to be hauled before an international court of justice as war criminals—especially if the war was based on false premises and conducted with an ineptitude that staggers the mind. It is an unnecessary, unjust, stupid, sinful war. The majority of Americans have assumed responsibility for the war. Therefore they share responsibility for all the Iraqi deaths.

OK, lets say there are only 50,000 extra dead. So that's not so bad, right? Americans are never going to have to render an accounting to their Creator for having supported such a massacre. Right?

I don't judge the conscience of anyone, leader or follower. I am merely saying that there is objective sin in the Iraq war, and our country as a country is guilty of sin. I'll leave it to God to judge the guilt, because that's God's job. I also leave it to God to judge whether there ought to be punishment for that sin. However, I think Americans—so serenely confident that the Lord is on our side—should live in fear and trembling about punishment.

The terrorists blew up the World Trade Center because they believed that the United States had done terrible things to Palestinians. The next explosion will be revenge for what we have done to Iraqis. We may not have been responsible for the plight of the Palestinians—though very few Muslims believe that. We are certainly responsible for what we have done and will do to the Iraqis during the next four years of folly. God help us all.

Because we are the only superpower, there is little chance that our leaders will be indicted as war criminals or that an invading army will punish the American people the way we punished the Germans after the war.

Don't give me that stuff that the Iraq war is not comparable to World War II. That argument deliberately misses the point that a country is responsible for the deaths it causes because of an unjust war, even if the deaths are numerically small compared to deaths from another war. An unjust war is an unjust war, and the deaths of innocents are the deaths of innocents. Where does one want to draw the numerical limit after which the unnecessary deaths of the innocent become a horrible crime? How many hundred thousand?

The United States has fought unjust wars before—Mexican American, the Indian Wars, Spanish American, the Filipino Insurrection, Vietnam. Our hands are not clean. They are covered with blood, and there'll be more blood this time.

The one faintly bright spot is that our victorious wartime president, now that he has been re-elected, might be able to extricate himself from Iraq more quickly than John Kerry. The war will never end unless and until the American government or the American people say that it's time to get out.

Will that require four more years?

(And before Catholics write me hate mail saying that I'm a disgrace for attacking the war, they should ponder writing a letter to the pope, who has made no secret of his opposition.)

December 3, 2004

Bush ignores intelligence reform

It didn't take George Bush long to become a lame duck president. While he was off in South America, two congressional Neanderthals, Representatives James Sensenbrenner and Duncan Hunter, at the urging of the Pentagon, scuttled the intelligence reform bill. All the years of work in establishing the committee and producing its lengthy report went down the drain, though it was supported by the president, the vice president and, somewhat weakly, by the secretary of defense.

There were plenty of votes in the House to pass the bill, but Speaker J. Dennis Hastert, something of a Neanderthal himself, refused to permit a vote on it lest it require Democratic votes for the compromise hammered out by the House and Senate to pass and go to the president's desk.

It is worth noting that the three Neanderthals do not come from districts that by any stretch of the imagination could be targets for terrorism. Come to think of it, the comparison of the threesome with the onetime denizens of the Neanderthal River Valley in Germany may be unfair to the latter.

President Bush was re-elected because the majority of Americans thought he was doing a good job in the so-called war on terrorism. Now it turns out that he doesn't have enough clout with the Republicans in Congress to win approval for an anti-terrorism reform that almost everyone in the country supports, including the Republican members of the commission that recommended the reform.

The three congressmen figure, doubtless correctly, that they'll be around much longer than Bush and they can do pretty much whatever they want because of their mandate to impose "moral values" on the rest of us. Strong president indeed! He can't even force two members of the House of Representatives to back down on a bill that he professes to believe is crucial for the country.

But does he really believe it? Might his support for reform of the nation's intelligence-gathering apparatus be of the same order of sincerity as his off-repeated support for a "strong dollar"? Perhaps it's only verbal— the kind of support that is expressed but not supported by any action. The Euro has appreciated 30 percent against the dollar, yet the president sustains his image by proclaiming he's for a strong dollar. Similarly, he supports intelligence reform but won't do anything to push it through Congress. He has been re-elected and thus surpassed his father. He doesn't have to worry about re-election ever again.

One must remember that Bush opposed the establishment of a commission to investigate intelligence failures at the time of the World Trade Center attack. He was forced into establishing the commission by the protests of relatives of the victims. At first he resisted the report and then caved in again when pressure from the relatives gained national media attention. Might it be that he's just as happy to let the issue die, now that it is not a possible re-election issue? Might it be that the Republicans in Congress sense that the pressure from Vice President Dick Cheney for passage of the bill is something less than enthusiastic and that he and the president would be just as happy to forget about the whole thing now that the election is over? Strange things happen in Washington all the time, especially when the national media have lost interest in a subject.

One might suspect that "now that the election is over" a lot of issues will slip down the drain—who made the bad decisions about Iraq intelligence; who leaked the name of a CIA agent to the media; who was responsible for the torture of prisoners in Iraq; how long the detainees are to be kept in Guantanamo; who made the decision that airport security should paw and undress women. These are fringe issues that must not interfere with the president's mandate to take more money away from poor people and give it to the rich.

The verbiage about the "war on terrorism" goes on, but in fact it must be over. Otherwise, the president would not permit intelligence reform to sink beneath the radar screen. Maybe the congressmen from Illinois, Wisconsin and California are not the only Neanderthals around.

January 28, 2005

Pray for successful vote in Iraq

Those of us who bitterly oppose the war in Iraq must hope and pray that the Iraq election is a success and that a strong and credible government will emerge from it. Even if we believe that the president's goal of establishing democracy in Iraq is madcap fantasy, we must still hope and pray that it can be done. Only if there is a semblance of an effective government will American troops begin to withdraw. The president must be able to spin the illusion of victory before he can announce the end of American occupation, perhaps at the request of a Shiite-dominated government. If the election is a failure, the killing will continue indefinitely.

Though it is unlikely, it is still legitimate to hope that democracy can be imposed on Iraq. Of 20 Arab countries, none is democratic according to the standards established by Freedom House. There seems to be a contradiction between Arab culture and democratic governance—any kind of democracy, much less American-style democracy. In Iraq the problem is compounded by the conflicts among the various tribal and religious groups in the country. Especially unpromising is the majority Shiite determination to wrestle power away from the Sunnis, who have dominated Iraq for most of its existence.

A democratic Iraq is the last remaining justification for war, now that the administration has been deprived of weapons of mass destruction and Iraqi complicity in the World Trade Center attack. Democracy in Iraq would not justify the war, but it would at least mean that all the deaths were not completely in vain. The administration could claim a victory in its campaign to bring "freedom" to every corner of the globe—even to places like Belarus and Myanmar.

A democratic government in Iraq need not have a lengthy existence. Once the administration has spun its "mission accomplished" theme, the American people will hardly notice that democracy has disappeared—just as they so easily forgot about the "weapons of mass destruction." Yet I would be happy to be wrong and happy if the memo-writing neo-conservatives were right that American power could firmly establish democracy in the Arab world. It is not a bet, however, that a sensible person would make.

The Bush administration is skillful at spinning away reality, I have come to believe, because it believes its own spin. Condi Rice replied with outrage when Sen. Barbara Boxer (D-Calif.) held up posters of the secretary-designate's warnings about weapons of mass destruction and suggested that loyalty had caused her to speak less than the truth. Rice insisted that she had never told an untruth and that she still believed it was right to try to create democracy in Iraq.

I have no doubt that she believed what she said, just as the president believes that he can dismiss the weapons fiasco by blaming the intelligence services of the world. Neither is deliberately lying. Both are firmly convinced that their own spin is the truth. The CIA, Americans must understand, failed to provide adequate intelligence, and thus the president was not to blame for the error. The president, you see, does not make mistakes. Democracy in Iraq alone justifies the war. It is unthinkable that the CIA told the president what he wanted to hear.

The late Herr Goebbels said that if you tell a big lie often enough, people will believe it is true. The Bush administration has modified the dictum: If your spin is outrageous enough and repeated often enough, people will believe it is true—and eventually you will believe it, too. Will the administration be able to spin a withdrawal from Iraq into a victory? It will get away with it, if only because the majority of Americans want to believe in victory.

The war will still be unjust, sinful, criminal. The people who re-elected President Bush will still have the blood of thousands of Iraqis on their hands. Spin cannot change those realities. Nevertheless, if spin can create clothes for the naked emperor so he looks victorious, Americans will no longer die in Iraq.

Iraqis will continue to die, but that has never bothered Americans and never will.

February 25, 2005

How long can Bush get away with lies?

As the criminal, sinful war in Iraq enters its third year, the president goes to Europe to heal the wounds between the United States and its former allies, on his own terms of course. The White House propaganda mill will hail it as another victory for the president and ignore the fact that most Europeans still consider the war dangerous folly and the president a dangerous fool.

One hears new rationalizations for the war on this side of the Atlantic. After the hearings on Secretary of State Rice, a Republican senator, with all the self-righteous anger that characterizes many such, proclaimed, "The Democrats just have to understand that the president really believed there were weapons of mass destruction in Iraq." This justification is not unlike the one heard frequently at the White House, "The president believed the intelligence agencies of the world."

Would it not be much better to have a president who deliberately lied to the people because he thought a war was essential than to have one who was so dumb as to be taken in by intelligence agencies, especially those who told him what he wanted to hear?

It is also asserted that the election settled the matters of the war and the torture of prisoners. These are dead issues that no longer need be addressed. Yet the president received only 51 percent of the vote and carried only one more state than the last time (picking up New Mexico and Iowa and losing New Hampshire). This is a validation of the war and of prisoner abuse? This is a mandate to do whatever he wants to do and whatever the leadership of the evangelical denominations want? A percentage point and a single state are a mandate for more war? Never before in American political history!

Finally, we are told that the Iraqi election confirms the Bush administration's policy in Iraq. The president's supporters must be in deep trouble to reach so far for that one. All the election proves is that the Iraqis want to run their own country. It also raises the possibility that Shiite clerics will deliver Iraq into the hands of the Iranians. Some kind of victory!

How do these kinds of arguments play in the precincts? The survey data suggest that war has become more unpopular. The majority of the American people now think it was a mistake, in a shift away from the 51 percent that endorsed it on Election Day. Admittedly, this is only a small change in the population, from a majority to a minority. Nor do the "changers" earn grace for their new opinions. They still endorsed the war on Election Day and are still responsible for it.

How long can the administration get by with its policies of spinning big lies into truth—as it has more recently done on Social Security?

Note the three most important Cabinet positions. Rice said that it was better to find the weapons of mass destruction than to see a mushroom cloud. "Judge" Gonzales said the Geneva Conventions were "quaint" and in effect legitimated the de facto policy of torture. Rumsfeld repealed the

"Powell Doctrine"—only go to war when you have the massive force necessary to win decisively and quickly. Brilliant businessman that he is (like Robert McNamara of the Vietnam era), he thought he could win with 130,000 (not at least 200,000, as the Army chief of staff insisted) and hence made the current "insurgency" inevitable.

The presence of these three towering giants in the administration certainly confirms that the president is confident that he is "right" on Iraq and that he has a mandate from the American people and from God that confirms that he is "right."

Nothing, in other words, has changed in the last two years. The war is still the "right thing to do," it is still part of the "war against terrorism," it is still essential to keep Arabs from blowing up our skyscrapers.

You can still get away with the "big lie" as long as Karl Rove and his team of spinners keep providing persuasive rationalizations. The American public is still supine, uneasy about the war but not willing yet to turn decisively against it. Will that still be the case next year when we "celebrate" the third anniversary of the war? Is the patience of the American people that long-suffering? Is there no outrage left in the country?

March 4, 2005

Bush a hypocrite to lecture Putin

Suppose that Russian President Vladimir Putin visited Canada and announced that the United States was retreating from its principles of freedom since the World Trade Center attack. The United States, he might have said, has denied due process of law to some American citizens. It has established a concentration camp in Cuba. It has tortured prisoners, indeed often and in many places. It denies aliens the right to trial by jury—indeed, it acts like the only ones who have Mr. Jefferson's inalienable rights are American citizens, and not always.

Then he says, while I'm at it, there are a lot of flaws in your democracy. You certainly don't think your Electoral College is democratic, do you? Neither is your Senate, with its disproportionate representation of smaller states. Rhode Island is as big as California? Gimme a break!

And what about your gerrymandered congressional districts (presumably he knows about Elbridge Gerry) that guarantee the re-election of incumbents, especially if they are conservative Republicans? What about Tom DeLay's open theft of Democratic congressional districts in Texas? Is your House of Representatives all that democratic?

And all the capitalist dollars that are poured into your campaigns? And the false attack ads aimed at the character of an opponent? And the endless spinning of the truth so that it no longer means anything? Would Mr. Jefferson and Mr. Madison approve of that?

How dare, he might conclude, the American pot call the Russian samovar black?

It is not my intention to say that Russia is more democratic than the United States. Patently it is not. Nor do I propose to argue that American democracy is far from perfect. Patently it is far from perfect. Rather, I am suggesting that for President Bush to come to the edge of Russia (Slovakia) and preach about democracy to Putin is rude, crude and undiplomatic. It is an insult to Putin and to Russia and to the Russian people.

It is also hypocrisy.

Putin seems by all accounts to be popular with his people. He is the strong leader that Russians have always wanted, most recently after the drunken confusion of Boris Yeltsin. The Russians show little inclination to imitate their neighbors in Ukraine. The Gulag is over, the rule of law is aborning. Russia has a long way to go, but it is struggling, however imperfectly, with the development of its own brand of democracy—and without much of an internal historical model to imitate.

Did Bush lecture the Germans and the French about their treatment of Muslims? Did he lecture the English about their continued failures in Northern Ireland? Hardly. He understood—or the people around him did—that it was inappropriate for him to intervene in the domestic problems of other countries. What made him think it was appropriate to lecture Russia about its failings as though it were a spoiled and obstreperous schoolchild?

Did he expect Putin to accept his insults and promise to do better? Did he think that the Russian people would say that it was time for the Russian leadership to shape up in response to the criticism of an American president? What good would come of his criticism? Why did he bother to make such a big deal out of it?

The answer is that his conservative base expected, indeed demanded, that he criticize Putin. Probably Karl Rove, his gray eminence, insisted that he do it. Conservative Republicans don't really believe that Russia has changed. They're waiting for Russia to renew the Cold War. They expect a Republican president to be "tough" with the Russians. Russians are still the bad guys, and Bush should "crack down" on them. For Bush, lecturing Putin on the failures of Russian democracy is a no-lose situation. He doesn't lose any votes in Russia and solidifies some votes in the United States. He enhances his cowboy image in Europe, but what's wrong with that?

Why not be rude and crude and patronizing? Why not act like an evangelical minister preaching to South American heathens? Why not act like the campus evangelist who tells Catholics that they are not Christian? Why not act like a Catholic bishop refusing the sacraments to a political candidate?

May 20, 2005

Bush is wrong on Yalta apology

President Bush continues the practice of the big lie as prescribed by Joseph Goebbels, Hitler's propaganda ace. If you tell a big enough lie often enough, people will believe you. Bush does not apologize even when he's caught in a falsehood. All right, there were no "weapons of mass destruction" in Iraq. But it was not his fault that he believed all the intelligence agencies of the world, was it?

The parents of the young men and women killed and wounded in Iraq as well as the relatives of all the Iraqis blown up since the American arrival might have a different view of things. They might be inclined to think that the buck stops at the desk of the U.S. president.

During his recent trip to Europe, when he wasn't telling Vladimir Putin how to preside over Russia, he retold one of the biggest lies of the 20th century. He apologized for the Yalta agreement that handed, as he said, Eastern Europe over to Soviet domination. Because one can hardly expect the president to read history books, one supposes that he does not realize that the serious studies of the Yalta conference reject that analysis. It's a Republican big lie that has become true because of 60 years of fervent repetition. It is still a lie, however—just like the claim in a *New York Times* article that the big powers had "carved up" Europe at Yalta.

The Yalta meeting occurred in February 1945. Consider a map of Europe at that time, such as the one opposite Page 246 of Max Hasting's book

Armageddon. By February 1945, Marshals Zukov and Konev were about to cross the Oder River, which was well inside Germany (and is now the border between Germany and Poland). Russia had occupied or surrounded every Eastern European capital except Prague. Stalin obtained nothing by the Yalta agreements that he had not already captured.

Despite President's Bush's willingness to accept American responsibility for Soviet occupation of Eastern Europe, this remains the Republican big lie of the 1940s: A senile President Roosevelt had given Poland and the Baltic countries over to Stalin.

Roosevelt was not at his best at Yalta. He still thought he could "get along with Stalin." However, there was nothing much he could do to extirpate the Red Army from those or any other countries they occupied except drive them out by brute force.

The Republican response then—and in Bush's apology even now—was that the United States should have driven the Soviet Army out of Eastern Europe. It is not clear now that it would have been possible; probably it would not have been. Moreover, there was still a war to be finished with the Japanese. Nor would the American people have been willing to accept the casualties of an attempt to push the Red Army back to its 1939 frontier. Napoleon and Hitler had learned the lesson of fighting a land war with Russia. Was the United States supposed to do a better job while at the same time defeating Japan, especially since—as few are willing to remember now—the public was already sick of war. Would a Republican president raise the battle cry "on to Moscow"?

Not very likely. Certainly, the Republican candidates in the 1944 election ("Get the boys home with Dewey and Bricker") were not calling for an invasion of Russian-occupied Eastern Europe.

Thus, Bush's "apology" was valid only if he believes that the United States should have driven the Red Army out of Germany (a geographically necessary first step) and then out of Hungary, Slovakia, Romania, Bulgaria, Poland, Latvia, Lithuania and Estonia (and Ukraine, for good measure). How many millions more would have died on both sides in this continuation of the war?

Why did no one ask President Bush if he would have gone to war with the Soviet Union in 1945? He could have used the Iraq excuse: to rid the world of a monstrous dictator. Like the Iraq conflict, such a war between the United States and Russia might have continued for a long time. Indeed, it might still be going on. Our cities would be in ruins. Most of us would be dead, and many of us would never have been born.

June 17, 2005

Expect terrorists to bring war to us

In May there were 90 suicide bombings in Iraq. That means that 90 young Arabs, mostly from Saudi Arabia, smuggled themselves into Iraq through Syria, fastened a jacket of explosives around their bodies, and blew themselves up in search for Islamic martyrdom, killing scores of other Muslims in the process. The war in Iraq, billed as an essential component of the war on terrorism, is creating more terrorists.

It is not unreasonable to expect that other young men will soon be destroying themselves in this country as they blow up Americans in shopping malls and restaurants and hospitals and churches. The chickens of the criminal war in Iraq will come home to roost. No matter that the majority of Americans disapprove of the war. It is too late for that now.

Since the end of World War II, the United States has fought three "small" wars—Korea, Vietnam, and now Iraq. We lost all three of them and for the same reason—hubris. We were the most powerful nation on Earth, we had the most advanced military technology, we could easily overcome the local peasants with their crude weapons. Then we found ourselves trapped in the Big Muddy with no easy way out.

The Arab martyrs have an effective strategy: Kill Iraqis to turn them against Americans. Americans are responsible for the chaos. If they leave, maybe it will end.

Our most recent exercise in hubris is by far the worst, the most irresponsible, the most appropriate to indict those responsible as war criminals. We could knock over Saddam Hussein with a small army; the locals would dance in the street and strew flowers on our tanks. Secretary Rumsfeld, the Robert McNamara of our day, repealed the Powell Doctrine—that we should attack only with overwhelming force and a clear exit strategy. Colin Powell must have known that this was folly but, good soldier that he is, he did not resign or become the Deep Throat of the present administration. However, good soldiers can also be war criminals. Both Rumsfeld and Powell were criminally negligent in their failure to consider the obvious possibilities for catastrophe after a quick and easy military victory.

The president, the vice president, the secretary of state and the coterie of "neo-con" intellectuals around them desperately wanted a war with Iraq even before the World Trade Center attack. The neo-cons whispered that the way to Jerusalem was through Baghdad, never thinking that suicide bombings could migrate from Jerusalem to Baghdad. None of these wise men bothered to worry about the aftermath of the war. The president is a risk-taker, we are told now, as he battles for his harebrained plan to re-form Social Security. The invasion of Iraq was a risk, a big risk, the potential costs of which were never seriously estimated. That's what happens when you have a reckless Clint Eastwood type for president. Are not the president and his immediate advisers war criminals for rashly plunging the country into the Big Muddy once again?

John F. Harris in his book *Survivor* describes in detail President Clinton's agonizing reluctance to engage in military action overseas. There were so many contingencies, so many things that might go wrong. The current administration has never worried about such problems. Convinced of our indomitable might, ignorant of the lessons of history, unconcerned about what might go wrong, it plunged blithely into the Bid Muddy. The rationalizations of weapons of mass destruction and Saddam's involvement in the World Trade Center attack were false.

Now the president, dismissing the revelations about the weapons of mass destruction (the vice president apparently still believes them), is content to say that he still thinks the United States has done "the right thing." However, the majority of Americans and even some Republicans want the United States out of Iraq. The military says it will take four years to train an effective Iraqi army. The Big Muddy gets deeper.

But what about the majority that once supported the war? Blinded by anger at the World Trade Center attack and terrified by terrorism, are they responsible for all the blood in Iraq? Will they be responsible for the Saudi martyrs who will begin to ravage this country? Were the Germans responsible for Hitler?

July 15, 2005

9/11 card losing its magic for Bush

The president's address on Iraq the week before last was, it seemed to me, a masterful political performance, a superbly orchestrated plea from a wartime president for support in a difficult political situation.

The attack on the World Trade Center—the essence of the justification for his foreign policy and for the invasion of Iraq—was mentioned five times. The people we are fighting in Iraq are the same people that caused the 9/11 catastrophe. The Iraq war is, above all, a war on terrorism. We must not yield to the terrorists. Americans should realize that we are fighting for freedom and that they must support the troops in Iraq, no matter how many of them have to die, because they are fighters for freedom of whom we must be proud.

Whether our swaggering, smirking president actually believes the argument is open to question. But he presented it with great force and powerful patriotic fervor before a captive audience of paratroopers. It was the argument that got him re-elected only a few months ago. There was no reason to think that it would not muster support at least in his base.

I wondered what the polls would show. Would support for the war rise above 50 percent? Would the president's personal popularity also rebound? I thought that both outcomes were likely. The 9/11 appeal had always worked before. It got the United States into the Iraq war and mustered support every time the president invoked it.

For reasons that I do not understand, none of the major media bothered to field a survey, perhaps one more proof that those who accuse the media of being supine in their relationship with the president are right.

However, there was one poll that had gone into the field the day before the president's speech and finished the day after the speech. The Zogby Group reported that the president's personal popularity stood at 43 percent all three days. The 9/11 card, played with considerable political skill, no longer worked.

Moreover, 42 percent of the respondents said that if the president had misled the nation about the reason for the war, Congress should impeach him—25 percent of Republicans agreeing with this judgment. That's not going to happen, not as long as the Republicans control the House of Representatives. If Democrats did, even now there would be stern investigations of the rationale for war. There are no checks and balances on a president who controls both houses of Congress and the Supreme Court—on which the apparently sainted Sandra Day O'Connor cast the deciding vote to put him in the White House.

The only checks left are the people who are now, it would seem, profoundly skeptical. The 9/11 card no long works. Presidential guru Karl Rove went to that well one time too many. Or, as Mr. Lincoln is alleged to have said, you can't fool all the people all the time. Yet it took a long time for the people to see through the 9/11 argument, and with little help from the media, which still treat the war on terrorism and the war in Iraq as though they were synonyms. If Zogby's data are accurate—and there is no reason to think they are not—the people now are way ahead of the media.

The "war on terrorism" argument will continue. The administration doesn't have any other argument for remaining in the Iraq quagmire. Doubtless we will hear it said that we must fight the war on terrorism to victory so that there will be no more barbaric attacks like those in London—as if the war in Iraq were not the cause of the attacks in both Madrid and London, and Bush were not the best recruiter that al-Qaida has. The president told the jihadists to bring on their insurgents, and they sure did. Almost certainly, the next step will be American commuter trains.

If the money and the energy and effort had been put into real national security instead of the useless and foolish war, Americans might be much safer. Fewer than 50 suspects have been convicted in the past five years. The CIA has kidnapped, tortured and killed suspected terrorists all over the world and not provided much safety in London or Madrid or anywhere else. The top guns of American leadership are still as obsessed with Iraq as they were the day after the attack.

July 29, 2005

Neck deep in the Big Muddy

The Big Muddy is deeper and darker. Two Pentagon reports this week show just how muddy. In a survey of the morale of soldiers in Iraq, the Pentagon found that more than half said that morale in their units was either "low" or "very low." Morale was especially low, as one would expect, among the National Guard and Reserve units. Only half of them said they had "real confidence" in their ability to carry out their mission, probably because they were not trained for the kind of war in which they are involved.

Another report raises questions about the development of the Iraqi fighting units. Half of the police units are still in training and cannot conduct combat operations. The other half and two-thirds of the army battalions are only partially capable of combat and then only with the help of Americans.

The American military, representing the combat power of the world's "only superpower," is patently unable to stop the murderous suicide bombers and seems clueless about a strategy that might stop them. Would-be "martyrs" have paralyzed our forces. One cannot use tanks or jets or predator planes or artillery, much less nuclear weapons, against a stream of dedicated young fanatics sneaking across a porous border.

In the meantime, the Iraqi parliament, working erratically on its constitution, has decided to abrogate most of the rights of women in the preliminary constitution and to subject them to "religious law." That means in the new "democracy" that we are supporting in Iraq, women will be more subject to male oppression than they were under Saddam Hussein. This is what our young men and women are dying for in Iraq?

People with yellow ribbons say we must support our troops. I agree completely. The best way to support them is to get them out of a war justified by falsehoods and carried out by incompetents who have tried to do it on the cheap with no idea of what they would have to face after Saddam's regime was knocked over. We must stay the course, President Bush says, but he won't specify what the course is.

One hears from the media military experts there will be a "drawing down" of troop numbers next summer. That would be just in time for the November election. The administration may by then have decided to follow the Warren Austin advice during the Vietnam war—proclaim victory and go home. It had better have a large supply of helicopters available around the U.S. embassy so we don't have photographs of large numbers of our allies desperately trying to climb on when the last copter takes off—as they did in Saigon.

The suicide bombs in Iraq kill Iraqis, but they are aimed at the American occupation and will end only when the occupation ends. Conservative columnists and editorial writers are screaming that the suicide bombers in London are not angry over Iraq; rather, they want to destroy our way of life. But their own testimony seems to be that they are protesting the treatment of Muslims in Iraq and Palestine. Tony Blair, the loyal junior partner in the Anglo-American alliance, is paying the price for this crazy war. When the coalition leaves Iraq, the bombings in England will stop, just as they will in Iraq.

The screamers will say that means the "martyrs" will have defeated us. That's precisely right. They are in the process of defeating us in a war that we cannot possibly win, the war that Bush needed so he could become a wartime president. Many of those who say the war was a mistake in the first place still argue that it would be wrong to leave now. Unless the Bush administration can find a way to stop the suicide bombers—other than the president's "disgust"—we have no choice but to get out of the Big Muddy now.

What idiocy not to expect that the attacks on Israel by suicide bombers would spread because of the war and occupation in Iraq. Why is anyone surprised? The president tells us that they "disgust" him. Hooray for him. His supporters call them crazy fanatics, as they may well be. But calling them names and demanding that the world denounce them will not put a stop to their attacks. They are beating us, and we are apparently unable to stop them, save by promising to stay the course. That is terribly frustrating to Americans, but that's a price they must pay for a criminal war.

August 19, 2005

Iraq course bound to end badly

Every time our smirking, swaggering, stubborn, dishonest president promises "to stay the course" in Iraq I feel sick, especially when, dressed in a sport shirt and standing comfortably under the blue Texas sky, he comments on the deaths in Iraq. Young men and women are dying, being maimed, suffering psychological trauma that will haunt them for the rest of their lives. All the president can do is mouth clichés.

What does "stay the course" mean? At one time it meant "regime change." Then it came to mean "weapons of mass destruction." Then it meant "war on terrorism." Now it apparently means an Iraq that is "democratic and free." Even for someone of the president's limited knowledge of history, that is nonsense. How many Arab countries are currently both free and democratic—from Mauritania to Saudi Arabia? Not a one. Does that not suggest that it would be impossible for the United States to impose on Arab culture what we mean by freedom and democracy? In fact, how many Muslim countries can boast of Western-style civil society and democracy? Turkey, maybe, at least up to a point. Iran? Pakistan? Bangladesh? Indonesia? Does that suggest that in its present form Islamic culture is not conducive to what we mean by democracy?

Have Karl Rove and Condoleezza Rice told that to the president?

In Iraq, even as the president babbles about "staying the course," the Shiite majority is struggling to create an Islamic republic on the Iranian model, more moderate, perhaps, but still a theocratic state in which the mullahs have supreme power—and women have almost no rights at all.

Indeed, "staying the course" seems to mean fighting Iran's war against Iraq with Chinese money (which pays for the part of the national debt the war is piling up through the purchase of American treasury notes).

I do not deny that there are elements in the Islamic heritage that are compatible with a civil and democratic society. I insist, however, that these elements do not dominate today in any Islamic country, again with the partial exception of Turkey. But President Bush is nonetheless going to create by sheer willpower and the blood of American troops such a society in Iraq?

Democracy does not mean the same thing to Muslims as it does to Westerners, it will be argued, just as Mr. Putin says that it does not mean the same thing to Russians as it does to Americans. Fair enough, I suppose, but there is no evidence that the president comprehends this fact. Most Americans believe that real democracy is something like our own. They believe that the president is promising that in Iraq. It is a foolish, ignorant, stupid promise.

Democracy does not mean merely that the majority of voters elects the rulers. It also means the rights of the minority are protected. It means freedom of the press, freedom of expression, freedom of religion, the right to seek redress of grievance, an impartial and independent judiciary; it means no street violence after an election, the right to presumed innocence and to appeal court decisions, respect for those who are different from you, protection of property and contracts, a stable and generally accepted civic culture, civilian control of the military and the police—all the precious and priceless freedoms and rights we Americans take for granted, however imperfectly they may be protected or honored.

Majority rule, without these kinds of safeguards, turns into tyranny, total power invested in the monarch or the general or the cleric or the caudillo or the maximum leader or whoever else claims at gunpoint to embody the will of the people. No matter how long Bush "stays the course" in Iraq, the history of that part of the world suggests that the end result of our "regime change" will be something like that. For this, American blood is being spilled?

Western democracy, far from perfect, is still the best there is. One may call what goes on in Cuba or Russia or China or Egypt or Algeria or Pakistan or Indonesia democracy not in the Western style, if one wishes. But the president should not deceive the American people. What will happen in Iraq will lead to something very much like what existed before Saddam came to power and eventually lead, in the name of the will of the people, to another tyrant who will rule with an automatic weapon in his hand.

September 2, 2005

Rationale for war dead wrong

There is yet another illogical and immoral argument in support of the Iraq war. It has emerged from that hard-line group—little more than a third of the American people—that approves of President Bush's handling of the war: We must support the troops fighting in Iraq. To support the troops means to support the mission. Therefore, we must support the mission. The argument has a certain appeal to the red states, especially to the poorest segment of the population that is the president's "base"—and whose children incidentally are the most likely white people to be fighting the war. Think of Jessica Lynch and Lynndie England.

It is not surprising, therefore, that the president, perhaps at the urging of his gray eminence Karl Rove, seizes this argument: We must continue to fight till we win in order to validate the sacrifice of those who have already died. More must die in defense of those who have already died.

The moral assumption behind the argument is "America, our country right or wrong!" This is an American war, a war entered at the order of our commander in chief. It is unthinkable that it would not be a just war. Thus wave the flag, don the yellow ribbon, shout "USA!" sing "God Bless America!" and support the troops. If you don't support the mission, you have abandoned the troops. Our country, right or wrong!

To be fair, Stephen Decatur, one of the great American naval heroes, was much more nuanced: "Our country, in its intercourse with other nations, may it always be in the right. But right or wrong, our country." There is a possibility of concluding from that formulation that our country might sometimes be wrong and that those who continue to revere the country must struggle to make it right. The fact that there are troops fighting and dying in Iraq does not mean that the war is right. Rather, it began for trumped-up reasons and has been run by stubborn and incompetent men and now clearly is wrong. To support the troops means to get them out of harm's way as soon as possible.

Bush's contention that because some men and women have died, others must continue to die demonstrates just how morally bankrupt the war is and he himself is.

The fractious constitutional convention in Iraq shows how absurd the war is. The likely outcome, whatever the words of the document may say, is a theocratic Shiite state, ruled by mullahs, and under Islamic law in which women and religious minorities have no rights, a state torn by civil war between the Shiites and the Sunnis. Bush apparently has not noticed it, but such a civil war is already going on. Not having been able to settle it thus far, there is no reason to think that America can ever put an end to that ancient religious conflict.

As Colin Powell wisely put it, "If you break it, you own it."

Only about one-seventh of Americans favor immediate withdrawal. However, if the Bush administration is unable to establish a credible time-table for getting out of Iraq—and it's hard to see how, given its goals, it can do that—then a tidal wave of opposition will sweep the country just in time for the 2006 elections. Given its track record, the administration may be able to steal that election, too. It may be able to sweep Iraq under the rug and make "patriotism," "freedom" and the "war on terrorism" the issues. The president may continue to persuade many people that Iraq is "central to the war on terrorism."

John Kerry lost in 2004 because he was unable to propose a credible alternative to the administration on national security. He lacked the for-titude to say that, even though he had voted for the war, he was mistaken. If the Democrats wish to win by running against the war, they'll have to be more ingenious in their slogans and their spin.

Then, perhaps one house of Congress will be independent of the ad-ministration, and there will be comprehensive investigations of Iraq. Then, the American people will understand why so many troops died unneces-sarily in an unwise and inept conflict. That would be the proper way to support the troops and to assure that others would not die in the future because of ignorant and reckless diplomacy.

November 4, 2005

Lying's just the tip of the iceberg

Since it is apparently not a crime to deceive the American people into supporting a foolish and unjust war, one must be content with the indict-ment of I. Lewis Libby for perjury and obstruction of justice. The indict-ment is an example of a mountain laboring two years to bring forth a molehill. Libby will have the best trial lawyers money can buy and stands a good chance of acquittal. If he is convicted, the president will surely grant him a pardon before he leaves office.

We are unlikely ever to learn who "outed" Valerie Plame and thus ruined her career. That the leak came from a cabal inside the White House has been evident for a long time. But if the special prosecutor was unable after two years of effort to find out the who-how-and-why of this gratuitous and vicious mischief, the historians of the future might not be able to tease out the truth. They might observe, however, that the scandal was proof of how far down the path of evil the Bush administration would go to defend its case for a war that has turned out to be foolish and unjust.

Did the president know what was going on? It is hard to believe that he did not—any more than to believe that President Ronald Reagan was unaware of the Iran-Contra deal. Libby's clumsy lies—attributing the "leak" about a CIA agent to journalists—were probably an attempt to protect the vice president, who is far too clever to be caught in any legal trap. Yet we know enough now to understand that the Iraq war is his war. He and the crowd of neo-conservatives around him and the secretary of defense planned the war even before the president defeated Sen. Al Gore (if he really did). They even tried to blame the World Trade Center attack on Iraq. A democratic Iraq, they argued, would transform the balance of power in the Middle East. The way to Jerusalem, they claimed, was through Baghdad.

Cheney proclaimed to the bitter end that weapons of mass destruction would eventually be found in Iraq and has never retracted or apologized for this claim, which was decisive in winning support for the war from the American people. More recently, he has claimed that the Iraqi insurrection (better called, perhaps, the Iraqi resistance) was in its "last throes," despite overwhelming evidence that it grows ever stronger. Is he lying, or is he the kind of true believer who sees the world differently from everyone else?

Who knows what the answer is to that question? In truth, it does not matter. The Bush administration, led by the vice president, systematically deceived the American people about the war and continues to do so. There were never any nuclear weapons, never any raw uranium, never any Iraqi involvement in the World Trade Center attack. The Iraq war was never part of a "war on terrorism."

The vice president is also supporting legislation that would provide the basis for the CIA to do what it is already doing—to torture people who are held outside this country. Granted Cheney's serious fear that jihadism has created another cold war situation, such legislation would still reduce the United States to a country that willingly supports savagery—an ineffective strategy at that. The war is Cheney's war, and the 2,000 American dead and the 32,000 Iraqi dead are Cheney's victims. The torture is Cheney's torture.

With this background, the indictment of Libby looks kind of silly. One relatively minor player in Cheney's war will have to suffer through a trial and perhaps some time in prison. The conspiracy to go to war pushed forward by the White House Iraq group will continue even if it has lost one of its more dedicated members.

There is nothing in the American legal system that permits the indictment of public officials for war crimes. Thus, perjury and obstruction of justice must suffice as a substitute. Yet it seems evident that both Cheney and Libby are war criminals. They fed the country false information to seduce it into a war that was both unnecessary and incompetent. And there is very little the American people can do to end the war for several more years.

November 11, 2005

War blurs lines between good, evil

They have rededicated the Lady Church (Frauenkirche) in Dresden. This baroque gem from the 1700s was destroyed—along with much of the city and 130,000 lives—by Royal Air Force bombers in February 1945, two months before the end of the war. This rededication comes as Germans ask whether they do not have the right to mourn their losses during the war— 600,000 civilians killed by the planes of Air Marshal Arthur "Bomber" Harris, also called "Butcher" by his RAF colleagues.

I fail to see how anyone can deny them that right, especially since research after the war demonstrated that the mass firebombing of German cities had no impact on the final outcome. The Germans started the war, it has been argued, and therefore they were to blame for what happened to them. The children who were killed in Dresden or in the fire storms in Hamburg were guilty? Or in the American fire raids in Japan?

I'm sorry, I can't buy that kind of moral reasoning. Collective guilt is a murky and messy concept, satisfying as rhetoric but dangerous in practice. The same logic would argue that because Israel took land from Palestinians, suicide bombers are morally justified in indiscriminate murder of Israeli citizens.

The raid on Dresden was unconscionable. There were no military targets there worth the destruction of the city. Winston Churchill is alleged to have approved the raid because of pressure from Stalin. He certainly approved of Bomber Harris's systematic obliteration of German cities. Both of them should have been subject to war-crime trials at the end of the war, just as were the German leaders. That the latter were far more evil in their deeds does not excuse the former. However, only the victors try the criminals, and they leave to history any judgments about themselves.

The lesson of raids on places such as Lubeck and Dresden is that, even in just wars, the side that has justice on its side is likely to do many evil things. War sucks everyone and everything into its vortex of wickedness. The wars against Japan and Germany were obviously necessary wars, and yet the victors (including the United States) emerged with bloody hands.

Moreover, wars are almost always longer than those who start them think they will be. In 1914, the German general staff predicted victory in 90 days after mobilization. The Confederacy thought that a few military victories would cause the Union to give up the fight. The British thought they could restore order in the rebellious colonies in a couple of months. Napoleon and Hitler both were confident they could knock over Russia in a single campaign. President Bush celebrated "mission accomplished" after a few weeks. Now the majority of Americans believe that he does not tell them the truth.

When good does evil to fight evil, it becomes—in T. S. Eliot's words—indistinguishable from the evil it is fighting. War blurs the lines between good and evil so they are hard to recognize and traps those who launch them in Big Muddies of self-destruction.

Yet humankind still enters wars with bursts of patriotism, self-confidence and desire for vengeance that blind populations to the risks they are taking and cause leaders to indulge in deception and—perhaps worse—self-deception about the terrible risks they are taking.

How could the leadership of this country not realize that an ineffectual war in Iraq would, instead of advancing the "war against terrorism," actually generate new generations of suicide bombers eager for, as the film title says, "paradise now"?

How could so many members of Congress and American voters be so influenced by the pseudo-patriotism stirred up in the wake of the World Trade Center attack that they would eagerly and enthusiastically rush into another Big Muddy? Even though "regime change" in Iraq might itself have been a good cause, why were there so many who did not realize the lesson of history that the war would be long and costly and ultimately pointless? And worse still lead the country down the path to torture and murder, which go against all the nation's ideals?

Why were there so few who said, "Hey, wait a minute! What are the risks? How long will it last?"

November 18, 2005

Dems distracted by wrong war

The elections last week proved that Democrats can still win elections. Recent surveys also show that solid majorities want a Democratic Congress next year and that a substantial majority of Americans think President Bush does not tell them the truth. The only problem is, there is little evidence that the Democrats' appeal goes beyond the fact that they are not Republicans. Do they need anything more than "turn the rascals out" as a campaign slogan?

Unfortunately for them, the Democrats are caught up in the "culture wars" mythology. The culture wars—over homosexuality, abortion and public school prayer, for example—are not issues that trouble most Americans. The majority of Americans tolerate the idea of civil unions for gays and legal abortion under some circumstances. Four out of five conservative Christians who believe in the literal inerrancy of the Bible think that abortion ought to be legal if a woman's health is in danger. Three of five Americans support prayer in public schools.

These "values" issues are important to the leaders of some denominations and organizations and to their activist members on both sides in the culture wars. But they are not crucial for most Americans. Unfortunately, because of the campaigns of activists, the obsession with these "values" by the media and the ineptitude of Democratic leadership, the Democrats are labeled by them. Hence, Democratic candidates don't seem to have the time or the energy to concentrate on the important issues such as national security (which means the war in Iraq) and economic justice. Nor do they seem to have the kind of leaders who can speak clearly and forcefully about them.

The presidential election in 2004 was not decided by "values" but by "national security," an issue that caused Sen. John Kerry to lose the gender gap—the normal Democratic advantage among women. He did not have a creditable alternative to administration policy with which to persuade women that his policy would keep them and their families safe from jihadists.

Even today, when he has been backed into a corner by public dissatisfaction with the war in Iraq, the president still links that war with the "war on terrorism." Democrats must provide a strategy and a policy for fighting terrorists that leave behind the "war" metaphor and disconnect the necessary struggle against terrorists from the foolish Iraq invasion. The bill the GOP pushed through the Senate this week on Iraq had no teeth in it. The Democratic version was much stronger. The Democrats can afford to be stronger still.

More seriously, the Democrats must return to their traditional themes of economic and social justice. They must rediscover the truth that their constituencies are not just the liberal activists (though their causes are important) but the hard-pressed working- and middle-class people. The Republican administration and the Republican Congress are presiding over a major shift in wealth from the poor and the middle class to the rich. Thus, they are trying to take $70 billion from food stamps, Medicare, education (loans and scholarships for college students) and veterans and give the money to the rich in increased tax deductions. Pension money and health-care money is being taken away from workers and retired workers to provide profits for badly run organizations (like United Airlines and General Motors) and their exorbitantly compensated executives.

Those who prognosticate about Christmas buying predict that "high end" (which means rich) patrons will buy more than ever, while "low end" (which means working-class and middle-class) patrons will buy less. This prediction will surprise no one who has watched the reverse Robin Hood style of the Bush administration. Yet Democratic leaders do not seem to be able to articulate a case against the administration's economic injustice—at least not one that gets across to voters through the national media.

Perhaps they can win 2006 and 2008 merely because Bush and his party have become unpopular. They have a much better chance if they run against a war that cannot be won and in support of the working people and the middle class, who are being robbed by the party of the wealthy.

November 25, 2005

Is Bush lying about his lies?

Not only did the Bush administration deceive the American people about the reasons for invading Iraq, it is now deceiving them about the deceptions. In a burst of political tantrums, the president and the vice president have shouted that it was "irresponsible" to assert that there had been deception and it was unfair to the troops fighting in Iraq.

Is the administration lying about its lies? That many of the arguments in favor of the war were false is beyond question. Nor can there be any serious doubt that the new argument that it is irresponsible to question the old arguments is also false. But if a lie is a conscious effort to deceive, then the charge that the president and those around him deliberately lied and are now lying again must be left to heaven. It is enough to say they spread falsehoods for three years because they had made up their minds that there had to be a war and are now spreading falsehoods about the original falsehoods. The president is not a man who likes to admit he was wrong. Therefore, one must cover up the mistakes.

Consider some of the evidence. Vice President Dick Cheney and the president both insisted that Iraq was trying to import "yellow cake" uranium for nuclear weapons. Then-National Security Adviser Condoleezza Rice and the vice president warned of "mushroom clouds."

Bush says that everyone agreed that Iraq had weapons of mass destruction. He has said in the past that it was not his fault that all the intelligence agencies of the world believed that they did. Therefore, the intelligence agencies of the world were to blame for the mistake, he wasn't. Everyone in Washington, he argues, supported the war.

In truth, many Democratic senators did, not realizing how much the case in favor of the war had been cooked. In the national intelligence estimate issued just before the war, the internal dissent was excluded. The administration had created an atmosphere of fear and deception that indeed won support for the war.

Now we realize that even before Sept. 11 the powerful people in the administration (Cheney, Rumsfeld and Wolfowitz) wanted a war with Iraq. The day of the attack some of them tried to find evidence that Iraq had attacked us. Now there was certainly going to be a war, and the challenge was to present a case to the American people to win their support for the war.

The search for evidence was essentially a search to make the case, not a search for the truth, much as one prepares a political campaign or garners support for legislation, or drafts a legal brief. One looked for evidence that would justify the war as preventing Rice's mushroom clouds. One took whatever one could find. Even Colin Powell says his sad attempt to be the Adlai Stevenson of his day was the worst experience of his life. The U.N. inspectors found no evidence of weapons of mass destruction. But that conclusion was dismissed, in effect, as a typical example of U.N. "waffling." No one in the administration, as far as I know, has ever said that the inspectors were right. It would seem such a suggestion is "irresponsible."

The buck stops in the Oval Office. If the president was not deliberately lying to the American people, he nonetheless presided over what was in effect and in truth a massive deception. He would be much wiser to admit his mistake and assume responsibility, but it is apparently not in his character to do so.

Moreover at least three-fifths of the American people now believe that he did in fact deceive them. The question arises as to whether he and Defense Secretary Donald Rumsfeld are also deceiving us on the certainty of victory in Iraq. Granting for the sake of an argument that we must train a functioning Iraq army, why will no one in the administration predict how long that will take? Why after several years of that effort is there only one fully capable Iraqi unit (of 750 men)?

James Fallows, in a long and careful article in the *Atlantic Monthly*, says that it would probably take 10 years, just as anonymous hints from the Pentagon assert. The alternative is to set a strict schedule for withdrawal, which Fallows admits would be a loss of honor.

Whose honor? That of the United States or those who fabricated the reasons for the war? What honor do Bush and Cheney have left?

December 30, 2005

"Cheney's law" gives absolute power

The controversy about spying on the American people fails to understand the implications of "Cheney's law"—the president of the United States has unlimited power in his role of commander in chief to do whatever he deems necessary in a time of war. He can intern prisoners without trial, approve the kidnapping of suspected enemies, send these suspects to prisons in foreign countries where they will be tortured, deny the right of habeas corpus, even nullify laws Congress has passed. He needs no permission from Congress or the courts to engage in any of these activities. The president, in other words, is the Maximum Leader at any time that he decides it is appropriate for him to exercise ultimate power in the United States.

Vice President Dick Cheney has argued this with considerable vigor and persuasiveness. Indeed, he argued it even before he was vice president. The current White House has obviously bought it.

Those who argue that it would not be difficult for the National Security Agency to obtain permission from the secret court to eavesdrop on American citizens miss the point of the controversy. The issue is not the National Security Agency. The issue, rather, is that those who revealed the domestic spying have dared to challenge Cheney's law.

There are historical grounds that lend some support for his draconian theory. President Abraham Lincoln suspended the right of habeas corpus during the Civil War. President Franklin Roosevelt interned thousand of Japanese Americans during World War II, acts of which later Americans became ashamed. Nonetheless, the response is that in times of crisis, a president must do what he has to do. And how long does the crisis last? Apparently, as long as the president says it lasts. When will the so-called war on terrorism cease? Arguably, never. Thus, the president will possess absolute power to ignore existing laws, Congress, the courts and the Constitution itself indefinitely.

There is political wisdom in Cheney's law. While law professors, liberals, some journalists and some clergy are deeply concerned about the Bill of Rights, it means very little to the average person, whose civil liberties have never been endangered. Moreover, when someone questions the absolute power of the commander in chief, President Bush can always play the "fear card." The successors of the 9/11 terrorists are still all around us. The absolute power of the presidency is essential to fight them off. Whether the "fear card" still has political clout remains to be seen. However, it has worked every time the president has played it. What better way to boost your approval ratings than by running against the American Civil Liberties Union and the Bill of Rights?

It would be very helpful to know how many conspiracies have been nipped in the bud by the measures justified under Cheney's law (and its spawn, the Patriot Act). The only answer seems to be Cheney's remark that it's not an accident that there have been no attacks since Sept. 11. National security, we are told, does not permit such chapter and verse.

How convenient. One might ask whether the founding fathers would agree that the commander in chief is in principle a leader with absolute powers. George Washington does not seem to have thought so.

Under Cheney's law, therefore, the president isn't a constitutional leader but in effect a military dictator, not notably different from Fidel Castro or Hugo Chavez—not to mention other military dictators in ages past. We must trust his virtue and restraint and that of those around him to assure us he won't abuse his absolute power. He is, after all, a God-fearing man who prays over all his decisions. This is pretty thin armor.

The only way to defeat Cheney's law is to elect a Democratic Congress and threaten impeachment for high crimes. Would the Democrats run on a platform of supporting the Bill of Rights? Are they capable of being so "unpatriotic"?

Could a commander in chief nullify such an election in a time of war? One would hope the president and vice president would not extend Cheney's law that far. A year ago I would have thought that such a suggestion was from the lunatic fringe of blog writers and e-mail nuts. Now I'm not so sure. Power corrupts, and absolute power corrupts absolutely.

January 6, 2006

Staying the course compounds Iraq war errors

Why did the administration pick Iraq as a target for the war it needed and wanted? Why risk death to more than 2,000 Americans and more than 30,000 Iraqis? As part of his current public-relations campaign, President Bush admits that much of the intelligence on which the Iraq war was based was faulty. He assumes responsibility but blames the intelligence services. However, he goes on to say that the removal of Saddam was the "right" thing to do. Saddam is a bad man. He has killed his own people. He caused instability in that part of the world. He hates America. He was always a threat. We had to get rid of him.

Many Americans are willing even now to swallow such obfuscation, even though it is a cover-up for the phony rationale propounded two years ago.

The proper question is why, of all the bad people in the world, was Saddam Hussein targeted? The president's charges could be leveled against many of the sociopaths on the loose in Asia, Africa and South America.

Who but far-out liberals would object to an attack on Fidel Castro? Or more recently Hugo Chavez? What about Kim Jong-il of Korea? Surely he is a greater threat to the United States than Saddam Hussein. Or the Muslim Arabs in Khartoum who have been practicing genocide against black Christians in the Southern Sudan and black Muslims in Darfur? Or the Shiite Grand Ayatollahs in Iran? Or the shifty Syrians who have been stirring up trouble for thirty years. Once we win "victory" in Iraq, who will be our next target? Not all these leaders, it might be said, are threats to the United States. But was Saddam a threat a couple of years ago? The president says he was, but where is the evidence that Iraqi terrorism was aimed at the United States? There is plenty of terror there now, but didn't our invasion and occupation create it?

With a wide selection of possible targets, why did the administration pick Iraq?

The first reason is that the administration needed a war as an excuse to enhance the wartime powers of the commander in chief. The United States had swept away the scruffy Iranian Taliban in short order. The "war" on terrorism needed another target. Secretary Rumsfeld was sure that Iraq would be a pushover. Shock and awe, some special forces and a compact expeditionary force would wipe out Saddam and all his troops in short order. Had we not driven them out of Kuwait as one would swat an annoying mosquito? It would doubtless be an easier job than even "taking out" Fidel Castro.

Moreover, the generally pro-Israel neo-conservative intellectuals assured the administration that a Democratic Iraq would "reconfigure" the situation in the Middle East. The way to Jerusalem, they insisted, was through Baghdad. So Iraq was the obvious target for another "war on terrorism," even though the evidence that Iraq had cooperated in terrorism against the United States or was even planning on it was thin—and we know now nonexistent.

Behind the administration's assumptions were two huge and costly errors. The first was that resistance in Iraq would collapse immediately. The president, the vice president and the secretary of defense were utterly unprepared for the "insurgency" and even now show no sign that they know what to do about it. The second was that Iraq was prepared for democracy. They assumed, and still do, that if you can organize a fair election and the majority wins, you have, ipso facto, a democracy. What you are more likely to have is a Shiite theocracy and a Sunni Caliphate in civil war. There is no tradition in Iraq of a civil society in which the various factions would share power and abandon their historic propensity to kill one another—a propensity that was recorded in all the history books about Mesopotamia that the neo-cons and the president had not read.

So the president's argument that America must "stay the course" in Iraq till "victory" is as worthless as his previous argument that Saddam possessed weapons of mass destruction. "Victory" will come only when Sunnis and Shiites stop killing one another, and that will not happen in the lifetime of any of us; that it is a hopeless task ought to be evident by now.

And, by the way, might one ask when the American bishops are going to follow the pope's good example and condemn torture, even when the victims are not American citizens?

January 13, 2006

Bush defenders use tortured logic

I receive a lot of nasty hate mail from Republicans. When I filter out the venomous obscenity and scatology, I find a theory not unlike that of the liberal left on separation of church and state. Stick with religion, these irate folk tell me, and get out of politics. Clergy have no business expressing political opinions. I wonder what they think of the great political movements that have swept the country—abolition, populism, prohibition, civil rights, "Reclaiming America"—all of which have had powerful and articulate clerical support. There was also, as best as I can remember, considerable clerical agitation for the impeachment of President Clinton, a sinner, as opposed to our present God-fearing president.

Unfortunately for the theory of the separation of religion and politics, many political issues are fraught with religious and moral implications. It may be that the religious heritages of those who complain about my condemnation of the present administration have no teachings about issues like just wars, lying to the American people, kidnapping and torture. They have every right to complain when a clergy person from another heritage comes along and condemns torture and denounces an administration that condones and even encourages it. I would appreciate it, however, if they'd tell me the name of their denomination.

Those who believe, like the pope and the Catholic hierarchy, that torture is a grave moral evil must be excused for taking a public stand against a president and a vice president who claim the right of the commander in chief to authorize torture that does not lead to death (in Mr. Cheney's euphemistic phrase) and want to extend that privilege from the CIA to the American military.

Published reports indicate that in the heady days after the World Trade Center attack the administration decided to assume that there were absolutely no limits to the power of the president, constitutional, political or moral. Thus a confederacy of thirteen CIA dunces kidnapped a Muslim imam from the streets of Milan, put him on a plane, and sent him to Egypt, which would certainly torture him. After months of abuse he was released with the explanation that he had been telling the truth all along. There have been many more "renditions" (which means the outsourcing of torture) to torture centers. No one in Congress has bothered to find out how many. The gumshoes from the CIA left their cell phones for the Italian police to find. The Italians now want, strangely enough, to indict the criminals who were working for the American government. Odd people, the Italians. Don't they understand that the commander in chief is a God-fearing man who can do anything he wants?

Torture has always been part of the human condition. The strong abuse the weak to seek information or to punish or for the sheer pleasure of it. The Nazis, the Communists and the Japanese did it during the war. Presumably some Americans did it too, though not as an instrument of national policy. Quantitatively, our current assaults on human bodies as a matter of American right are much fewer than those of our former enemies. Qualitatively, if even one man or woman is tortured by implicit or explicit consent of the president of the United Stares, it is a grave sin and must be condemned. Don't try to tell me that a president who approves of such behavior is a God-fearing man. "Rendition" disgraces the president, his administration, the American people and our heritage as a free country. And don't tell me that I'm just arguing the politics of the Democratic Party (which left it to Sen. John McCain to take on Mr. Cheney). I'm arguing for basic American and Christian principles. As T. S. Eliot once wrote, when good does evil to fight evil it becomes indistinguishable from its enemy.

T. George Harris, the distinguished editor and publisher, fibbed to get into the Army at the age of seventeen during World War II. From Normandy to the Battle of the Bulge he flew as an observer in an artillery spotting plane for which he was awarded a medal and a battlefield commission at Bastogne. He wrote me recently that Mr. Bush's approval of torture spreads slime over the traditions of the American military.

I agree with Mr. Harris. Today we stand covered with the slime of George Bush and Richard Cheney for all the world to see.

February 10, 2006

Mideast still hostile to democracy

How could anyone have been surprised by the Hamas victory in the Palestinian election? The Palestinians are a people who feel oppressed and aggrieved. They believe that their land was taken from them. Perhaps they shouldn't feel that way, but in fact they do. Why would they not vote for a party that advocates the destruction of Israel? All the agreements and "road maps to peace" change very little as far as they are concerned. Peace will never be possible so long as terrorists flourish in Palestine. After more than a half century that should be obvious. Voting Hamas into power may have been folly, but the folly is real and it's not likely to go away.

How could one be surprised that Iran elected a populist demagogue who threatens to obliterate Israel? It's madness, you say? Perhaps it is, but the militant nationalism of Iran is a madness that is not likely to go away.

Does anyone seriously believe that with Palestine in the hands of Hamas and threatening sounds from Hamas's sponsors in Iran, nervous Israeli voters won't turn to right-wing extremists in their next election?

Almost certainly Iran is developing nuclear weapons to destroy Israel, as its president suggests. Almost certainly Israel will attempt to strike first. Insanity? Certainly, but that does not mean that it will go away.

How could one be surprised about the size of the plurality of the theocratic parties in the Iraq election? The Shiite majority has been oppressed for a long time. Why wouldn't they strive to regain the power that they feel was theirs by right?

Does anyone think that if the Saudi royal family should be so imprudent as to permit a real election in the country that produced all but one of the World Trade Center terrorists, the radical Islamists would not win?

The point of these dire observations is that the president's madcap policy of promoting "democracy" in the Middle East is folly. Democracy means to him "free" elections and majority rule. But majority rule often means the tyranny of the majority. A man or a party wins a majority or even a large plurality (as did Hitler) in an election, and that is the last election there will be for a long time.

Other conditions have to prevail for majority rule to serve the cause of what we in America would consider democracy. There must first of all be respect for the minority that lost the election, for its right to exist, its right to oppose, its right to criticize. Then there must be concern about the rule of law that survives majority rule, which means an independent judiciary. There must be clearly stated rights and liberties that the majority cannot abrogate.

Not all countries are capable yet of the civic culture that these conditions create. Most European countries are, but some of them achieved such a climate for democracy only recently, and only imperfectly. When one considers that the Republic of Ireland is the sixth oldest continuing democracy in Europe, one realizes what a tender plant it is.

In Russia, for example, just now the most troubling question is whether Mr. Putin will step down after his second term. Majority rule often is the first step to tyranny.

The Middle East will have to muddle along without democracy for the foreseeable future. Tyrannies of one sort or another, either of the leader or of the majority party, will continue to be the only possible form of government, except in Israel, Turkey and perhaps Lebanon.

How could the president of the United States believe otherwise—unless spreading the democratic faith around the world is in fact a useful electoral slogan in this country, many of whose citizens believe that majority rule in elections means that everything has been settled. For that reason, did not James Madison and Co. create a system of checks and balances in the Constitution? The founding fathers feared the power of an uncontrolled majority.

It's worth nothing that the current majority of about 1 or 2 percent has begun to dissolve the American civic culture. Citizens can be held indefinitely without trial. Their phone lines and e-mail can be invaded. Torture is tolerated. The filibuster restraint is in jeopardy. Minorities within the majority can dictate Supreme Court appointments. The Congress is dominated by ideological polarization. The executive claims the privilege to ignore congressional quests for information. One party seeks in its K Street project control of all lobbying and lobbying money.

Our civic culture is not as weak as that of Palestine, or Saudi Arabia, or even Russia. But it is beginning to fray around the edges.

February 17, 2006

Two mistakes: Homeland Security Dept., Rumsfeld's Iraq

Last week, as the congressional hearings on Hurricane Katrina droned on, I happened to read George Packer's memorable book on Iraq, *The Assassins' Gate*. Sociologists are fascinated by bureaucracy because Max Weber, one of sociology's founding fathers, studied them closely and wondered whether they would work. Could any governmental bureaucracy have coped with Katrina.

The committee of House Republicans (you don't want Democrats on such a committee because they might suggest that something was lacking in the president) lambasted the Department of Homeland Security from top to bottom for its past and ongoing failures. Could a more nimble and alert bureaucracy have responded better than a hastily assembled and ill-fitting hodgepodge of disparate agencies, each jealous of its own freedom, presided over by political hacks?

DHS came into being so that the Bush administration might seem to be doing something constructive about homeland security when in fact it was merely manipulating organizational charts. The underlying rationale was that an agency designed to protect Americans from terrorists would also be able to protect Americans from natural disasters. Clearly it could not do the latter, and it seems unlikely that it can do the former.

Could a more focused agency, led by highly trained and charismatic specialists—or supervised by a sophisticated and intelligent president—have done a better job? We will never know the answer to that question as long as critical positions are filled by individuals whose talents are based on political loyalty and personal financial contributions or skill at bureaucratic infighting. Could a corporate CEO who has been in and out of administrations for twenty years and learned the art of pleasing presidents, preside successfully over a war in a distant country about which most Americans—including himself—know practically nothing?

The answer is that a man like Donald Rumsfeld could certainly take charge of such a war. He elbowed aside Secretary of State Powell, ignored National Security Adviser Rice, turned CIA Director Tenet into a babbling sycophant, and browbeat the military leadership into submission. All he needed were memos from the neo-conservatives to fight such a war. As should be patent by now, he made a terrible mess of it. The American military contingent was too small by half, ill prepared in equipment and training to contain the early looting and the ongoing guerilla war it is still fighting, uneducated in the history and the ethnic politics of Iraq, unable to restore and sustain the country's oil industry, and generally insensitive to the hopes and fears of the Iraqi people.

The United States was the only superpower in the world. It possessed a mighty array of military technology, from smart bombs to killer drones. With the help of friendly local support and ingenious special force units, it would be relatively easy to institute a democratic regime in Iraq and thus (to the joy of the neo-conservatives) take pressure off Israel. It did not have to plan in minute detail what should be done after the war was over.

Packer admits that he tended to support the war at the beginning and still thinks it could be won. He has great sympathy for the hard work and bravery of the Americans. An extraordinarily gifted writer, he portrays the Iraqis with sensitivity and sympathy that one rarely reads in shorter and more simplified accounts of Iraq.

Yet the war has been a series of blunders from beginning to end. The worse crime was not the deception of the American people in the reasons for the war but the failure to plan for the postwar situation, to describe what really went wrong, and to take responsibility for it.

"I came to believe that those in positions of high responsibility for Iraq showed a carelessness about human life that amounted to criminal negligence. Swaddled in abstract ideas, convinced of their own righteousness, incapable of self-criticism, indifferent to accountability, they turned a difficult undertaking into a needlessly deadly one."

What kind of a man should preside over a war, if there is to be one? The lesson of both Vietnam and Iraq is that the last sort of person to be responsible for war—especially with a president who admits no mistakes—is a brilliant, hard-charging corporate executive. Of such men war criminals are made.

March 10, 2006

Evil of war brings unending pain

A clergy person often encounters paralyzing grief. Death is a savage blow to a family, especially to the closest relatives of the victim, spouse, parent, child, sibling, usually in that order. Joan Didion in her book *The Year of Magical Thinking* describes her grief after the death of her husband, John Gregory Dunne, with searing honesty. She depicts the denial, the anger, the guilt, the refusal to let go, the paralyzing vortex of emotions that is often triggered by a single memory, the "magical thinking" that somehow he is going to come back. At the end of the book she suggests that maybe she will shortly pass beyond grief to mourning, a state of sadness but not paralysis. You miss the lost love and always will, but you will get on with your life.

Some people are unable to make that leap definitively. They cannot let go because that would be a betrayal of the lost love. The guilt and anger and magical thinking continue indefinitely. They cannot accept the harshness of Jesus on the subject: "Let the dead bury their dead." A firm religious belief that death does not end life is not much help—the raw emotional pain exists at a level of the soul deeper than intellectual conviction and maybe deeper than faith. No one can rightly judge those who are trapped in a miasma of grief. The most another person can do is listen, or maybe only be present.

Every time I see a picture of an American killed in Iraq, I wince. I think of the agony that the death will cause, shattering, rending, paralyzing pain, and the stress and the strain it will introduce into family relationships. I wonder if the family will ever be free from this suffering. In most cases it probably will; mourning will replace grief, more or less. In some families the trauma will be too much, the guilt and anger and magical thinking will persist and blaming will increase—purgatory now, self-created purgatory. The rationalization that he (or she) died defending American freedom, given bravely to the privacy-violating TV journalist, sounds hollow and will seem more hollow as the years go on.

And what of the Iraqi lives, the men and women and children killed so casually by their own kind and even by Americans. On a day when 50 Iraqis are killed, but no Americans, we tend to breathe a sigh of relief. Iraqi grief is not the same as American grief. The Muslim "rag heads" have brought the disaster on themselves. Besides, their noisy lamentations are not in good taste. Yet if we believe in American religion we must mourn with them too as best we can.

Why 2,200 Americans dead? The reasons keep changing—Iraqis were probably involved in the Sept. 11 attack, they possessed huge stores of weapons of mass destruction, we had to get rid of Saddam Hussein, we have to keep our promises to the Iraqi people, we must keep faith with those Americans who have already died. We must establish democracy in the Middle East.

Some Americans still believe these arguments. Many do not. You cannot fool all the people all the time.

The real reasons for the war are too harsh to be fully accepted. The vice president wanted to tighten up on civil liberties. The secretary of defense wanted to wage a new kind of war. The neo-conservative memo writers wanted to take pressure off of Israel. "Our president" wanted to reap the glory of being a wartime president. The majority of Congress wanted to be seen as patriotic Americans. Many, perhaps most, Americans wanted revenge for the World Trade Center attack. Many, perhaps most, Americans believed that the war in Iraq was part of the "war on terrorism."

The only consolation the grief-stricken families can fall back on is that their lost loved ones died doing their duty. This is certainly the truth, and it is certainly an admirable way to die. Some of the families already want to know why a death at the hands of a roadside bomber or a suicide bomber was a necessary duty. One can only pray that God brings peace to them. As for those who caused the war, how can they sleep at night?

April 28, 2006

Generals trying to stop new fiasco

Many military officers for reason of conscience criticize the political leadership of the armed forces, even after they've retired, on the grounds that the behavior of the leadership is immoral. As Marine Gen. Gregory Newbold said, the "decision to invade Iraq was done with a casualness and swagger that are the special province of those who never had to execute these missions or bury the results." This judgment does not differ from that of George Packer, an early supporter of the war, in his extraordinary book *The Assassins' Gate*. Two men with different backgrounds and perspectives come to exactly the same judgment and use the same word, "casual."

One may be prepared to agree that the protesting generals should have resigned from the services if they thought that the war was being run by civilian cowboys. But, should they not, like Colin Powell, have maintained a stoic silence about their discontent? One hears two arguments in favor of this position: regard for the morale of the troops and respect for the American tradition of civilian control of the military.

It seems to me that if an officer is convinced that his civilian leadership is reckless with his soldiers' lives, then he must resign and speak out. Otherwise he is cooperating in evil and is just as much a war criminal as the "casual, swaggering civilian leadership."

The "support our troops" theory is a much weaker one. If "our troops" are in an impossible situation, devised by arrogant and incompetent civilian leadership, then the best support is to demand that they be removed from the situation into which folly has placed them. Taken literally, "support our troops" means the same thing as "our country, right or wrong."

The issue becomes not whether it is right to criticize the leadership but whether the criticism is valid. If it is, then there should be a resignation, but of the president instead of the secretary of defense. Another book on the war—*Cobra II* by military historians Michael Gordon and Bernard Trainor—addresses the same issue. Their craft requires a careful and detailed description of the battles, major and minor, of a campaign that future generations of cadets will study in the service academies. Such men have no particular ideological bias. They are diagnosticians whose duty is to describe what worked and what didn't work.

There can be no doubt after reading the 500 pages of battlefield reconstructions in *Cobra II* that American soldiers and Marines fought with tenacity and courage and that their non-commissioned officers and lower-level commissioned officers were resilient and ingenious, even up to regimental, brigade, and divisional commands, as they always have been in American military history. The problems were at the very highest level—Franks, Sanchez, Bremer, Rumsfeld, Cheney, Wolfowitz.

As Gordon and Trainor sum up their work:

The Iraq war is a story of hubris and heroism, of high-technology wizardry and cultural ignorance. The bitter insurgency Americans and British forces confront today was not pre-ordained There were lost opportunities, military and political, along the way. The commanders and troops who fought the war explained them to us. A journey through the war's hidden history demonstrates why American and allied forces are still at risk in a war the president declared all but won on May 1, 2003.

The hubris and devotion to high technology and total ignorance of the enemy are not the problems of either the officer corps or the troops. They are problems at the very top level of the country, from the president on down.

Why have the generals spoken out now? Doubtless because they see the same group that created the mess in Iraq preparing to incite a war against Iran, using the same techniques of stirring up fear and pseudo patriotism. They actually seem to believe that they can carry it off again, despite their failures in Iraq. It is almost as though there is a Karl Rove scenario. As part of the war on terrorism we begin to create shock and awe in Iran during October. The Republicans are the party of victory and patriotism. We must keep them in power to support our brave troops and our brave president, and to avenge the heroes of 9/11.

As Mr. Cheney is alleged to have argued to the president: If we don't finish Iran now, no future administration will be able to finish it.

June 2, 2006

New motto for Bush: Semper fiasco

God, our Muslim brothers remind us, is the merciful and the compassionate. Therefore we do not make moral judgments on the morality of others. It is up to God to make such judgments. So the moral guilt of the American Marines who apparently murdered perhaps two dozen civilians in Haditha, Iraq, last November must be left to heaven. Yet in the objective order these murders of men, women, and children are a disgrace to the United States and to the Corps and to all the dead we honored last Monday. Their actions are likely to lead to the murder of many Americans by Islamic terrorists, who are not quite as compassionate and merciful as God.

Yet questions must be asked. What are the Marines doing in Iraq, much less riding in patrols down isolated, dusty desert roads? The Marines are an elite unit. They charge through Belleau Woods, they land on beaches at Tarawa, they climb Mount Suribachi on Iwo Jima and raise the American flag, they push toward the Yalu River in North Korea in the depth of winter cold and then, cut off from main American force, "redeploy" from the Chosun Reservoir and out of the trap.

During this epic retreat Curtis Kiesling, one of my seminary classmates, only a few months out of Notre Dame, volunteered to storm a Chinese machine gun above his platoon of the 11th Marines. He silenced the gun and fell back among his comrades dead. That's what Marines are trained to do. They are not trained to be bait for terrorists. They do what they're told to do, of course, and try to live up to the ideals of the Corps. Yet, without excusing what happened, one must ask what in the world they were doing on patrol in western Iraq, where they would be an excellent target for an ambuscade, many of them on their third deployment to Iraq. Indeed, what are any Americans doing dodging roadside bombs in that country?

It will be said that they were defending American freedom. Doubtless they believed that they were. Yet there is no evidence that Iraq was ever a threat to American freedom. Or, it will be contended, they were fighting in the cause of democracy in Iraq. Anyone familiar with the disasters of the early 1920s when the English tried to civilize the new and artificial country (using poison gas, as Saddam Hussein did) will understand that democracy in that tribal society is a pipe dream.

In fact, they were there because the president of the United States "decided" that God wanted him to invade Iraq and the secretary of defense declared such an invasion would require only a small force—less than half the size his military leaders said would be necessary—and that there was no reason to provide an elaborate plan for the time after the war was over. So Reservists and National Guard and elite groups like the 11th Marines were deployed and redeployed and redeployed again and 2,400 Americans (so far) died in a war that has turned out to be folly. We sank into the Big Muddy again.

I will leave to God the most merciful, the most compassionate, to decide about the moral guilt of Messrs. Bush and Rumsfeld. Doubtless they acted with good intentions and confidence that God was on their side. In the objective order, however, the only one we can know, they are in part responsible for the murders at Haditha. I doubt that they will be troubled by the TV clip of the young girl who hid under the bed while the Marines executed her family.

They will never be held to this responsibility. The buck no longer stops in the Oval Office, as it did in President Truman's day, or at the Pentagon. It stops with the young men who cracked under strain and their superiors who tried to cover it up. They will be punished and the leaders of the country will proclaim their own great virtue for serving justice. They will not ask themselves, nor will the country ask them, if they might be in part responsible for war crimes.

As for the cover-up, I am part of a group of men who covered up for abusive brother priests. In great part we deny responsibility for what our colleagues did, even though we knew about it or should have known about it. And our leaders, our commanding officers, if you will, still exercise their offices and still presume to prescribe proper morality for the laity.

No one is responsible anymore. For anything.

June 16, 2006

Americans don't want an empire

The United States of America is a paper tiger. It reverses the dictum of Theodore Roosevelt. It speaks loudly and carries a small stick. Americans are told by their leaders that their country is the last superpower in the world, that we have the duty to bring democracy to the rest of the world, that we have the might and the right, the power and the virtue, to impose by ourself our will on the planet.

This is rubbish, not to use a more scatological word. The United States is not much good as an imperial power because it lacks two of the qualities essential for effective imperialism: a population that is ready to absorb serious casualties in the cause of the empire and leadership that is sufficiently cynical to abandon moralism when there is a chance to deal.

It will do no good to lecture the American people on their obligation to endure substantial loss of life in a cause that the leadership thinks is a national duty. Americans will rise up in righteous anger if they have been attacked and destroy the foe, make no mistake about that—as the Japanese did in 1941. But they quickly become impatient with the endless, small wars, in which young Americans die without any clear purpose and without any "light at the end of the tunnel."

That may be immature of Americans, but that's the way we are. We lack the stern moral determination that the *Wall Street Journal* preaches to us several times a week. We are not exactly pacifists, but we are isolationists. We always have been isolationists. Tell us that we must do something about Darfur or Kosovo or Rwanda and we ask: Why us? If the rest of the world is interested in doing something, OK, but don't expect us to go it alone for long. After Korea and Vietnam, that should have been clear. We went along with the Iraq invasion because our leaders were able to persuade us that it was a war to punish the Sept. 11 terrorists when in fact it was about the belief that a "democratic Iraq would shift the balance in the Middle East. The *Journal* likes to compare us with the Western Europeans who have been spoiled by prosperity and the failure of their virility. They want peace at any price, so they can continue to enjoy the socialist comforts of their consumerist lives. But such a description applies to Americans too, save for a birth rate that is a bit above replacement. Prosperous countries have no stomach for war, especially when they realize that the people they are fighting are not the people who attacked them. Americans never voted to become the enforcers of democracy and justice everywhere in the world all by themselves. Hence, wars like Korea and Vietnam and now Iraq always end badly.

After the Great War of 1914 to 1945, the idea of collective security emerged. The nations of the world would band together to protect one another. In practice this meant that the United States protected Western Europe's fragile emergent prosperity from the Russians. That notion has deteriorated into a theory that America is the great policeman of the world, with an occasional tiny "coalition of the willing" tagging along until the party in a given country that sent troops to Iraq was voted out of power. Iran is not perceived as a threat now, so former English Foreign Minister Jack Straw called our plan to bomb Iran "nutty"—which it surely is. If the rest of the world, including those most likely to be threatened by fanatical mullahs are not concerned, why should Americans be worried?

Since 1916 the United States has fought in five wars (excluding the first Iraq war). In each of these conflicts we came to the rescue of others and gained nothing for ourselves. Nor did we receive much gratitude for our efforts. How just those wars were is open to question. Some probably were, others certainly were not. But they were not self-serving conflicts. Somehow the hubris of power, which seems to possess our leaders every couple of decades, seduces them into conflicts they can never win. They cannot admit to themselves that the world's most powerful country is a paper tiger because its people are not imperialists.

June 30, 2006

Suddenly, the key isn't security

"Homeland security" was the slogan for the election four years ago. This time around there are two clichés—"Global War on Terror" and "Freedom and Democracy for Iraq." Yet, the commission that reported on some of the 9/11 mistakes is back, now as a private group, to report on whether the country is any more secure than it was. No one is listening. We are preoccupied with the killing of a terrorist leader who had lost some of his power, a dubious Iraqi cabinet, and another grandstand presidential flight, this time to mark corners turned rather than a mission accomplished.

"Homeland security" isn't mentioned any more, not after the Katrina debacle. Is there any reason to expect that the collection of clowns in that ramshackle, jerry-built, Rube Goldberg department can protect the nation from terrorists? The 9/11 Commission reports that there is no adequate list of terrorists to compare against airplane passenger lists, that the Transportation Safety administration is poorly managed, and that the FBI, after years of trying and billions of dollars, still does not have a functioning computer system.

The CIA has a revolving door for its directors and spends much of its energies in a struggle to protect its turf from another all-encompassing superstructure—the National Intelligence Agency. We read in the papers that al-Qaida canceled its plan to spread nerve gas in the New York subway because it wasn't big enough. If the real terrorists feel the need to top their World Trade Center victory, what must they be planning? Is there any reason to think that our disorganized, stumblebum, muscle-bound gumshoes will be able to figure out what they're up to? What might they try on September 11, 2006?

I see by the papers that the Chicago Transit Authority has a lovable golden lab named Ryan who wanders through mass transit locales charming customers as she politely sniffs them. After the attacks on Madrid, why are there not hundreds of her sisters and brothers prowling around? Costs too much I guess.

Might they be scheming to plant "dirty bombs" on container ships in several American ports that will go off at the same time? Despite the warnings about the inadequacy of port protection, five years later they remain a dangerous weakness in our cockamamie security system. Stay away from them this September 11.

Or what about simultaneous attacks on jumbo jets as they're taking off from five major airports? Stinger anti-aircraft missiles are readily available on the international arms black markets. The military possesses weapon systems that will deflect attacks from its planes flying out of Baghdad, but, we are told, it would be too costly to mount such defenses on commercial jets. So the American fleet of jets is an inviting target. It would require only 10 or 15 men to launch a Stinger attack from side roads a short distance from five airports. Maybe, just maybe, a couple of the missile teams would be discovered and destroyed. Maybe, just maybe, some of the missiles might misfire. All right, only two or three 747s blow up. What does that do to the American economy?

No one seems ready to ask why some of the money diverted to rich Americans as tax reductions is not used to protect jets. Or why a few of the billions that are poured into the Big Muddy of Iraq are not available to prevent such a disaster.

Last week we heard much about the pathetic wannabe Haitian terrorists who weren't Muslim, had no guns and no money and pledged their allegiance to al-Qaida as administered by a government informant. Doubtless such folk shouldn't be permitted to play their games, but as evidence that the country is cracking down on terror, it is pretty thin.

The president plays fast and loose with the truth when he says that the war in Iraq is a crucial front in the war on global terrorism. In fact, Iraq was not a base for terrorism before the World Trade Center attack, and the war itself has created more terrorists than there were five years ago. Victory in Iraq, should it ever happen—which seems unlikely—would do nothing to divert al-Qaida and its imitators from their goals of punishing the United States. Instead of increasing our national security, we put our bet on the wrong enemy: the fictional weapons of mass destruction in Iraq.

July 7, 2006

Cheney really wants U.S. dictator

In the winter of 1933, before Franklin Roosevelt's first inauguration on March 4, there was a clamor in the United States for a military dictatorship.

The banks were closing, a quarter of Americans were unemployed, rebellion threatened on the farms. Only drastic reforms, mandated by the president's power as commander in chief, would save the country. Something like the fascism of Mussolini's Italy—viewed benignly by many Americans in those days because it worked (or so everyone said)—would save the country from communist revolution.

As Jonathan Alter reminds us in *The Defining Moment*, his brilliant book about FDR's first hundred days, men as different as William Randolph Hearst, financier Bernard Baruch, commentator Lowell Thomas and establishment columnist Walter Lipmann argued for the necessity of dictatorship to reorganize the country's economy. Both the *New Republic* and the *Commonweal* (a Catholic liberal journal) advanced the same thesis.

The call for a military-style dictatorship is the ultimate temptation to the greatest treason of a democratic society. Fortunately for us, FDR resisted the temptation and reformed the American economy by a mix of gradualist changes (like Social Security) and magical "fireside chats." Unfortunately, years later he yielded to the temptation to a military dictatorship when he interned Japanese Americans simply because they were Japanese. In the first case he resisted the demands of the American people. In the second he caved in to their racist demands, just as Lincoln caved in to such demands and abolished habeas corpus during the Civil War.

The United States is currently caught up in a new campaign for a military dictatorship—rule by a military chief with absolute power. The White House, inspired by the vice president, has argued that in time of great danger, the president has unlimited powers as commander in chief. If he cites "national security" he can do whatever he wants—ignore Congress, disobey laws, disregard the courts, override the Constitution's Bill of Rights—without being subject to any review. Separation of powers no longer exists. The president need not consult Congress or the courts, only the vice president, the attorney general and God. Moreover, the rights of the commander in chief to act as a military dictator last as long as the national emergency persists, indefinitely that is and permanently.

Many, perhaps most, Americans don't mind. The president is "tough on terrorists" and that's all that matters. What is the Bill of Rights anyway? Mr. Bush, his supporters will argue, is a good man, even a godly man. He won't misuse the power, even if the power he claims is no less than that which Don Hugo Chaves exercises in Venezuela

The Supreme Court in its ruling about a Guantanamo detainee just before Independence Day was a sharp rebuke to Cheneyism (fascism American style). It dealt with only one case and left the president wiggle room. He could consult with Congress about new legislation that would provide more rights for the detainees in a military trial. But that violates Mr. Cheney's first principle that the commander in chief doesn't have to consult with anyone on matters of national security. If the president is to be consistent with the Cheney theory and the Alberto Gonzales memos, he should defy the Supreme Court and insist that he has the right to establish whatever judicial process he deems proper for these potentially dangerous people without any interference from anyone. He may still do that.

Republicans who will seek re-election in November already suggest that they will run against the Supreme Court decision. The court, they will tell the American people who want the detainees to be shot at sunrise tomorrow, is soft on terror, just like Democrats in Congress. They could probably get away with this nonsense because fear will cause the voters to forget that this is the Republican court that elected Mr. Bush to the presidency.

Richard Cheney is a vile, indeed evil, influence in American political life. He is a very dangerous person who would if he could destroy American freedom about which he and his mentor prate hypocritically. His long years in Washington have caused him to lose faith in the legislative and judicial processes of the government. The country, he believes, requires a much stronger executive. Such concentrated power would have been necessary even if the World Trade Center attack had not occurred. He uses the fear of terrorists as a pretext to advance his agenda of an all powerful president, a military dictator. So long, of course, as he is a Republican.

July 14, 2006

Iraq war was lost the day it started

If we "cut and run" from Iraq, the Republican senators argued recently, we will lose our credibility, dishonor the memory of those who have already died there, break our promise to the Iraqi people, and settle for something less than victory. The United States does not quit that way. So Republicans will run in November against dishonor, flag burners, gay marriages, the *New York Times*, the Supreme Court, and the Democrats who want to lose Iraq (just as they ran a half century ago against Democrats who "lost" China). Will it work? Sure it will.

In fact, the United States did cut and run in Korea and Vietnam. It did settle for something less than victory in these two wars. The United States did abandon the North Korean and Vietnamese people. It did dishonor the dead soldiers, if withdrawing from an impossible conflict does dishonor those who have died. Some of the senators know that. Most of the American people, ignorant as they are of history, have forgotten.

However, the truth is that Iraq was "lost" the day the war started. It was an artificial country like Czechoslovakia and Yugoslavia, stitched together after the Great War. The British forced its rebellious tribes together with bombs and poison gas (still a popular form of killing in that country). They left in charge the minority Sunni tribes, who ruled brutally through eight decades, viciously suppressing the Shiite majority and other tribes, particularly the Kurds in the north. Saddam Hussein was merely the logical conclusion of the cruel dictators who had ruled before him. When the American invasion brought him down, it destroyed the Sunni establishment and gave power to the Shiite majority. It also confirmed the Kurds' determination that they didn't want to be part of Iraq any more. Moreover, they had 100,000 well-trained and well-armed troops who would defend Kurdistan from any invaders.

Thus, as Peter Galbraith writes in his *The End of Iraq*, Iraq ended for all practical purposes when the Americans arrived. To exacerbate the centrifugal forces, the United States did not send enough troops, did not try to stop the looting—particularly of weapons—did not plan for a postwar policy, and sent arrogant amateurs to administer the country.

However, the Kurds already have an independent country, the Shiites have established their own regional governments with close ties to Iran, and the Sunnis have launched a civil war. Eventually the Sunnis will form their own enclave and continue the civil war in areas they share with the Shiites, especially Baghdad. No foreign army is capable of policing these areas of continuing conflict. The central government that we have created will at best be able occasionally to mediate among these independent enclaves.

Those who knew anything about the history of Iraq were predicting this outcome before the war. The president, the vice president, the secretary of defense and the swarm of neo-conservative intellectuals around them did not know Iraqi history and paid no attention to those who did. The pretense now that the war in Iraq can still be won displays the same criminally arrogant ignorance of the Bush administration before the war. Messrs. Bush, Cheney and Rumsfeld are still not speaking the truth, perhaps not even to themselves. Neither are the senators who will run against the Democrats (and probably win) on the platform of victory in the war.

Peter Galbraith has been around Iraq long enough to know that the first Bush administration supported Saddam in his war with Iran, providing weapons, equipment and intelligence, some of it in support of poison-gas attacks on the Iranians. He also remembers that the previous Bush urged the Shiites and the Kurds to rise up and revolt against Saddam after the Persian Gulf War. He and his advisers did not believe that they would take him seriously. Hundreds of thousands died. The people of Iraq have very good reason for hating Americans.

Most Americans will not read books like *The End of Iraq*. They know almost nothing of the history of this artificial country, which is all right because they don't know much about the history of their own country either. The president doesn't even read memos his staff prepares for him. Most of the important people in the government don't have time to read. Therefore, having ignored the lessons of history, they repeat its mistakes. Americans will continue to die in Iraq because no one making decisions could bother reading its history.

July 21, 2006

Why Dems strike out like the Cubs

The national Democratic Party is just like the Chicago Cubs. Both organizations are lovable losers. Come to think of it, neither is all that lovable any more. Both have become just losers. For the Cubs we used to blame the Wrigleys. Now we blame *Tribune* (as it calls its corporate self). We used to blame the stingy salaries. Now they pay good salaries and still lose. Through the years since Frank Chance, they have let people go to other teams, where they do better. Not only have they utilized all the traditional ways of losing, they have invented some highly original ones—like messing up young pitchers. They disgrace the city, their loyal fans (a matter of faith as Cardinal George once said) and baseball.

The Democratic Party has elected three presidents since the death of FDR—John Kennedy, Jimmy Carter and Bill Clinton—and only Clinton was re-elected. (Presidents Truman and Johnson were re-elected after succeeding presidents who died in office.) They have served up to the American people such losers as Adlai Stevenson, George McGovern, Walter Mondale, Michael Dukakis, Al Gore and John Kerry. Jimmy

Carter won by a close vote (against the man who pardoned Richard Nixon) and became a loser the day he took office. None was very lovable, with the exception of Governor Stevenson, who had to run against a war hero.

The Democrats sealed their doom at the 1972 convention when they threw out Mayor Daley and union leader George Meany, cutting themselves off from their working-class and urban-ethnic bases. Since then Democratic leaders (mostly from the East Coast) have been so concerned with feminist activists, gay activists, African American activists—though not with Latino American activists—that they have lost any sense of their own identity. They don't ask themselves where the activists will go if they don't vote Democratic. Nor do they give a hoot about Catholics, who are the second largest minority in their party, because they conclude the "Catholic vote" is an anti-abortion vote.

Now they have apparently decided that the war is not to be an issue in the fall campaign. The surveys show that both the Republican president and the Republican Party are unpopular with substantial majorities of Americans. Almost two-thirds of Americans think the war is a mistake, a substantial majority believe they weren't told the truth when the war started, and about half favor an immediate schedule for withdrawing the troops. As the situation in Iraq deteriorates, opposition to it will grow. It is the critical issue among the American people and one on which the Democrats can win.

So what will the amiable losers do? They'll do their best to keep the war out of their campaigns. They won't emphasize the deliberate deceptions, the terrible mistakes—not enough troops, inadequate training of the troops, lack of planning for the postwar months, incompetent American civilian administrators, ignorance of fractured Iraqi society, torture, cover-up, numerous civilian deaths, torture, rape, murder (sometimes involving soldiers who should never have been sent to Iraq), the decline of American prestige around the world, the increase in the number of potential terrorists, the resilience of the Taliban because the Iraq mess has distracted American leaders from Afghanistan. Above all, the senseless deaths and maiming of young American men and women in a war that was doomed to defeat before it began, young men and women who were at risk because Mr. Cheney and Mr. Rumsfeld wanted a war to demonstrate American power and because the president didn't like Saddam Hussein.

Why won't they campaign on these issues? Because they fear that Karl Rove will accuse them of "waffling," defeatism, dishonoring the dead, pessimism, betrayal of promises, supporting the enemy, lack of patriotism and treason.

Why won't they campaign against preemptive wars based on Mr. Cheney's 1 percent doctrine—if there's only 1 percent chance of weapons of mass destruction in Iraq, we take them out?

The flag-draped-coffins spat illustrates their propensity to lose. Republicans screamed that the ad was in bad taste, and the Democrats withdrew it. Is it not worse taste to pretend that Americans are not dying in Iraq in a futile war?

Candidates who cave in at the threats of name calling or are afraid to fight back by telling the truth don't deserve to win. And they won't win. The Cubs have their billy goat curse, the Democrats are cursed by their own cowardice.

July 28, 2006

Who grieves for dead Iraqis?

What is the worth of a single Iraqi life?

The *New York Times* reported that during recent months a hundred of them die violently every day, 3,000 every month. In terms of size of population, that is the equivalent of 300,000 Americans a month, 10,000 every day. Yet the typical television clip on the evening news—an explosion, automatic weapon fire, bleeding bodies carried away, dead bodies on the streets, adults and children screaming in agony, wounded bodies in inadequate hospitals—has become as much a cliché as the weather report or another loss by the Cubs. The dead Iraqis are of no more value to us than artificial humans in video games. The Iraqis seem less than human, pajama-wearing people with dark skin, hate in their eyes, and a weird religion, screaming in pain over their losses. Weep with them, weep for them?

Why bother?

Rarely do Americans tell themselves that the United States of America, the land of the free and the home of the brave, is responsible for this slaughter. In a spasm of arrogance and power, we destroyed their political and social structure and are now unable to protect them from one another. Their blood is on the hands of our leaders who launched a war on false premises, without adequate forces, without plans for the time after the war, and then sent in inept administrators who could not provide even a hint of adequate public services.

As Colin Powell, who knows something about war, unlike the president and his top thinkers, told Mr. Bush, "If you break it, you own it." If you shatter a society, it is yours, and you're responsible for it. The United States shattered Iraq, and we are responsible for the ensuing chaos that we are unable to control. So a hundred human beings are killed every day, and the most powerful military in the world (as Messrs. Rumsfeld and Cheney insist) is unable to stop the killing.

On most of the standards for a just war, the invasion of Iraq was criminally unjust. Messrs. Wolfowitz, Cheney and Rumsfeld wanted to invade Iraq the day after the World Trade Center attack. They tried to persuade the people that Iraq was somehow involved in the attack. They insisted that the Iraqis possessed weapons of mass destruction. Their arguments for the war, we all know now, were not true.

There was, therefore, no just cause, no attempt to exhaust all possible alternatives short of war, no real hope for victory, no postwar plans, and no ability to prevent the postwar butchery that was easily predictable to those who understood Iraq. The war leaped from slogan to slogan—weapons of mass destruction, the critical front in the global war on terrorism, stay the course, freedom and democracy in Iraq. All these slogans are false.

Were America's leaders deliberately lying? Did they really believe that the Shiites and the Sunnis would not murder one another, or did they know better? One must leave the state of their consciences to God. However, they should have known and in the objective order they are criminally responsible for the hundred deaths every day. They should be tried for their crimes, not that such trials are possible in our country.

The hundred who die every day are not merely numbers, they are real human beings. Their deaths are personal disasters for the dead person and also for all those who love them: parents, children, wives, husbands. Most Americans are not outraged. Iraqis are a little less than human. If a hundred people were dying every day in our neighborhoods, we would scream in outrage and horror. Not many of us are lamenting these daily tragedies. Quite the contrary, we wish the newscast would go on to the weather for the next weekend.

Is blood on the hands of those Americans who support the war? Again, one must leave them to heaven. But in the objective order it is difficult to see why they are not responsible for the mass murders. They permitted their leaders to deceive them about the war, often enthusiastically. How can they watch the continuing murders in Iraq and not feel guilty?

How would you feel if the street were drenched with the blood of your son and daughter, if your father were in the hospital with his legs blown off?

We cannot permit ourselves to grieve for Iraqi pain because then we would weep bitter and guilty tears every day.

August 4, 2006

Dehumanizing others is no virtue

To hate other humans or to feel no pain at their suffering, it is necessary to dehumanize them, to write them off as less than human. The Nazis are the classic example of this dehumanization. Germans were the *obermensch*, the master race. Jews, Slavs, Gypsies were the *untermensch*, the inferior peoples who barely had the right to exist.

The Puritans dehumanized Native Americans, white Americans dehumanized African Americans, Irish Protestants and Catholics in Northern Ireland dehumanized one another, as do Jews and Arabs in the Middle East, and Shiite and Sunni Muslims. In every case, one attributes to the "other" characteristics that prove that they are not fully human by the use of stereotypes—"illegals," for example. The American soldiers who tortured, beat, raped and murdered Iraqis dismiss their victims as "rag heads." The rest of us are able to ignore the pain and the grief of ordinary Iraqis, as I learned from responses to my last column, by arguing that Iraq was involved in the Sept. 11 attack or that Saddam killed far more than have died under our inept and unplanned "occupation."

The first argument is ignorant. Bush administration officials have admitted in whispers that no evidence has been found of a link between al-Qaida and Iraq. It is also immoral because it assumes that revenge is appropriate. Some of them killed some of ours, and therefore it's all right to permit the killing of many of them.

The second argument reveals twisted immorality. Because Saddam was a mass murderer, Americans are not responsible for our failure to protect Iraqis when we have taken charge of their country. He was worse than we are. He killed through commission; we kill (for the most part) through omission. Our only sins were to make war on the basis of false arguments with little understanding of the people whose social system we destroyed and to establish an occupation of arrogant incompetence. Thus the ineffable Paul Wolfowitz, the intellectual architect of the Iraq war, could say, "I think that there are ethnic differences in Iraq, but they are exaggerated."

Right! The Kurds, Sunnis and Shiites will be too busy celebrating our liberation to begin killing one another. All of which proves that a Ph.D. from the University of Chicago does not protect a person from folly. It is unlikely that Mr. Wolfowitz assumes any responsibility for what went wrong.

So you see, the e-mail that makes this argument implies, why should we feel any guilt because Saddam was much worse than we are? Baldly stated, that argument is nonsense and immoral nonsense at that. Yet many Americans are still ready to use it to wash their hands of the pain and suffering, the fear and the horror of innocent Iraqis whom we have betrayed.

Joel Preston Smith, one of my e-mail commentators, writes that he was in Iraq before the war and after it began. "If I hadn't been treated so well, maybe I wouldn't feel so connected to the families and friends who sheltered me, fed me, helped me do my work. But I see the vast majority of Iraqis as incredibly kind, thoughtful people. And it is a knife in my heart, every day, to see them suffer." Many Americans do feel a similar knife, but many others (for the most part, it would seem from my e-mail, ardent supporters of the Bush administration) dispense themselves from any feelings of grief or responsibility.

Moreover, when Americans finally "cut and run"—as Ronald Reagan did in Lebanon—there is no reason to think that Baathist leaders of the insurgency (from the safe haven of Syria) will not re-install Saddam or someone as bad as he was.

The man who was to lead the military police contingent into Iraq was promised 20 battalions of MPs. At the last minute, to prove Mr. Rumsfeld's point that not many troops would be needed to dispose of Saddam (Wolfowitz argued that only thirty-five thousand troops could do the job), his contingent was cut to three battalions. If he had his full complement, he might have been able to prevent the looting that provided weapons for the insurgency. Mr. Rumsfeld dismissed the looting as something that was inevitable and not important. "Stuff happens."

Are all Americans responsible for the administration's ignorance and arrogance in Iraq? Surely not. Yet those who still defend the war with clichés and phony arguments despite all the published evidence to the contrary are whistling in the dark as they pass the graveyard.

August 11, 2006

Arrogance, ignorance invite disaster

In a war, as Secretary Rumsfeld says, "stuff happens." Things go wrong, sometimes a lot goes wrong, on occasion everything goes wrong. Then you have a fiasco (the title of the best book yet about Iraq, written by Thomas

E. Ricks). Military history is filled with fiasco stories—the French army at Agincourt, for example, or the Union Army at Fredericksburg. A more recent fiasco was Operation Market Garden in the autumn of 1944, a scheme cooked up by British Marshal Bernard Law Montgomery.

The Germans, driven out of France, were falling back behind the Siegfried line. Montgomery desperately wanted to win the war by himself. The plan was that his British Second Army would run around the end of the line and go on to Berlin. Three airborne divisions (two American, one British) would secure bridges over the Rhine at Nijmegen, Enthoven and Arnheim. The armored corps of the 2nd Army would drive up the road, cross the Rhine and strike into Germany. It was an ingenious scheme, at least on paper. It turned into a fiasco (recorded in the book *A Bridge Too Far* and a film of the same name). The American airborne divisions captured the first two bridges. The British division failed to capture the bridge at Arnheim and their armored corps moved too slowly. The English paratroop division was destroyed, and the war went on.

Why the failure? Market Garden was a hasty plan, developed in less than two weeks. The intelligence was inadequate. There were more German troops moving into Holland than Montgomery realized. There were not enough paratroop divisions. There should have been two at Arnheim, but there were no more available. The armored corps was not strong enough and moved too slowly. The causes: arrogance and ignorance. The result: fiasco.

This paradigm matches the Iraq war: terrible intelligence, inadequate planning, not enough troops, underestimating the enemy. More arrogance and ignorance. Only the size of the fiasco is much larger, a terrible blow to the American military and to American prestige for the next decade. The pessimism among American leaders at the Senate Committee last week was palpable. There might be a civil war and, if there is, there is little the United States can do but get out of the way. Probably the worst fiasco in American history, worse than Bull Run, the Little Big Horn, Pearl Harbor. In the years to come people will ask, Why did they do it? They had been warned about what would happen and they went ahead anyway. The Congress and the media did not protest. Were they out of their minds?

The answer, I suspect, is yes, we all were out of our minds. Osama bin Laden in his wildest dreams could not have imagined that the United States would have responded to the World Trade Center attack with such madness. Ricks, the *Washington Post*'s Pentagon reporter, points out that the columnists and the editorial writers at his paper and the *New York Times* supported the war at the beginning, and the *Times* carried Cheney's falsehoods in its news columns (courtesy of reporter Judith Miller).

Most of these writers, sentinels against government failures, have changed their minds now as sanity begins to return, but they have yet to admit their mistakes and take responsibility. Thomas Friedman of the *Times*, its all-purpose pontifical expert on the Middle East, has finally announced, yes, it is time to call a peace conference among Iraq parties and get out. Where was he three years ago? Why doesn't he admit flat out that he was wrong and apologize? Why doesn't he say that he was swept along by the 9/11 frenzy and the blatant lies of the administration, and that he ought to have known better? Why doesn't he credit those of us who warned all along that Iraq was another Big Muddy, worse even than Vietnam? Why doesn't he concede he, too, failed the American people by not standing up to the frenzy sweeping the country? Why doesn't he criticize the media, which propounded the false cliché that America would never be the same again and the misleading shibboleth "war on global terror?"

Arrogance and ignorance were not limited to the administration. Friedman and David Brooks and Robert Kagan and James Hoagland failed in their duty to cry "hold, enough!" We should not permit them to change their minds until they admit full responsibility for the fiasco, which has given bin Laden his biggest victory yet.

August 18, 2006

"War" doesn't describe threat to America

The "War on Islamo-fascism" is replacing the "War on Global Terror" as the favorite Bush administration buzz slogan. It is a good slogan because it appeals to the "nuke 'em" segment of the population as an election approaches and because it means nothing at all. The very word "war" has been misused so often that it has lost all its meaning—the war on drunk driving, the war on drugs, the war on obesity, the war on pornography, the war on calories, the war on autism, the war on gay marriages, the war, as I saw in a newspaper recently, on cervical cancer.

"War" used to be reserved for military battles between powerful armies, as in the Civil War or World War II. Now it means anyone and everyone's favorite cause. The word is a victim of linguistic corruption. Since in some fashion we think with words, linguistic corruption corrupts our thought and indeed destroys thought because it eliminates the necessity and the possibility of thoughtful distinctions—just what knee-jerk, right-wing haters want.

Thus "war on Islamo-fascism" enables both Vice President Dick Cheney and the senator from Connecticut to lump the Iraq war with the plot to blow up transatlantic flights and blinds the victims of such slogans to the facts that in Iraq most of the killing these days is Muslim on Muslim and that there is no evidence of an Iraqi trying to attack the mainland United States or indeed any American until we invaded their country and messed it up. The transatlantic terrorists are English citizens of Pakistani origin who resent the way England treats them. The World Trade Center terrorists were mostly Saudis who resented U.S. support of Israel and American presence in their country. Different people, different anger, different exploitation of a religious heritage.

There's an old Latin saying, "Qui nimis probat, nihil probat"—he who proves too much proves nothing at all. If you lump too many phenomena under one label that is also a slogan, you create confusion for yourself and bar serious thought. You justify a fiasco in Iraq on the grounds that it is somehow connected with plans of religious fanatics to blow up airplanes. More seriously, you sink enormous resources into the former and neglect the threat of the latter. You do not invest some of those resources in airport screeners that detect the liquid materials from which bombs could be created—though you have known for 10 years about the possibility of such bombs. You do not equip airliners with defenses against anti-aircraft rockets, you do not improve the Arabic language capacity of your intelligence services, you do not force your various intelligence agencies to combine their efforts despite bureaucratic inertia against cooperation, you do not cover the gaping holes in protection of sea ports, chemical factories, and mass transit systems.

The only thing that the various forms of terrorism have in common is angry resentment based on fanatical religious vision. You do not respond to that threat, which takes different forms in different contexts, by invading a country and destroying its social structure. Rather, you mobilize your resources of technology, talent, planning and intelligence to defend yourself against crazy zealots. Most Americans feel, quite correctly, they are not safer than they were five years ago. They are probably less safe because the next wave of crazy terrorists may well be Iraqis who resent the fiasco we imposed on their country.

There is no reason at all to believe that the Department of Homeland Security has notably improved our defenses against the crazies. Otherwise it would be working on the scanners that track liquid explosives instead of relying on Pakistani intelligence (who got the first tip about the transatlantic terrorists).

Americans will have to live for many years with the same unease as do the Israelis—some crazy might blow me up in the next minute. We will eliminate most of that possibility by being quicker, smarter, more ingenious and more determined than they and not by grandiose talk about "war" and not by seeking out new Big Muddies into which to sink our resources.

August 25, 2006

5 years later, he's Osama has-been Laden

Back in 2004 during the ill-fated John Kerry campaign, the Massachusetts senator laid out for the *New York Times* magazine an intellectual sketch of how he would deal with terrorism and terrorists. It should be "primarily an intelligence and law-enforcement operation that requires cooperation around the world." In effect, he believed that the appropriate model was police work and not military invasions.

He did not go public with this scheme, however, probably because his handlers thought the Republicans would accuse him of being soft on terror. His advisers apparently felt such a campaign stance would be grist for Karl Rove's mill. Perhaps that was the right decision, because the public had yet to turn against President Bush as it has for the last eight months.

However, when the English cops broke up the plan to destroy U.S. jets with liquid bombs, the White House celebrated the close cooperation among police forces in Pakistan, England and the United States. Conservative columnist George Will, of all people, seems to have been the only journalist who noted this strange comment sounded pretty much like Kerry. A White House source told him that Kerry was wrong. "The police method does not work." Will notes ironically that such a response assumes that the war in Iraq does work.

In fact, the oft-repeated presidential insistence that the war in Iraq is the central front in the war on terrorism is just one more of the many White House lies, though one might argue that the president is not smart enough to perceive that the police work of the English had nothing to do with the war in Iraq (save perhaps that the crazies wanted to blow up the planes to punish the United States for invading Iraq) and therefore was not lying. Similarly, his repeated insistence that the terrorists want to take away our freedom is on the face of it false. They don't give a hoot about our freedom. They care only about punishing us. If we have lost some freedom in the last several years, it is the president who has taken it away from us by his claim to have unlimited powers.

The president believes a lot of things that are not true—such as that it was all right to paw German Chancellor Angela Merkel in a television scene that seemed almost like an episode from "Deadwood."

The same point about the negative impact of the Bush war rhetoric was reported by James Fallows in a major article in the current *Atlantic Monthly*. Fallows interviewed some 60 experts on the Middle East, half of them Americans. To his surprise, there was a general feeling that the United States had basically won the war with al-Qaida. America had destroyed its training camps, killed thousands of its fighters, deprived it of command and control apparatus and holed up its leaders in the mountains of Afghanistan. Moreover, it has established a worldwide intelligence and police network that is increasingly effective in preventing many attacks by imitation al-Qaidas.

One cannot say that the United States is safe, but it is a lot safer than it was five years ago. This country should declare victory in the war on terrorism, Fallows argues, and continue its determined intelligence work and cooperation with police authorities in other countries.

Lawrence Wright, in his account of the World Trade Center attack, leaves no doubt (if there still is any) that the disaster might have been avoided if the various American police agencies—FBI, CIA, NSA—were talking to one another instead of protecting their own turf.

The ideas of Kerry, Will, Fallows, and Wright converge around one theme: Total safety from terrorists is not possible, but large military campaigns do not and have not enhanced the safety of Americans. Why was it necessary to invade Iraq? Sometimes I think it was a blind lashing out at enemies. America had suffered a terrible loss. Improved international police and intelligence work did not seem an appropriate response. If there was a war on terrorism, America needed a real war so that the punishment would fit the crime.

September 1, 2006

Blame 9/11 on airlines, Congress, Bush

The fifth anniversary of the World Trade Center attack is coming up soon. It should be a time of national disgrace and shame. It never should have happened. Americans have been so busy for the past five years in the search for revenge that they have not bothered to ask why it happened and not asked seriously who was responsible for it. Why was a ragtag band of religious fanatics able to humiliate this country? What did we do wrong? Until we admit our shame, we will not be able to avoid another such national ignominy.

The primary responsibility belongs with the airline industry and the Republican-dominated, big-business-serving Congress. In 1996, a commission chaired by then-Vice President Gore recommended a number of regulations to protect the safety of airline passengers. Among the recommendations was that steel doors separate the flight deck from the rest of the aircraft. Characteristically, the airline industry lobbied against the legislation on the grounds that such doors would cost too much. The absence of the doors, however, cost almost 3,000 lives.

The airline presidents and lobbyists responsible for the defeat of the steel doors ought not to be able to sleep at night because of this deadly betrayal of their passengers. Similarly with the media, which did not denounce the greed of the airlines at the time or even after the Sept. 11 attack. If the terrorists had known that they could not gain access to the flight decks, they probably would not have tried to execute their plot. If they had, it would not have worked.

Corporate greed and congressional cowardice and media silence were the primary causes of the destruction at the World Trade Center. To deny this is to lie, one more lie in five years of terrible lies.

The most guilty individuals were President Bush and National Security Adviser Condoleezza Rice. They wrote off the warnings about al-Qaida they inherited from the Clinton administration as just one more element of the Clinton years they wanted to discard. We won't give terrorism as high a priority as the previous administrations, Rice told Richard Clark. In a work of prestidigitation worthy of the greatest political crooks in history, the administration excused itself from responsibility and shifted the blame onto President Bill Clinton. Again the national media let the Bush administration get away with it.

Bush promptly assumed the mantle of a wartime president, which, as the *Wall Street Journal* crowed, destroyed the controversy over the dubious Florida vote in the 2000 election. He used this mantle of a nation at war to claim leadership in a global war on terrorism and, with Rice, indulged in an aggressive, go-it-alone foreign policy that alienated almost every other country in the world. Egged on by his coterie of neo-conservative intellectuals, he launched a frivolous and foolish fiasco in Iraq in which thousands of Americans and tens of thousands of Iraqis have been slaughtered. Yet precisely because of the myth of his success against terrorism, he won the congressional election of 2002 and the presidential election and will almost certainly win the election this November, once more in the name of war on global terror—more recently the war on Islamo-fascism. Now it would seem he and the vice president are planning a war against Iran.

Historians will doubtless say that the attack on Sept. 11, 2001, was a national tragedy. They will also contend that the nation's response to that tragedy was even worse. The American people were not responsible for the former, but they will certainly be judged guilty for all the evil of the latter.

If I were Osama bin Laden and I wanted to hit America with an anniversary attack, I'd look for more weaknesses like the absence of steel doors—such as, for instance, the inadequate screening of checked luggage. This time the guilty will not only be the airlines and Congress. It will be the rest of us who have settled for inadequate security because real security costs too much.

September 15, 2006

Presidents don't end wars they start

Much of the history of the United States in the last half century has involved wars that the country should not have waged and from which it could not extricate itself. In Korea the United States mistakenly decided to take on China after it had won a great military victory in the legendary landing at Inchon. If it had ended the war when it drove the communists out of South Korea, American casualties would have been light and the communists humiliated. Unfortunately, General MacArthur made the terrible mistake of assuming that China could accept an American army on its Yalu River boundary.

One can generalize that mistaken wars will end only after there is a change of administrations. Korea was Mr. Truman's war, Vietnam was Mr. Johnson's war, and the Iraq war is Mr. Bush's war. Only when the president who started the war leaves can this country manage to end the war that was identified with him.

President Eisenhower promised that if elected, he would go to Korea, though that promise was hardly enough to persuade the Chinese army to go home. President Nixon had a "plan" to end the Vietnam war, though in fact he did not. While he and Henry Kissinger messed around in search of a dignified withdrawal and caused more American casualties than in Truman's years, he (and President Ford) could finally end the war that President Johnson could not end. It is clear today that President Bush cannot (which means will not) end this most foolish of the three wars.

Why is it so difficult to extricate American troops from an impossible situation?

The commander in chief was in each case personally responsible for the decision. Moreover, to rally support for the decision that in retrospect was a serious mistake (underestimating the enemy in each case) the president had to rally the national will with appeals to patriotism, honor, and American self-interest. His emotional involvement in "victory" increased as the number of casualties did—and in the case of Lyndon Johnson and George Bush some kind of identification with Abraham Lincoln took place. Finally, the president's political party resisted the temptation for a long time to criticize him.

Moreover, a substantial segment of the American public, especially Southern and evangelical, believes that patriotism demands that the nation emerge clearly victorious no matter what the price. These people wave flags, talk about the threat to the United States (of a much weaker enemy) and accept the patriotic appeal that we simply don't lose wars and we must stand by our troops. When they are told that we will not defeat the enemy because we cannot, they scream defeatism, surrender, betrayal. They also suggest that we should nuke the enemy. The pathological super-patriots always fall back on the power of nuclear weapons to obliterate the enemy. Those who argue for withdrawal from an impossible situation are accused of cowardice and infidelity to our fallen heroes. A substantial segment of the officer corps of the military—mostly out of harm's way—becomes furious, though its members were the ones who provided the advice on which the war was based.

It would seem, sadly, that we have learned nothing since the Inchon landing. A successful imperialist power (which the United States is not, cannot and should not ever be) has to be able to override a public turn against the conflict. Nor does the myth of American power, which is indeed great but not invincible, especially against peasant guerrillas, cause the leadership—military and political—to consider carefully all the risks of charging off to an easy victory against weaker opponents. One would hope that, this time, the three-strikes-and-you're-out theory would supersede the moribund Powell Doctrine (attack with maximum strength).

Indeed those, like Messrs. Bush and Cheney and Rumsfeld, who ignore the lessons of history are doomed to repeat its mistakes.

A war will probably not end when the party whose war it is loses a congressional election. That is not likely to happen in November anyway because the fear/patriotism/betrayal campaign will keep Republicans in control of Congress.

September 22, 2006

Exploitation of 9/11 was shameful

The remembrance of the World Trade Center last week was an unbearably ugly event, a national disgrace, another blot on the integrity of the country. Under the deft direction of the administration and the supine cooperation of television, it was turned into an event for the Republican congressional campaign, whether the individual candidates wanted such help or not. The imagery was designed to stir up anger and the desire for revenge. What ought to have been a national liturgy of reconciliation and rededication became an exercise in opening old wounds and pouring salt on them. In its wake, those who disagree with the president—even senators of his own party—become allies of the terrorists.

Do he and his advisers have no shame at all?

Most obnoxious was the exploitation of the grief of the survivors. Anniversaries are always difficult for the bereaved. They should be permitted to suffer in privacy supported by their faith and their families. Long ago, however, those behind the TV cameras lost all taste and sensibility. Grief, like sex, is no longer a private matter. The pain must be emblazoned across the television screen so a voyeuristic public can revel in it. Have TV journalists no shame at all?

In the wake of the attack we were told that everything had changed, that America would never be the same again, that the threat of death and destruction would forever hang over us. We must smoke out the terrorists and get rid of them, but they would always be out there waiting for us. We must get even with them, but we must always be afraid of them. The response to this doomsday rhetoric was a mixture of sadness, fear and a deep need for revenge. The administration, not able to find Osama bin Laden, now plans to drag some of his henchman—tortured and illegally imprisoned—before kangaroo military courts to prove how tough on terrorists it really is before the election.

Do the marketers of such propaganda have no shame at all?

The memorialization of death and destruction also contributes to the ambient self-pity and self-righteousness that often paralyze the nation. New York City, where there has been for a long time a plenitude of both these vices, now has extra reasons to indulge in them. After five long years of unseemly squabbling, its citizenry has been unable to agree on a replacement for the World Trade Center. Do the battling partisans of different plans in the Big Apple have no shame at all?

The various experts in Washington tell us that the terrorists will be back. Homeland Security Secretary Michael Chertoff and Vice President Cheney warn us often that they are out there waiting and we must not let down our guard. They do not explain why not a single person in this country has died because of terrorist action in the last five years. Having it both ways, they claim that their secrecy has prevented more terrorism and that there still is an overwhelming danger—hence, we must prevent known terrorist sympathizers from entering the country and expel those who are already here. When one asks what triumphs we've had so far because of their vigilance, their routine answer is that they can't answer that question for reasons of national security.

Have Messrs. Cheney and Chertoff and their fellow criers of "wolf" no shame at all?

We have been told often since the attack and we heard it ad nauseam on the anniversary celebration that America will never be the same again. Rarely does anyone examine this sick cliché—which promotes the self-pity—to see that it corresponds to reality. However, the *Wall Street Journal* (in its news section) did reexamine it last week and found that it did not correspond with reality. The American economy has bumbled along and American consumers continue to consume. Only the airline industry suffers, and that in part because of the fiendish harassment of its customers by a government that apparently takes satisfaction in treating every passenger as a potential terrorist. Do the cliché mongers and the passenger harassers have no shame at all?

October 13, 2006

Will Republicans lose control of Congress?

My Democratic friends are counting up the number of seats they're going to win in the election: 16, 20, 35, 50. I hate to disappoint them, but the Republicans will win in the sense that they will not lose. Democratic overconfidence, as American as cherry pie, happens every election year along about now.

The Republicans will win because they are tough and the Democrats are weak. The average American does not care a hoot about the Bill of Rights, privacy or torture. Quite the contrary. Typical Americans are afraid of terrorists. How could they not be with the cliché "war on terrorism" heard constantly in the media and from the president every day?

President Bush has always been tough on terrorism. He's perfectly willing to approve torture (though he doesn't call it that), eavesdrop on phone lines, repeal the Bill of Rights and suspend habeas corpus. While folks don't like the war in Iraq anymore, they half-believe that the president is telling the truth when he says it is the central front in the war on terrorism. The typical voter, cowering with fear, wants to know what habeas corpus means. The Republicans may not in fact be tougher, but they sound tough (tough on illegal immigrants, too—Build a wall!).

Second, the Republicans are smarter. They've spent the last year and a half digging up dirt about potential opponents and have developed slogans against them to which they are unable to respond effectively. Thus, in one district in the Chicago area, the Republican candidate says on every possible occasion that his opponent (a veteran who lost both her legs in Iraq) wants to give $6 billion of Social Security money to illegal aliens. The allegation is absurd but effective. Democrats don't have the gall and the guts to say such things. Therefore, they lose.

Third, the Republicans are richer. They have piles of cash to pour into the closing days of the campaign to fill TV screens with negative ads that a harsh person might call lies. None of these ads will discuss the Iraq war or weapons of mass destruction. But they will emphasize toughness on terrorism, which the Republicans have made the issue of this campaign. They will emphasize the flabby-minded liberalism of their opponents, who are as bad as the terrorists. How do you establish that you're not a flabby-minded liberal? Easy! Become a Republican!

Fourth, the public does not want to hear about the National Intelligence Estimate that the war is producing swarms of new terrorists all over the world. Nor does it want to hear about the delicious tidbits in Robert Woodward's new book. No one cares whether Secretary of State Rice remembers or does not remember meeting with CIA people two months before the World Trade Center attack, a meeting in which she was warned about an imminent attack on the United States.

Fifth, nor do the voters care about Mark Foley's folly. They understand, as the media prophets do not, that the only sex scandals that matter in contemporary politics are Democratic scandals. It may be a shame, but that's the way the rules are written. The Republicans, members of God's party, are all godly men. Accusations against them are the result of Democratic pre-election leaks. Besides, an "overly friendly" or "naughty" e-mail to a teenage page is not a serious matter compared with national security, is it?

Someone tries to point out that the memories of both Rice and House Speaker Hastert seem to be failing: So many events that everyone else remembers, they can't seem to recall. The response is obvious. They're so busy at work protecting the security of the nation that they can't be expected to remember unimportant matters like a warning about a major attack or an e-mail to a stupid page.

The Democrats will snipe at one another after the election, exchanging blame for one more loss. Why didn't they run a vigorous campaign—on such matters as health care, college education, the decline of the middle class? The answer is they did, but no one heard them. The three simple words "war on terrorism" drown out everything else. We knew that six months ago. All else was Democratic wishful thinking.

And young American men and women continue to die in Iraq.

October 20, 2006

How White House undercut Blair

After reading my colleague Roger Ebert's review of "The Queen" (and it is wonderful that he's writing reviews again!), I decided that I must see the film at once. I was not much interested in the royals, empty and useless folk—though the Brits are welcome to them as a symbol if they want. But I was very interested in Tony Blair.

Blair is the most fascinating British prime minister since Winston Churchill, and he does not consume a tumbler of bourbon for breakfast every morning, as Churchill did. Blair brought Labor into the mainstream of English politics, won three overwhelming victories and reshaped much of English political life.

The House of Lords has been shorn of its last vestiges of political power. He devolved home rule, of a sort, to Scotland and Wales. His intense efforts have ended the violence in Northern Ireland, and just this week seemed to have persuaded the Rev. Ian Paisley to enter a political alliance with the Catholic Sinn Fein (keep your fingers crossed!). The previous week Paisley actually visited Sean Brady, the Catholic Primate of All Ireland—an unthinkable event until very recently. (Paisley once shouted "heretic" at the pope!)

The film is the story of how Blair prevented the monarchy from self-destructing by its silent response to the death of Princess Diana. The drama comes from the personal ambivalence he felt about the queen's stubbornness. He was not a fan of the royal family, either as persons or as an institution. Yet he believed, rightly or wrongly, that the royals were still a critical element of English life. So at the beginning of his term of office, he saved the royalty against their wills and against some of his own instincts—though also with considerable respect for the queen's half-century commitment to her duty as she saw it.

Similarly, at the end of his years as prime minister, Blair remained loyal to the Anglo-American alliance, one suspects with considerable doubt about the American leader with whom he was yoked. He had been able to moderate and restrain the queen; President Bush was another matter altogether. He knew that Bush was already unpopular in England and that a war in Iraq would be equally unpopular. Yet the alliance, he felt, was essential to both countries. He gambled and, sadly, he lost the gamble.

Animosity toward Blair increased during this decade in office. The English chattering class (professors and journalists) never much liked him. He was too smooth, too articulate, too adroit, too charming. The rest of the country became rather bored with his wit and his smile.

Many people were looking for an excuse to take him down—nothing fails like success. Blair was tagged with the label "Bush's puppy." He had gambled and lost. Whether Labor can win an election without him is problematic. There is no one else in any party on the English political stage who can compare with him in talent, energy and ideas. As we say across the Irish Sea: We'll not see his like again.

Was the alliance worth saving? Surely it was. However, it will be a long time before a prime minister risks his career by allying himself with an American president. Blair not only lost, he lost big. He watched the institution he believed in so completely disintegrate. He did not realize, I suspect, just how incompetent were the neo-cons and the evangelicals in the Bush administration and how clueless, if well-meaning, Bush was.

Most Americans have begun to realize what a tragic mistake the Iraq war was and how many men and women—Iraqis and Americans—have died needlessly. Against such a background, the destruction of an agile and able foreign ally may not seem to matter much. Yet, if you do in your closest friends, pretty soon you will not have any friends left, only enemies. In years to come, this country will come to regret what Bush did to Blair.

(Ireland, by the way, is such a large country that it needs four primates: two Primates of Ireland [in Dublin] and two Primates of All Ireland [in Armagh Northern Ireland]. The luck of the Irish!)

October 27, 2006

Will voters buy latest twist in Iraq tale?

It would appear that two weeks before the election, President Bush may be revising the course as well as staying it. Perhaps this is the ultimate Karl Rove scam: We will stay the course until victory in Iraq, but we will set up "milestones" that will in effect be a schedule for withdrawal. We will have our cake and eat it too. After all, as Defense Secretary Donald Rumsfeld himself has said, Iraq belongs to the Iraqis; it's up to them to take it over.

The implicit message to voters who are fed up with the nightly scenes of mass murder on television is that the administration has a better way to get out of Iraq than the Democrats—who don't have any milestones—and this better way at the same time will be tough on terror.

Will the voting public buy this double talk? It has accepted all previous spinning of the truth, why not this one, too? How can the Democrats who have demanded a scheduled pullout from Iraq attack the "milestones"?

If it works, it will be the greatest shell game in political history. The only problem with it is, while it might win another election, what will happen when the bloody killing in Iraq continues despite the milestones? Never fear, the administration will find one more scam, even if it proves to be the ultimate repeal of the principle of contradiction.

The chairman of the committee devising the strategy is former Secretary of State James Baker, who managed, with the aid of the ineffable Nino Scalia, to turn defeat into victory in the 2000 presidential election. There are few prestidigitators inside the Beltway who possess his skills.

If it all works out, the killing may continue in Iraq, but at least Americans will have left, flushed with victory no doubt. The president will be able to say that this is what God wanted him to do all along. Mission accomplished!

As Bob Woodward makes clear in his *State of Denial,* there is a bureaucratic logjam that protects the president from the truth of what is happening in Iraq and thus enables him to talk about staying the course until victory. The iron law of oligarchy is that one always tells one's boss what the boss wants to hear instead of what he needs to know. (The law applies in all human organizations, including corporations, churches and universities.)

Many layers of bureaucracy intervene between the men and women who fight and die in the war and the Oval Office—the generals in Iraq, the generals at Central Command, the Joint Chiefs of Staff in the Pentagon (handsome men in tailor-made uniforms and loaded with medals who have seen very little combat and have very little influence), the secretary of defense, the National Security Council at the White House, the secretary of state (one of whose main responsibilities is protecting the president and keeping him happy), and then finally the Oval Office. As the facts go up the ladder, they are transformed unless the man at the top makes Herculean efforts to find out what he needs to know.

Woodward argues that rarely does this president hear from anyone who would disagree with him and almost never does such a person say what he thinks. Woodward depicts the president as often shallow, vulgar, petulant and vindictive—not the kind of boss that even a three-star general might want to take on.

So Baker and the others who want to change Iraq policy have their work cut out for them. At no point dare they say, "We made mistakes." Rather, they will have to argue that the new policy is nothing more than staying the course in a different fashion.

One is reminded of Ronald Reagan's reaction after he withdrew the Marines from Lebanon (where more than 100 had been killed by suicide bombers). He took full responsibility. If anyone were to face court-martial, he said, he should be the one. John Kennedy after the Bay of Pigs fiasco also assumed full responsibility, even though it was a scheme he inherited from the Eisenhower administration. Those were the days, however, when the buck stopped in the Oval Office.

November 3, 2006

U.S. is casualty in Bush's vanity war

Why did the United States invade Iraq? The administration, still claiming to be "tough on terrorism," dances around in its search for a credibility-saving way out. Bloody bodies and great clouds of smoke appear every night on television. American casualties increase. President Bush no longer uses the words "staying the course." He still seems to insist that the Iraq war is the central front in the war on global terror. The issue on this election eve ought to be: Why did we invade Iraq in the first place?

We no longer hear that Iraq had weapons of mass destruction aimed at us. Or, as Secretary of State Condoleezza Rice put it, that the invasion was the "right thing to do." Or that the American goal is to make Iraq safe for democracy. Or that we must fight to the end to preserve the honor of those who have died.

What, then, was the reason for the war, other than that the rage and fear of the American people after the World Trade Center attack made it easy for the administration to sell the war?

George Packer, in his book *The Assassin's Gate*, observes that "it is impossible to be sure" why the country went to war in Iraq and quotes Richard Haass, an aide to the president, as thinking that he would go to his grave "not knowing the answer." Frank Rich in *The Greatest Story Ever Sold* suspects that Karl Rove's desire to build a permanent Republican majority was a major factor.

My hunch is that the answer can be found in the president's words when he was told about the attack: "This is war!" In point of fact, it was not. It was a vicious assault by a gang of international criminals, not a war in any sense that the word has traditionally meant. The president's spontaneous eagerness to find a war where there was only a terrible crime marked the genesis of such phrases as "war on terrorism," "war on global terror" and "war on Islamo-fascism."

They were catchy phrases and crept easily into the national vocabulary. They made Bush a national hero that some in the media could compare to Abraham Lincoln. They made him a "wartime" president who could fly out to an aircraft carrier (within sight of the California coast) and proclaim "mission accomplished."

Unfortunately, after the quick cleanup of Afghanistan (as we thought then), there was no war around. Bush needed a war—another quick, easy victory that would eliminate any discussion of the possibly stolen 2000 election. Whatever the motives of the other chicken hawks, like the neocons who wanted to go to "Jerusalem through Baghdad," ultimately the reason for the invasion of Iraq was that the president at some level in his personality wanted a war, needed a war. He also wanted and needed an enemy, and Saddam Hussein was the ideal enemy.

Alas for everyone, Bush and his advisers, most notably Vice President Dick Cheney and Secretary of Defense Donald Rumsfeld, miscalculated the reaction of the Iraqis to the invasion. They especially misunderstood the propensity in that deeply troubled society for Muslims to delight in killing other Muslims as well as young Americans.

I do not question the president's sincerity. He undoubtedly persuaded himself that the war was what God wanted him to do. Yet, we can now understand that the war is kind of a vanity war; the president wanted to prove he was a good wartime president. He isn't. The vice president wanted to prove that he was the toughest man inside the Beltway. He isn't, save possibly when he has a shotgun in his hands. The neo-cons wanted to reshape the Middle East and take pressure off Israel. They didn't. The national security adviser (and now secretary of state) wanted to prove she was an astute diplomat. She isn't.

The war has become the main issue in the election. Americans will vote on Tuesday on whether they support the war or oppose it. Have they come to realize that it is a vanity war, or do they still want revenge on terrorists and are they still afraid?

November 10, 2006

Iraq disaster finally caught up with Bush

Even the "born-agains" may have been part of the Democratic revolution last Tuesday. In its final pre-election poll, the *New York Times*, with its usual religious tin ear, presented but did not comment on a graph that showed this Republican "base" was evenly split between Democrats and Republicans in its voting plans. While exit poll data is necessary to confirm this finding, it was a strong hint that the house of cards Karl Rove had created was falling apart.

In our book on conservative Christians, Professor Michael Hout from Berkeley and I questioned whether the "evangelicals" were a strong component of Rove's coalition. We had calculated that they added at the most 1 or 2 percentage points to the "base" provided by the white Protestant population. The influence of their religious leadership on Republican politics was based on what former House Speaker "Tip" O'Neill called "shadows and mirrors."

Another component of Rove's alleged magic was "patriotism" and fear of the terrorists. President Bush claimed during his madcap campaign that the Democrats were in fact on the side of the terrorists, creating much enthusiasm among the partisan crowds to which he spoke. As Abraham Lincoln may have said, you can fool all of the people some of the time and some of the people all of the time, but you can't fool all of the people all of the time. Enough of the people were fed up with the Iraq war that Rove's black magic did not work as it used to. It took a long time for the electorate to move beyond the fear and anger of the World Trade Center attack, but move it finally did.

The Republican leadership continued with all the old dirty tricks—vicious negative ads, harassing phone calls, targeting candidates who seemed particularly vulnerable, hassling voters, especially if they were black, identifying themselves with "our brave troops," wrapping themselves in the American flag. They took particular pleasure in going after war hero Tammy Duckworth in the 6th District just as they had destroyed amputee Sen. Max Cleland in the 2002 Georgia election. Cleland was not a patriot because he opposed the Homeland Security Department. Duckworth planned to take Social Security money from elderly white Americans and give it to Mexican illegals. Such lies call to heaven for vengeance. But the administration has told so many lies in the past six years that lies are not enough to win an election anymore.

Sixty years ago the Republicans got even with Franklin Roosevelt by forbidding third terms to a president through the 22nd Amendment. A president elected to a second term is a "lame duck" on Inauguration Day because he has lost the power of running again. Oddly, four Republican presidents became lame ducks—Eisenhower, Nixon, Reagan, and now George W. Bush. Nixon was forced to resign. Eisenhower and Reagan were the victims of the 22nd Amendment, forbidden a third term by Republican animus toward Roosevelt.

Bush, then, is a lame duck. After this week's election he has become a very lame duck—indeed, a dead duck. He chose to make the election a referendum on the Iraq war and on himself. He lost. Overwhelmingly. He has spent all the capital that he claimed from his 2004 victory.

Commentators already are telling the Democrats that they must compromise to get along with the president. Bush is making nice noises about working together—which means in his version of English that they must do what he says. The war in Iraq must go on till victory, no matter how long it takes and how many Iraqis and Americans die.

The new Democratic Congress must resist the temptation to be "responsible" on Iraq. It was not elected to be responsible. It was elected to end this stupid and immoral war. James Baker, who in Florida in 2000 showed how skilled he is in turning defeat into victory, may well provide a face-saving way out for the president, but even that will not hide the truth that his legacy will be the memory of a scarred battleground presidency, devastated by vicious partisan politics and a deadly blend of ignorance, arrogance and incompetence.

Latest disastrous plan: More GIs to Iraq

Many of the wise people in this country who supported the Iraq war at the beginning now contend that the answer to the problem is to send more troops to Iraq. Sen. John McCain says that 20,000 more should be enough. Some of the military "experts" on television are hinting that 100,000 more will do the job. Rumors are being leaked from the Iraq Study Group established to shape "new strategy" that it will recommend more troops, too. The *New York Times* editorial page recommends more troops temporarily in Baghdad.

One begins to wonder who won the election and whether McCain plans to seek the presidency two years hence with the blood of more American men and women, to say nothing of Iraqi women and children, on his hands. One has to ask all these wise people how they know that more troops will prevent Iraqis from killing one another or merely provide more targets for snipers and roadside bombers.

What serious neutral expert could possibly predict that more troops will solve the problem? Does not all the literature on guerrilla war suggest that traditional military force, no matter how large, cannot cope with dedicated shadow warriors? There were a half-million Americans in Vietnam and they could not end the war. Gen. Earle "Bus" Wheeler asked for 200,000 more troops without any guarantee that they could find the light at the end of the tunnel. Lyndon Johnson finally said "no" and in effect resigned from the presidency.

Is McCain prepared to stake his reputation for "experience" in matters military on the promise that 20,000 more American targets would win the war? Is the new secretary of defense (a member of the Iraq Study Group) willing to risk becoming a new scapegoat for more failure and more death in Iraq?

What reason is there to think that there is more that the United States government can do to "win" the Iraq war? Or to retreat from it with its dignity not in tatters? Or to provide some cover for the president's soiled legacy?

The only strategy that makes sense is that of Ronald Reagan when suicide bombers blew up a Marine barracks in Lebanon. He promptly removed the Marines and took full responsibility for the disaster. That's what brave and honorable men do when they have produced a fiasco. They don't worry about American credibility or honor. They don't talk about sending in more troops. They "cut and run," taking full responsibility for their mistakes. They don't ask more Americans to risk senseless deaths so that their leaders can try one last foolish attempt to save face.

The war is lost. It was lost before it began. The majority of the American electorate knows that. I daresay the majority of the Iraq Study Group also knows that. Some of its members probably know that the only way George W. Bush can emerge with any honor from a terrible blunder that is finally his responsibility is to imitate Reagan (and John Kennedy after the Bay of Pigs or Lyndon Johnson after the Tet Offensive).

There was a sign on the Oval Office desk of Harry Truman when he was president that said, "The buck stops here." It hasn't stopped there for the last six years. Is there any chance that President Bush will abandon his conviction that he is God's agent and make a brave and honorable decision to withdraw from the Big Muddy into which he has led this nation? On the basis of his words after the election, there seems very little likelihood of that.

Might the Iraq Study Group, stuffed as it is by Bush family retainers, have the courage to recommend such a decision? How can it?

Only the president can salvage his own honor. Only he can save some of his legacy. Only he can free the Republican Party from the taint of Iraq. Those of us who have opposed the war from the beginning because it clearly could not be won (and for other reasons, too) ought to pray that God can touch his hardened heart.

November 24, 2006

What is the point of American deaths?

My mother used to tell me when I was very young a story about the last American to die on Nov. 11, 1918, at 10:59 in the morning. It was an urban folk tale of that era, doubtless, though indeed there was an American who was the last victim of the war. His death was pointless, that was the sentimental irony of the story. But so was the death of everyone else who died in that absurd, insane mass murder. The "Great Powers" of Europe stumbled into the war because of a toxic mix of arrogance and ignorance and couldn't find a way out of it. Nothing was settled, the war went into a recess to be renewed 20 years later with even more demonic fury.

I found myself pondering as I watched the heartbreaking Veterans Day ceremonies on television, what the government will tell the family—parents, spouse, children—of the last American to die in Iraq. Or the families of all the men and women who have died there. What was the point in their deaths? They fought bravely for their country. They did their duty. They will be missed. Their courage is an honor to their sacrifice. That should be enough and that's all there is.

They died defending American freedom? But American freedom was never at issue. They died to protect the country from weapons of mass destruction, to create a democracy in the midst of the Arab world, to win a victory that would enhance American credibility, to keep faith with those who had already died, to get rid of Saddam Hussein, because the president said it was the right thing to do, because Iraq was the central front in the war or terror?

Or should the families be told the real truth? Their young people died because of the arrogance and the ignorance of the American government, because of mistakes and blunders, because some of our leaders thought the war was a good thing, because it would take pressure off of Israel, because of Arab oil.

What can we say to the additional survivors between now and the day the last American dies there, all those lives erased in a lost war our leaders could not end? Should we tell them what Henry Kissinger said of Vietnam casualties after President Nixon took office—they died in the name of American credibility?

Every time I hear on the radio of new casualties or see bereaved families on television, or open newspapers with massed photos of those who have died, I want to scream "all these losses, all this suffering, all these shattered families were unnecessary." I sense from a great distance the pain and the grief.

President Bush and Vice President Dick Cheney killed them.

Most Americans agree that the war was mistaken in its inception and mismanaged in its execution. If some of that majority do not also feel the grief and the pain and the rage, the only reason is that they have hardened their hearts in the name of patriotism or party loyalty or the words of the Bible. God have mercy on those with hard hearts.

The issue now is whether the new coalition of leaders can find the quickest, safest way out. We must hope and pray that it can, that the hubris that led the country into the war will not prevent us from getting out.

Will God punish the United States for all the deaths, both Iraqi and American? I don't believe that God works that way. However, our intervention in that chaotic, broken country will certainly have created hundreds, perhaps thousands of would-be martyrs who will seek vengeance. We will have brought it on ourselves.

God forgive us for the war, especially those who voted for it in 2004, and especially the pundits, the commentators, the editorial writers who supported the war until almost the last moment and are still willing to accept more casualties so this country and its president can escape with some dignity.

It's a shame there will be no war-crimes trials.

December 1, 2006

Moral health tip to America: Stay out of draft

Rep. Charles Rangel (D-N.Y.) celebrated the Democratic election victory by proposing to renew the military draft. His oft-repeated argument is that the draft would produce an army with social and racial equity. White, college-educated young men and women would have to serve as target practice for Shiites, Sunnis and other murderous tribes in Iraq when they take time out from killing one another.

Others jumped on the bandwagon. If President Bush had college men and women wading into the Big Muddy, young people would have rioted, wealthy parents would have complained, the war would have stopped.

Just like the Vietnam War stopped in 1968, right?

The war will stop because people voted against it and against the president. (Eighty percent would vote against him if he could run again.)

Rangel's argument is patently sick. It assumes that Bush would be cowed by riots in the street. Moreover, there is no successful appeal from the ballot to the bullet in this country, from elections to street demonstrations (except maybe in Florida, where ballots don't count anymore). To create social unrest through a draft is to shortcut the electoral process.

Moreover, if there had not been a draft to provide unlimited young bodies for the jungles of Vietnam, that war would never have started—nor, for that matter, would the Korean War. As the world should have learned in 1914 and 1939, the availability of conscript armies is an open invitation to leaders to make war. If Bush could have mustered conscript armies of men and women, he might have taken on Iran and Korea, too—whatever was required for victory.

The suggestion of "National Service" brought a lot of authoritarian liberals out of the woodwork. All young Americans, they argued, should be obliged to do two years of service either in the military or in some other form of indentured servitude to the government. They owe the duty of such service to their country.

To which the only valid reply is, "Who says?" Isn't this the United States of America, not ancient Sparta? The government has no claim on the time and life of anyone, except the people who volunteer for military service (often, alas, because they have not many other choices in life) and convicted criminals. Conscription is just barely tolerable in times of great national emergency, if then. The government doesn't own Americans simply because they are young. The late economist Milton Friedman argued that the draft was an inequitable tax levied against the young and in favor of the middle-aged and the old.

The editorial writers of the *New York Times*, who have often had a soft spot in their hearts for national service, lament that Rangel's proposal will fail. Like most authoritarian liberals, they think it right and proper and orderly that young men and women be pushed into adulthood by government pressure to do good. It will teach young people, they imply, maturity and responsibility and self-control (and get them away from video games and beer bashes!).

In fact, volunteer-service rates among young Americans are the highest in the world. The generosity and the merit of volunteering are diminished if it becomes compulsory and is destroyed altogether when the young people are forced to work for an inept and incompetent government.

Moreover, volunteering as a requirement for graduation is a perversion. Humans grow in virtue not by being forced to repeat virtuous actions but by freely choosing such actions.

Veterans of military service usually weigh in on this issue by announcing that the military "made a man out of me." What kind of man, I wonder, has to brag that military brutality was essential to his manhood? Will it make a woman out of his daughter?

One should ask Rangel, if the draft created such racial and social equity in the 1960s, how the president and vice president managed to avoid combat. How could such draft dodgers be elected to high office? And don't tell me that the president served in the Texas Air National Guard. That's like serving in the Nebraska Navy.

December 15, 2006

Bush doesn't seem capable of admitting his serious errors

The long-awaited report of the Iraq Study Group was dead on arrival. It was designed as a proposal by a bipartisan commission of wise men that would provide President Bush with a way out of the Big Muddy into which he had led the country. There was no particular reason to think that any of the major recommendations would in fact change the situation in Iraq.

Certainly, the Shiites and the Sunnis must reconcile, but they've been fighting each other for 12 centuries. Attempts to force the Iraq government to end the conflict are doomed from the beginning. Patently, the conflict in Palestine must end for the Middle East to settle down. However, hard-liners on both sides don't want to pay the price of peace, as the failure of President Bill Clinton's Camp David negotiations confirmed.

Clearly, there cannot be peace in Iraq without some kind of cooperation between Iran and Syria. But there is little reason to think that either country wants to take the United States off the hook—and it is unlikely that the president would negotiate with those countries even if Secretary of State Condoleezza Rice would permit him. James Baker and Lee Hamilton were quite clear that there was no guarantee that any of these efforts would work or even be accepted by the president.

However, they would provide the administration with something to do for the next year before the president begins to "draw down" American troops in the first quarter of 2008, just before the presidential campaign begins in earnest.

The president and the residual hawks in his administration could say, "Look, we tried to do everything they suggested and it's just not working." Presumably Baker, who helped the president steal the election in 2000, thought that his protégé was flexible enough to take that route out of the Big Muddy.

It seemed obvious from the beginning that the president was not about to buy in to such a scenario. He is still the commander in chief, his spokesman told us. He was still the "decider." The ISG members were repeating, in muted language, the criticism of the "liberals," who are cowards who want to cut and run. His scary behavior at the press conference with Tony Blair, in which he verbally assaulted a British journalist, left no doubt that he was not backing off from his previous views. Jabbing his fingers, shouting, swaggering, smirking, he was fighting off all his enemies. When he feels he is under attack, the president digs in and strikes back.

It is late in the day to wonder if the president has the character required of a man who must play his role. Strength for him means single-minded stubbornness and very little else. He does not seem capable of admitting that he has made serious mistakes—which presidents such as Kennedy, Johnson, Reagan and Clinton were able to do. He is innocent of his father's suave flexibility, to say nothing of the evasiveness of FDR, for whom there was no hole deep enough that he could not slip out. Even if the country and his party and his legacy are deep in the Big Muddy, there is nothing in his personality that permits this president to lead the way out until the mission is accomplished. He will certainly not change his goals merely because the Democrats won a mid-term election.

The "new strategy" that he is going to unveil as a Christmas gift to the nation will likely be a spin on the old strategy. He will tell us that he has read all the recommendations and this is what he has decided. This spin might well hearten some of his faithful followers and win him a few points in the polls for a while, but it will not stop the killing in Iraq.

It will be interesting—and horrible—to keep track of how many Americans die in Iraq during 2008.

New York Times columnist Thomas Friedman, who strongly supported the war in 2003, now says that it will take either 10 minutes or 10 years to end the Iraq incursion. One must end it by ending it. Despite the caution and the hopes of the ISG, it will require a different president to grasp that overwhelming truth.

January 5, 2007

Saddam execution is stain on America

Americans cheered enthusiastically last week for President Ford, who pardoned Richard Nixon. Simultaneously they celebrated the fact that President Bush did not insist on pardoning Saddam Hussein—in fact didn't even think of it. Those who wanted Nixon behind bars only wanted revenge. Those who wanted to see Saddam attached to a rope just before he died were not seeking revenge.

Go figure.

He was once our man in the Mideast, the Republican Party's man. Indeed, American Republican intelligence services provided support for his killing of Kurds and Shiites before the first Gulf War. Should those American leaders who supported such efforts be put on trial and hanged?

The present incumbent of the White House often spoke of his personal anger at the Iraqi president. Well, now he has had his revenge, not that it does him much good.

Those who take the Christian scripture seriously must believe the words of God in the epistle to the Romans, "Revenge is mine, says the Lord, I shall repay!" God claims a monopoly on revenge, but the need for it is a powerful human passion. Many of the relatives of victims at the time of American executions tell us that the death of the hated person brings closure. In fact, it is only a hollow closure that cannot endure. Many countries reject the death penalty as unworthy of humans. They are right, and the United States is wrong.

The papacy has been leading Catholics in that direction during recent decades. Thus the pope's "foreign minister," Cardinal Martino and his official spokesman, Federico Lombardi, spoke out against the execution of Saddam, the former saying that it was a crime following another crime and the state has no right to kill a human being. It's interesting that so many devout "papal Catholics" feel free to dismiss this teaching. It is also interesting that so many evangelical Protestants also feel free to ignore it—including our president.

Does that mean mass murderers should go unpunished? Should Saddam have been freed to kill more thousands? Certainly not, no more than Nixon should have gone unpunished for his crimes against the Constitution. Nixon should have gone to prison; Saddam should have spent the rest of his life in an American jail—to protect the world from him.

It was the Iraqi government that hanged him, it may be argued. He was captured by American troops, kept in an American prison and led to the gallows by American guards. The Iraqi government is still a pathetic creature of American military might. Perhaps many Iraqis were glad to see him dead. Yet those who were not can claim with good reason that the Americans killed him. It would be foolish and presumptuous to assume that Arabs will not try to kill an American president. Revenge and more revenge and yet more revenge.

The English, who have had a long history of hanging those who caused trouble in their colonies (including Ireland), are properly horrified at the barbarism of American executions. They have come to understand what Cardinal Martino said about the state taking human life. Why do Americans not perceive the same truth? Are we still barbarians? Or does the troubled history of killing African Americans and Native Americans and hanging horse thieves and cattle rustlers in the Old West still make us a bloody-minded people? Why did so many of us rejoice in the killing of Saddam? Why were so few evangelical voices in this country raised against it—with the notable exception of the voice of Rev. Jesse Jackson?

Should not the Nazi and Japanese leaders have been executed after World War II? If we believe revenge is justified and that it is not a monopoly of the Lord's, we would say yes. Would the rest of his life in prison for Hitler, should he have been captured, not been a better punishment? From the perspective of the present, only the most bloody minded would say no.

Our president has the "regime change" that was the rationale for the war. Now he proposes to send tens of thousands more American troops to continue it. How many more on both sides will have to die for no other reason than his need for victory?

January 12, 2007

Unjust Iraq war raises painful question: Why?

TUCSON—I become angry every time I see a spread in a local newspaper of the recent military casualties. They are mostly young, their lives still ahead of them, victims of a stupid, unjust, criminal war. Many more have been maimed for life. I think of the suffering families, parents, spouses, children whose lives will be forever blighted by the pain of the death of someone they love.

I ask myself why, and the answer is always a new cliché: to protect America from weapons of mass destruction, to punish al-Qaida, to change the balance of power in the Middle East, to defend democracy in Iraq, to protect the honor of those who have already died, to achieve victory.

I thought of these ever-changing justifications and became angry again as I flew out here. There were a dozen or so young people on the plane—all in their from-another-planet fatigues. They were bound for Fort Huachuca, where they would learn the skills of military intelligence and then return to their airborne division and thence to Iraq. They would be part of the "surge" President Bush is planning to win the war in Iraq. They would be targets for roadside bombs, for snipers, for suicide bombers, for kidnappers who would behead them. Most of them were young—in their teens or just barely beyond. They were quiet, polite, innocent. Some of them would die, others would be maimed.

Again I asked why. The answer is that after the election and the report of the Iraq Study Group, our swaggering, smirking president had the choice of withdrawal or escalation. Since he is an almost pathologically stubborn man, he chose escalation. He chose to listen not to the wise men of the Iraqi Study Group, but to the last remnant of the neo-cons, William Kristol, and the always-con, Henry Kissinger. The president is the commander in chief, the "Decider," the leader who does not make mistakes. If he sticks to his principles, is true to the will of God whom he encounters in his prayers, and stays the course, then he will achieve victory. He may face intense criticism, but like Harry Truman and Gerald Ford, history will vindicate him.

And young men and women will die.

The long period of alleged reflection is the same game the president played before he announced that he had decided that there was no choice but to invade Iraq. We now know that the time for decision-making was window dressing. He had decided on the invasion months before.

The military and civil leaders on the ground did not endorse the "surge" enthusiastically enough, so they were replaced by those who would hitch their kites to the president's comet. You agree with the Decider or you are recalled. And you had better be loyal, as Gen. Colin Powell was, or you will not be a good soldier.

How many troops will eventually "surge"? The answer seems to be more than 20,000. (Powell, finally showing some courage, has said that all the American military would not be enough.) How long will the "surge" last? Anywhere, one hears, from one to three years. Will it really work?

Will the Sunnis and the Shiites really stop killing each other? The lesson from previous "surges" seems to be that as long as the American military occupies a neighborhood in force, the killing slows down. When it withdraws, the "bad guys" return.

How long will young Americans, untrained for the work, have to play cops and robbers in Baghdad to "pacify" the city? How many centuries have these two tribal religious factions been fighting one another? Whenever the Americans leave, presumably in the next administration, they will begin their internecine murders once again.

Through the whole Iraq fiasco, the United States has messed up—from "shock and awe" through the failure to stop the looting ("stuff happens," as then Defense Secretary Donald Rumsfeld called it), the elimination of the Iraqi Army, the various pitched battles, the poor body armor and unprotected Humvees to the bungled execution of Saddam Hussein. Can the American military finally do something right? The wise person—or even the person with a memory—will remain skeptical.

January 19, 2007

Bush is a picture of defeat

The presidential address last week was pathetic enough to make one feel sad for the poor dear man, as they say in the old country. With little emotional affect he read a lecture about his "new strategy," which was in fact nothing more than a new tactic, growled at Iran and Syria, threatened the Iraqi government, and promised that the United States would emerge the winner in Iraq.

The notion that 20,000 more American troops would pacify Baghdad was farcical. If one really intended to stop internecine war between two religious tribes, one would have had to promise a lot more Americans. John Keegan, the famous English military historian and commentator, estimated that pacification would take 50,000 troops. Various American military experts suggested that it would require at least 100,000 soldiers and Marines. If one calculates two American soldiers or Marines for every 1,000 people in a city, as does the Army's counter-insurgency manual, 140,000 fighting men (which excludes the half of the troops in Iraq who are not combat soldiers) would be required.

The mountain labored and gave birth to a mouse.

Some of President Bush's allies in government and the media (David Brooks in the *New York Times*, for example) contend the "new strategy" must be tried, if only because there's nothing else to do. Republican senators insist the Democrats in Congress must suggest an alternative strategy if they expect to be taken seriously. How are we going to solve the "Iraq Problem" unless we have a strategy?

There are two answers to such idiocy: (1) There isn't an alternative strategy or any strategy that will clean up the Iraq mess, and (2) the Democrats do have a strategy: phased withdrawal, beginning now.

In fact, no one knows what will happen when American troops leave or what Iran or the Arab countries would do. One does know that the Arabs and the Persians don't particularly like one another and that the Sunnis want to run Iraq again and have little interest in reestablishing a Caliphate presided over by Osama bin Laden.

In any event, the Middle East is always unstable. The Iranian president is unpopular with his people because he has not been able to transform the economic chaos in his country. The various Islamic factions are not likely to try to induce stability in their part of the world as long as a U.S. army is occupying one of their countries.

The president's apocalyptic descriptions of Iraq after "we" leave are transcriptions of neo-conservative memos. The neo-cons are high-level thinkers and brilliant memo writers. They provided the ideas that the president and his aides (none of them high-level thinkers) needed to justify the war. Although many of them are distinguished graduates of the University of Chicago and similar institutions, they seem to know very little history. None of them anticipated what a cursory reading of Winston Churchill's book on Iraq would have predicted: the present civil war.

The most pathetic part of the president's talk was the peroration, a listless reprise of all the neo-con clichés from the last six years: war on terrorism, enemies who want to destroy our way of life because they fear our freedom, global cultural confrontation, the crucial battle of our time. For motivation to support his "new strategy," the president had to fall back on the conventional wisdom of talk-radio hosts, conservative editorial writers and the gurus of the Fox network.

No one ever offers hard proof that these horrors would occur. The battling Shiites and Sunnis are interested in killing each other in a struggle for power for themselves in Iraq. They may hate Americans, but they hate each other more. The only ones who can destroy American freedom are government officials who claim the right to read our mail, listen to our phone calls, bug our e-mail, and deny some of us the right to have lawyers to defend us. They are the real enemy.

For all the bravado of his words, the president did not seem to have his heart in the speech. He tried to sound tough but really seemed like someone who knew deep down that he was a beaten man.

February 9, 2007

U.S. needs the strength to be patient

We are told that it is a time for Americans to demonstrate courage, strength, power. We must not accept defeat in Iraq and the "dire" (favorite new word) consequences of failure—such as region-wide chaos in the Middle East. It is not clear who these "we" are. Not the senators or columnists or editorial writers who are calling on us for sacrifice. They are not in combat themselves, they do not have children in combat. By what right do they lecture those who do and those who now perceive that it was the wrong war, carried out in the wrong way?

President Bush and his swagger, either in his walk or in the "Bush Doctrine," emphasize America's power. We can do what we want because we have the power to do so and God is on our side. The United States should not negotiate with Iran or Syria as long as it remains powerful and its people steadfast and courageous. It dialogues with other countries only in the modality that Cardinal Egan of New York described to his priests as dialogue Roman style—"I talk, you listen." In fact, it seems unlikely that the president or the vice president or the attorney general is morally capable of dialogue. Once the arrogance of power is abandoned, they would become mute.

I suggest that what the United States needs is not power or strength, but ingenuity and honesty.

"Frontline" last week did a program about the Berlin airlift, one of the great diplomatic triumphs of the Cold War. Since no one pays any attention to history, it means as much to leaders today as the battle of Lookout Mountain. In 1948 Stalin imposed a blockade on Berlin, hoping to force the Allies out of the city and to integrate it into the socialist empire. It was suggested to President Truman that we send a convoy of tanks through the blockade and force open the road to Berlin. Truman, unlike the current White House crowd, had been in a war. He realized that the Russians might back down (as they often did in subsequent crises), but that they might not and that something could go wrong, which would launch another war. He decided that the United States would supply the 2 million people of Berlin and the 20,000 Allied troops by air. No one, not least Stalin, thought it would work. However, American ingenuity and organizing skill made it work. After two years Stalin backed down—the first defeat he had suffered since Stalingrad.

The current crowd, spoiling for a war with Iran while bogged down in the Big Muddy of Iraq, would have sent that tank column right down the road and God only knows what would have happened. It would have bombed the Russian missile sites in Cuba in 1963. It would have refused to negotiate with the Russians. It would never have gone to China, as President Nixon did. It would still be fighting in Korea or Vietnam. It would not have broken the chill with Khrushchev. It would not have negotiated with Gorbachev, as did Reagan.

The history of the United States in the last half century shows that the country loses nothing when it minimizes risks, is open to negotiations, and exits impossible situations with grace. In those times the leaders of the country urged patience but never strength. They feared the dangers of war. They never equated power with moral right. They never lied to their people. They made mistakes, but because they were more or less sane and not unintelligent, they were never reckless.

The revelations of the I. Lewis Libby trial reveal a very different environment. The office of the vice president emerges as something like a cross between a story by Franz Kafka and one by Lewis Carroll. The vice president and Libby, respectively, play the Mad Hatter and the March Hare in their efforts to cover up a cover-up.

The president and the vice president and the secretary of state, having learned no lessons from one war, seem ready to risk another. They urge courage and strength and power but are innocent of such traditional American instincts as realism, pragmatism, restraint and ingenuity, to say nothing of honesty.

February 16, 2007

Be cautious about impeaching Bush

Impeach the president? Impeach President Bush? We learned from the attempt to oust President Bill Clinton that there are few rules for indicting and convicting a president.

A high crime and misdemeanor can be anything that a majority of the House of Representatives says is a high crime or a misdemeanor, and proof of guilt is anything that two-thirds of the Senate says is proof. Thus, a man can be indicted (impeached) for an alleged perjury in a civil trial over private sexual behavior (usually meriting only a civil punishment), and he could be deposed if two-thirds of the Senate accepted the evidence. There is no appeal, no higher court that can declare that such perjury, while lamentable, is not a high crime. To get rid of a president, all you need to do is to have enough votes.

The only president ever forced out by an impeachment proceeding was Richard Nixon, and he was never indicted or convicted, but quit (wisely) before votes could be taken. For there to be a successful impeachment, the Congress and the public have to conclude that there is no other choice. There was no such consensus in 1998. Three-fifths of the American public approved of the way Clinton was doing his job, and everyone knew there were not enough votes in the Senate. The House voted for impeachment because, as Newt Gingrich said, "We can do it." It was an empty, partisan and vindictive choice. The national media hyped it into a big deal when it was only a shabby political trick.

What, then, about increasingly frequent cries for impeachment proceedings against Bush? There are certainly enough votes in the House to indict him, just as the Gingrich House indicted Clinton, but hardly enough in the Senate to convict him.

What would the charges be? Launching a war based on lying to the people, incompetent and corrupt administration of the occupation after the war, deceiving the people about conditions in Iraq and refusal to begin removing the troops when the public had made it clear that it wanted an end—all substantially more serious than perjury in a civil trial. Not valid reasons for removing a president? If a majority of the House should say that they are valid reasons, then they become valid reasons. What better cause for dumping a president than monumental and stubborn incompetence that has caused tens of thousands of deaths?

Neither the country nor the Congress is ready for such a battle now—though three-fifths of Americans wish his term were over. When U.S. Rep. Bob Drinan of Massachusetts, a Jesuit priest, introduced a motion to impeach Nixon in 1973, it was quickly shunted off the agenda. Yet, a year later it was voted out of committee, and Nixon left the White House. The public and Congress had all they could take of the man. Should Iraq keep deteriorating until the end of the summer, impeachment might make more sense than cutting funds for the war, although both the president and the vice president would have to be convicted of high crimes at the same time.

I am not advocating the deposing of the president by congressional vote. Nor would I, unless the country was ready for it and enough of those senatorial Republicans up for re-election were eager for such a vote lest their future be tied to the fate of that swaggering, stupid man.

The firing of a president is a traumatic event. It would cause a deep wound in the body politic. It took a couple of decades to recover from the shock of deposing Nixon, though after the trivialization of the process by Gingrich it might be less shocking. It may be necessary to strike back at the pernicious claims of extra-constitutional presidential power by the administration. It is not true, as Garry Wills has reminded us, that the title "commander in chief" magnifies the constitutional power of the president. Indeed, his title of commander in chief of the Army and the Navy is limited by the constitutional powers of the president. He is not the commander in chief of all of us, and perhaps that needs to be made clear. Yet, deposing a president is a savage and blunt instrument to be used only when absolutely necessary and at the risk of poisoning the political atmosphere for decades.

February 23, 2007

U.S. keeps making mistakes in Mideast

The collapse of the shah in Iran was the beginning of American troubles in the Middle East. The shah was "our guy," an absolute ruler who was secularizing the country and freeing his people from the shackles of religious superstition and obscurantism. It never occurred to our foreign-policy thinkers and experts that the people of Iran wanted their obscurantism and old-fashioned religion. The American leadership did not see the ayatollah coming and was unprepared for the defeat of the shah. Educated as they were in the great secular universities, our foreign policy gurus did not have a clue about the importance of religion in Middle Eastern countries.

The same gurus or their successors have made the same mistake again. They expected the Iraqis to welcome our appearance on the horizon, like the 7th Cavalry riding to the rescue in the old Western movies. They expected the various factions in Iraq to band together in the formation of a stable democracy that would be a beacon of hope to the Middle East. As

Paul Wolfowitz, the leader of the neo-cons, remarked, too much was made of the difference between Sunnis and Shiites.

A few other scholars ominously predicted a civil war between these two largest religious factions. The Shiites were the majority but had been ruled for centuries by the minority Sunnis. Indeed, the avowed followers of Ali (the Prophet's son-in-law) and his grandson never ruled in any Arab country till the arrival of the Americans in 2003, when our leaders in the name of democracy in effect turned the country over to the Shiite majority. The Sunnis, followers of Saddam Hussein, who had kept them in charge, began the insurgency against Shiite rule.

The other Arab nations, with their own internal Shiite minorities, could not help but wonder why the United States was following such a stupid and dangerous policy. The Iranians, who are Persians, not Arabs, and right next door to Iraq, rejoiced. It was natural for them to ally themselves secretly with their Shiite brothers across the border. They wondered why the United States was following such a foolish policy yet were delighted that the Americans had eliminated the two most serious threats to Iranian security: Saddam on their western side and the Taliban on their eastern side.

The great victory for American democracy was in fact a great victory for Iran. Now the president and his babbling secretary of state are shocked that Iranian power has increased, apparently unaware that American foreign policy is responsible for that increase.

The neo-cons are apparently gone from Washington, but there are still some of them around, still writing memos, and still influencing policy. The memos for the so-called surge came from William Kristol and Robert Kagan, lesser lights than I. Lewis Libby and Douglas Feith and Paul Wolfowitz, but still neo-cons. Despite all their mistakes in understanding the importance of religion in that part of the world, the president still is apparently willing to listen to them.

Now he is doing all he can to prepare the public for a shooting war with Iran. He certainly has no illusions about the 1st Cavalry riding into Tehran to a flower-tossing welcome while statues of the ayatollah are pulled down for American television. All he needs to build up his reputation for toughness and to restore some of his popularity among the nutmeg segment of the population is to "take out" a couple of Iranian bases. You can't believe he would be dumb enough to try that? He was dumb enough to get us into the Big Muddy in Iraq, wasn't he?

In the meantime, Iran, noting how reasonable the United States has been in its most recent conversations with North Korea, is sending out signals that it might be nice to sit and talk. The babbler-in-chief keeps telling us that the Iranians know what they have to do.

That's what passes for foreign policy in Washington these days. Russian President Vladimir Putin's recent protest against American unilateralism— albeit a case of the pot calling the kettle black—seems eminently reasonable.

March 9, 2007

Betraying the truth betrays the troops

I see by the papers that Senators Barack Obama and John McCain have been "dinged" by the "researchers" (mud collectors and mud throwers) because they have asserted that lives and money have been "wasted" in Iraq. How dare they say that the lives of "our troops" were wasted? Have they no respect for the feelings of the survivors of "our troops"? Must one maintain the illusion that these brave men and women died for something important, like American freedom or democracy or to prevent another World Trade Center attack?

The truth is that they died because of loyalty to the armed services and to their duty. That ought to be enough. One ought not to pretend that the war was waged for any other reason than that the president, the vice president, the secretary of defense and their coterie of neo-conservative intellectuals wanted a war and exaggerated intelligence data to justify it.

The members of the administration talk endlessly about loyalty to our troops and the duty of all Americans to support them. In fact, once they had the congressional resolution justifying the war, they showed precious little concern for the troops. They did not send enough troops to ensure immediate victory, nor did they train them for the kind of war they would have to fight. It was supposed to be over in a couple of weeks. You could win with substantial numbers of Reserve and National Guard personnel, weekend soldiers who were yanked away from their families and jobs and sent off to war.

They did not equip the troops with adequate body armor or adequate vehicle armor. They did not devise a way to protect the troops from roadside bombs. They played games with their paychecks. They deployed and redeployed and then redeployed again, as though they were yo-yos, without any concern for their personal and familial stress. They assigned them to duty in prisons like Abu Ghraib for which they were totally unqualified.

And Donald Rumsfeld delivered himself of the brilliant military dictum, "stuff happens." And remarked that "you don't fight the war you want to fight but the war you have to fight."

Then, when the troops died in substantial numbers, they forbade pictures of flag-draped coffins being unloaded by the score from transport planes. They boasted of great progress and then redeployed troops again beyond human endurance.

As the casualties mounted, the president mouthed meaningless clichés like, "Iraq is hard." Hard on whom, one wonders? On himself or the vice president? On Secretary Rumsfeld or Secretary Condoleezza Rice or on the wives and children, the mothers and fathers, the sweethearts and the friends of those who died in a foolish war that has been bungled at every deeper step into the Big Muddy? Hard on the men and women whose lives will be forever blighted by unnecessary deaths? But those of us who wanted all along to remove them from harm's way are accused of not supporting the troops when the leaders who sent them into this military miasma clearly don't give a hoot about them, save as a political talking point.

Now we have the revelations of how the returning troops are treated at Building 18 in the Walter Reed Hospital complex, the inadequate treatment at most VA hospitals around the country, and the cover-up of statistics about brain injuries and post-traumatic stress disorder. The returning troops, it would seem, were relegated to a status similar to victims of Hurricane Katrina.

To those of you preparing to write your usual letters telling me I am a traitor for not caring about the troops, I reply that you betrayed them by your silence about the intolerable expenditure of American blood and money (some of which might have gone to VA hospitals) so that President Bush could play-act at the role of a wartime president. And he wasn't even the kind of wartime president who would tour the hospitals or appoint people to make sure the hospitals were decent places to come alive again.

In an administration where spin, doublethink and lies have replaced the truth, why is anyone surprised about mistreatment of injured troops? Why do we still think that the buck stops in the Oval Office as it did in Harry Truman's day?

March 30, 2007

Bush team is adept only at bungling

The Bush administration reminds me of Jimmy Breslin's comic novel, *The Gang That Couldn't Shoot Straight*. The premise of the novel was, what if you had a Mafia gang whose members were incompetent at the things that mafiosi are supposed to do. Similarly, the Bush administration has often shot itself in the foot because its key players are not qualified for their jobs. They make a mess of the job and are protected by secrecy, or if that isn't possible, by spin. The current example is the selective firing of U.S. attorneys for reasons that are not yet clear. The gnomes who created the mess are two of President Bush's old cronies from Texas: Alberto Gonzales and Harriet Miers. Neither, as is now patent, is a heavy hitter. Gonzales has been involved in controversies over the Geneva Conventions (which he called "quaint") and legal memos that appear to involve approval of secrecy, torture, imprisonment without trial and spying on Americans without legal warrants. Small wonder the president does not want him to testify under oath.

Another example of not being able to do the job were the men who were supposed to deal with Hurricane Katrina: Michael Chertoff and Michael Brown (of Homeland Security and FEMA, respectively), neither of whom had the intelligence to deal with a catastrophe or the experience of responding to major disasters (unlike Brown's predecessor, Edward Witt). However, they were loyal Republicans, so no other competence was required. New Orleans continues to be a mess; FEMA continues to be unable to spend the money. No heavy hitters in this mess.

Then there is the Coalition Provisional Authority, which was supposed to govern Iraq in the years after the war. L. Paul Bremer, the head of the CPA, did not speak Arabic and had never served in the Middle East. He had been a staff aide to Henry Kissinger and ambassador to Norway. The members of his staff, mostly younger Republicans, seem to have been even less qualified, and according to journalists covering Iraq, did not speak Arabic and rarely left the fortified Green Zone. Whatever Bremer's intentions, he and his staff must share the blame for what came after the new government was installed. None of them seems to have been a heavy hitter.

The worst example by far of the gang that could only shoot itself in the foot is the president's foreign-policy team. Condoleezza Rice had been provost at Stanford University, which might have qualified her to become president of a state college in the California system, but scarcely the president's top foreign policy adviser or now secretary of state. Donald Rumsfeld was a hard-driving and arrogant corporate executive skilled at bureaucratic infighting who ignored the advice of the experienced military officers and ran the Defense Department as his own fiefdom. He used the war to prove his hypothesis that a small American military force would easily triumph, and he made no preparations for reconstruction after the war—two tragic mistakes, the results of which are still with us.

Vice President Dick Cheney, on the basis of the "Scooter" Libby trial, seems an angry man with paranoid tendencies who may even now suspect an Iraq link with al-Qaida and weapons of mass destruction hidden away somewhere. Mixed in were a clique of neo-cons: Paul Wolfowitz, Douglas Feith and Libby, who could write strong memos. The only heavy hitter, who might have been able to prevent the mistake of the war, was Colin Powell, whom Rumsfeld and Cheney marginalized. No wonder the war went terribly wrong and tens of thousands have died.

Gonzales, Miers, Chertoff, Bremer, Rice, Cheney, Rumsfeld, Wolfowitz: Could any of the members of this gang have been expected to shoot straight? Besides Powell, where were the wise men (and women) who could have protected the country from a string of disasters?

Bush is a victim of his bad taste in advisers and staff, his propensity to Texas cronyism and his inclination to cover up and spin the truth. There is no reason to believe that he is better advised about the "new" strategy in Iraq, or that the mistakes will not continue till Jan. 20, 2009. No heavy hitters need apply.

April 13, 2007

Endless war, endless spin

Most of us thought that the last election settled the Iraq issue. The voters by a substantial majority rejected the Iraq war. It now appears that Iraq will be the focus of the presidential election next year. In an exercise of political legerdemain almost as ingenious as that which launched this stupid, inept and immoral war, President Bush has somehow reintroduced it as the focus for political debate this year and next year.

Despite the sentiment of the voters and the wise advice of the Iraq Commission, victory is still possible in Iraq if only we have the patience and the courage (are willing to accept more deaths of other people's children). We must protect Iraqi democracy. The consequences of failure are unthinkable. We must keep faith with our dead troops. If we don't fight the terrorists in Iraq, then we will have to fight them here at home.

There is nothing new in any of these arguments, and nothing true either. Yet they are advanced as new insights to support a "new" strategy and they are propounded by White House spokespersons, Republican members of Congress, commentators on the Fox network and conservative columnists and editorial writers as if they were wisdom that has not been heard before. Now at last, they seem to be saying, we've finally got it right.

The war is lost. It was lost before it started. It is immoral and it was immoral before it started. The Republicans running for re-election know the public is fed up with the war but they are caught in recycled old rhetoric and cannot slip out of it.

More disturbing, however, are the arguments being advanced by the three musketeers who are the major Republican candidates. They are still spinning the war in Iraq as the real war on terrorism. Rudy Giuliani seems eager to take on Iran. That might not be fair to Alexander Dumas's gallant warriors. Perhaps they should be compared to the "see-no-evil-hear-no-evil-speak-no-evil" trio of simians.

If the jingoistic militarism of the candidates persists for another year, the public will have to choose between support for a war it doesn't like anymore and the charge that it is cowardly and traitorous. It seems unlikely that this "framing" of the issue could win the election. But in the last couple of decades American voters have been erratic in their responses to the constant spinning of slogans and fallacies, and especially those spun by the words "Sept. 11, 2001." The Iraq war, solidly beaten in 2006, could bounce back again and win in 2008. That would mean that a new Republican president would have waded full into the Big Muddy and taken the baton from his predecessor.

The "endless war" would continue. More flag-draped coffins would be flown in during the dead of night, more maimed bodies turned over to the dubious care of military and veterans hospitals, more National Guardsmen fired from their civilian jobs, more traumatized veterans wandering about in an emotional fog, and more life-ruining tragedies imposed on Americans, young and old.

I do not want to question the motivation of the Republican candidates. They need the support of hardcore Republicans to win the primaries—men and women who will put great emphasis on loyalty to "our" president. Yet the picture of Sen. John "Straight Talk" McCain standing in a marketplace in Baghdad, wearing body armor, with helicopters buzzing overhead, celebrating the new safety in the city suggests that he is already trapped in the Big Muddy.

Conclusion

A minimal statement of the Catholic theory of the just war is that war should be the absolute last recourse. This perspective was acceptable in the United States in the years after 1945. The two small-scale wars (as distinguished from big wars like World War II) the country fought mostly because it blundered into them and couldn't get out. However, the Bush Doctrine reserved the right to start a preemptive war, a war against anyone who might attack you some day. The United States was the world's only remaining superpower, and therefore it had the right to strike out against a perceived threat even if its rockets were not already on the launching pad. Nor was this country bound to consult with anyone who would be opposed to such a war. We informed Germany and France, for example, what we were about to do. If they disapproved, that was their problem.

The Europeans learned in the early 1940s that modern war was horrific, even if it turned out to be necessary. Hence, they resisted involvement in America's preemptive strike against Iraq. The American government couldn't care less. All it needed to do was to persuade the American people that Iraq was a more or less imminent threat. National Security Adviser Condoleezza Rice summed up the argument. We could not wait for the smoking gun in Iraq because it could turn out to be a mushroom cloud. In the combination of fear and fury after the World Trade Center attack, the American people bought into the Bush Doctrine of preemptive war. The change in national policy became official without any serious discussion. The Republicans won the 2002 and the 2004 elections because the president had persuaded the public (with the help of ingenious if diabolic spinning by Karl Rove) that the war in Iraq was necessary and would end in victory.

However, as the situation in Iraq deteriorated, the public changed its mind—as it has been known to do before. You can't, as the saying goes, fool all the people all the time. The excuses for war had been deceptive. The United States had no plans for dealing with postwar Iraq. The leaders of the country had misled the people. The killing went on and increased. The national leadership had no idea how to cope with the mess.

The voters turned against the war in the election of 2006. By May 2007, the president's popularity rating had fallen to 28 percent. The public was disgusted and angry and wanted out of the Iraq mess. Promises that we could still win fell on deaf ears.

In the midst of this dramatic change there was little discussion of the Bush Doctrine or the theory of preemptive war—shoot first and ask questions later. The ultimate mistake of the Bush administration was not reliance on slanted intelligence, not the failure to consider postwar problems in Iraq, not the incompetents chosen to administer postwar Iraq, not ignorance of the religious conflicts in the country, not the pretense that the situation was improving when it was not, not the naivete about the ability of the American armed forces to win the war. The most fundamental failure was the adoption of the theory of preemptive war, a failure both moral and strategic.

War is too complex, too problematic, too murky to be entered in haste. Only when the moral principle that war should be the last resort is taken seriously will there be the time and the concern to make sure that all the imponderables are at least pondered. In 2002 and 2003 there was apparently no one in the White House capable of demanding that the administration think through the ramifications of an attack on Iraq (as the Kennedy Brothers did during the Cuban Missile Crisis). It would be a piece of cake, a slam dunk, a road to Jerusalem through Baghdad.

A preemptive war, as the Bush Doctrine defined it, left no time and no opportunity to consider at least some of the things that might go wrong— a civil war between the Sunnis and the Shiites, for example, and possible responses to such an event. Undersecretary Paul Wolfowitz simply and confidently commented that he did not think it was a serious problem. If he and his neo-con intellectuals had read a few books of Iraqi history, they might have known better. But there was no time. The mushroom cloud might appear the day after tomorrow.

The cowboy/patriot myth that is a critical part of American culture said, in effect, "Let's go get the so and so and be done with it." The temper of the times supported such a battle cry.

Has the country learned its lesson? It didn't learn the lesson of Vietnam about the mistake of fighting the Vietcong as though it was the Wermacht. Nor did it learn the lesson of the "Powell Doctrine"—attack with maximum strength. If another occasion when the nation has been injured and infuriated should arise and there is another president who wants a war ("this means war," were his first words when told about the attack on the World Trade Center), will shallow intelligence and "patriotic" clichés and battle cries lead to the same disastrous errors in judgment? It is not at all

clear to me that the American people would be prepared to insist on restraint and caution as Europeans did after 1945.

All the norms I described in the introduction have the same two-sided
implications—what is moral is also usually the best strategy and best as-
surance that the negative effects of war will not cancel out its positive goals.
The United States had no choice but to respond to the attack on Pearl
Harbor in 1941. But the Japanese military did not apply the norm that war
should be the last possible choice. Its fanatical patriotism blinded it to the
possibilities of defeat and destruction.

Are all Americans guilty of an unjust war, even those who opposed it
from the beginning? I would not absolve columnists, editorial writers and
others who changed sides in midstream—a stream that turned out to be the
Big Muddy. But I cannot accept the argument of James Reston, Jr., that
since it was done in our name we are all responsible. The theory of collective guilt is abhorrent. As Hannah Arendt said, if everyone is guilty then
no one is guilty. Yet those who supported or still support the war should
demand of themselves, when they wake in the morning to the news of several hundred more Iraqis blown to pieces and pictures of blood on the
streets, whether some of that blood is on their hands.

I am often asked why the church and the hierarchy did not speak out
against the war. I would reply that both the American bishops and the
Vatican did speak out, but their voices were not heard, perhaps because in
the midst of the sexual-abuse crisis no one was listening to the bishops any
more.

I have wondered how many priests preached against the war? My impression is that priests were generally silent. Were their sermons about the
principles of a just war? Perhaps, but they didn't make the Catholic or the
secular press. Should not priests stay out of politics? Was their silence not
proper? Was not opposition to the war evidence of political support for
Democrats?

A war is not politics. It is a catastrophe of human suffering about which
a priest has no choice but to speak out. I'm not altogether sure that the
Vatican, for all its reservations about the war, would have approved of a
priest in the United States who condemned it from the altar at a weekend
mass. The "patriots" would have denounced him to the Vatican for "politics."

Yet to paraphrase the founder, if we remain silent, the very stones will
cry out.